W9-BCT-732

THE BASKETBALL CLINIC'S COMPLETE BOOK OF

Defensive Fundamentals and Drills

THE BASKETBALL CLINIC'S
COMPLETE BOOK OF

Defensive Fundamentals and Drills

Compiled by
the Editors of
THE BASKETBALL CLINIC

Parker Publishing Company, Inc.
West Nyack, New York

PARKER PUBLISHING COMPANY, INC.

West Nyack, New York

Library of Congress Cataloging in Publication Data
Main entry under title:

The Basketball clinic's complete book of defensive fundamentals and drills.

1. Basketball—Defense—Addresses, essays lectures. 2. Basketball coaching—Addresses, essays, lectures. I. Basketball clinic. II. Title: Defensive fundamentals and drills.
GV888.B35 796.32'32 81-5115
ISBN 0-13-072199-9 AACR2

Printed in the United States of America

How This Book Can Help You Win

If offensive basketball comes easy to your players, then defense is just plain hard work—dirty work at that. Offense gets all the attention but without defense you don't win.

The Basketball Clinic's Complete Book of Defensive Fundamentals and Drills is the book that gives you the know-how for stopping your opponent, for making your defense more effective. Put simply, this book shows you how to win with hard work.

The 33 outstanding coaches who are assembled in this book have proven their defensive ability over and over again. With over 6000 career wins, their knowledge is something that you can use as you prepare to do league, district, conference, and state championship battle.

This book can be the cure for all that defensively ails your team. If you have problems with your adjustable area man-to-man press, consult Burrall Paye. If you need a system of multiple defense, then Frank Pasqua is your man. Having problems with your 2-3 zone variations? Dick Hitchcock has the answer. Trying to decide how best to use your personnel? Give Bill Peters a chance. And if you need drills to improve individual defensive skills, then Bill Leatherman has the know-how.

This book is not to be taken lightly, because the coaches collaborating here have worked on the junior high, high school, college, and professional levels. So they know what it takes to stop your opponent.

Even if your offense is so high-powered that you blow out your opponent night after night, this book is still for you. On those days when your offense sputters, it makes sense to have an ace up your sleeve to hamper your opponent from blowing *you* out. And that ace is defense!

If your star player has picked up a few quick fouls and you have to sit him down, your team can still be effective if they concentrate on defense and make the other team work hard just to take a shot.

By no means will this book guarantee victory—no book can—but it sure can make your job a whole lot easier. All coaches are human, and they make mistakes, but this book can help minimize the mistakes and it can be an extension of you. It can be another brain working for you—a library of defensive knowledge.

THE BASKETBALL CLINIC'S COMPLETE BOOK OF DEFENSIVE FUNDAMENTALS AND DRILLS is what you need to give you a well-rounded attack. If coaching defense is not your favorite area, then let this book help you become the defensive power you want to be.

Board of Editors
THE BASKETBALL CLINIC

Contents

Part 5

DEFENSIVE DRILLS

Part One

ZONES

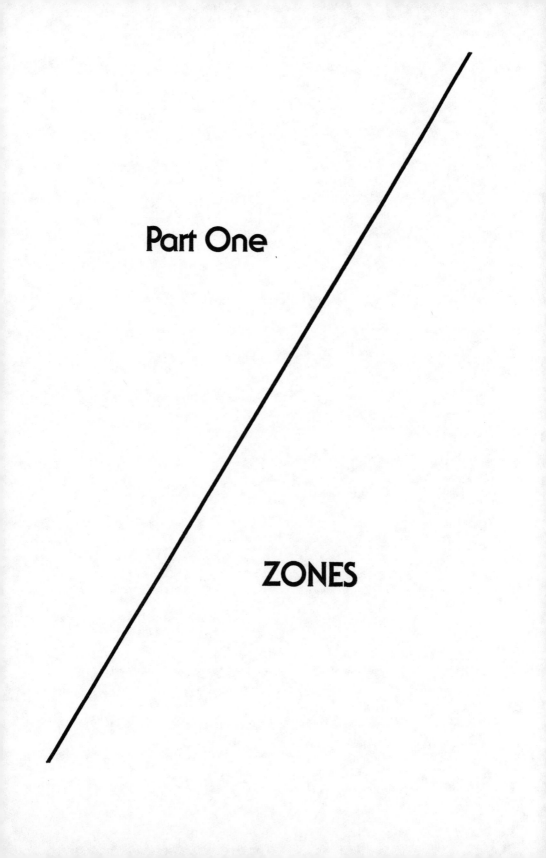

1

The 2-1-2 Offside Zone Defense

by Gilman E. McKinnie

Former Head Basketball Coach
Coulee City High School
Coulee City, Washington

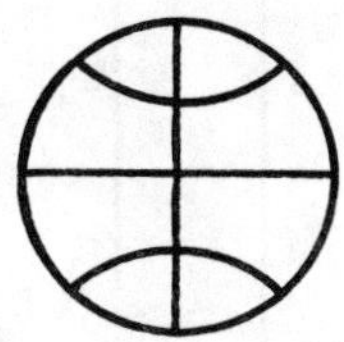

Gilman E. McKinnie was the head coach at Coulee City High School (Coulee, Washington) for five years. In that time, Coach McKinnie compiled a 97-33 won-lost record, including two district championships. In state tournament play, he led his squad to a 9-3 mark with second, fourth, and third place finishes. Currently, he is assisting the basketball program at Lake Stevens High School (Lake Stevens, Washington).

After emphasizing the 2-1-2 zone defense for two consecutive years, many teams were able to devise offenses that were sometimes effective against the standard 2-1-2 zone (see Diagram 1). So, to prevent using the man-for-man defense or a 1-2-2 zone, neither of which permits effective use of personnel, we came up with the offside zone defense (see Diagram 2). This defense merely emphasizes aspects of the 2-1-2 that are not normally employed.

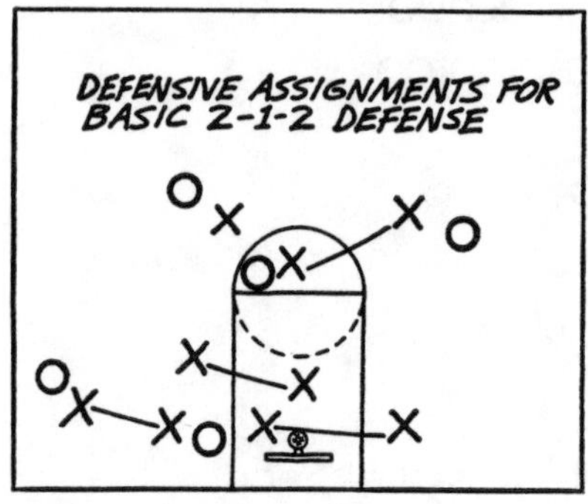

Diagram 1

Diagram 2

NOTE: The offside zone defense is a supplement to the 2-1-2 zone. We have used it for an entire game many times, or for a quarter or two depending upon the opponent's offense. In any case, it has proved effective.

The offside zone defense naturally emphasizes the positions of the two offside or weakside defensive players. Against certain zone offenses, with proper use of the weakside defensive men, an almost man-to-man situation is created.

Alignment and Assignments

Under a normal 2-1-2, the middle man is not normally responsible for the low-post or baseline player. In the offside zone formation, he drops down to the base on the strongside (ball side).

The baseline defensive player will take the opposition's wing man, whether he is in the corner or on the side.

The strongside guard will pick up the strongside guard of the offense.

The offside guard will be free to take the high post (in fact, he must defend him). The offside guard may front the high post or play behind him, depending upon how you want to defend him.

The offside (weakside) baseline defender will then be responsible for the offensive player on the weakside. He must even check the weakside player if he goes to the top of the key.

Defensive Responsibilities Illustrated

The defensive responsibilities for the 2-1-2 offside zone defense are illustrated in Diagram 2.

1 & 2: offensive guard on his side when ball is on his side of the court. Otherwise, he will have the high post.

3: will defend baseline player under basket or roamer in basket area.

4 & 5: will take wing man in corner or on side when ball is in his half of court. Otherwise, he will control player on the weak or offside portion of the court when ball is on other side or strong side of the court.

NOTE: As can be seen in Diagram 2, weakside defensive players are more effective.

Basic Keys to This Defense

The basic keys to this defense are as follows:

1. Constant pressure on the high post is especially effective if your key is to stop the high post.
2. Big man on defense can always defend the low post.
3. Opposition's weakside shooter should be neutralized by the offside defensive forward.
4. Unlike most zones, the offense cannot burn you with the fast repetitious pass.

5. The basic 2-1-2 is never more than a step or two away, and is always used as a point of reference.

WEAKNESS & STRENGTH: The offensive point guard may be able to create a problem or two. If he is an extremely effective outside shooter, one defensive guard may be assigned to him and the other defensive guard can take the high post. The basic strength is that it combines the best aspect of man-to-man defense (pressure) and the best aspect of the zone (organization and control).

Summary

Emphasis on defensive play is essential to the development of a good basketball program. We have found that the zone defense can lead to less-than-desired performance by some team members because of the built-in aids that the defense provides.

FOR EXAMPLE: Constant help in the middle, shutting off the offensive drive to the basket.

With the use of the offside 2-1-2, the defensive ball player must demand of himself his very best effort because you have given him specific responsibilities that most zones don't have.

The offside zone has also proved to be much more rewarding to the defensive attitude of the player because each member of the team must depend upon himself, yet he can always get some help.

The offside zone is very flexible. We have had success with it against good outside shooting teams and also against those teams that emphasize the inside game.

If you feel that you can match up with the opposition's big man, this defense is particularly effective. The strongside defensive forward can often sag in and help out underneath.

2

The 1-3-1 Zone Defense: Ideas, Techniques, Drills

by Carl Peal

Former Head Basketball Coach
Petersburg High School
Petersburg, Virginia

Carl Peal's outstanding coaching career came to an end in 1975 when he retired. In 20 years of coaching he compiled a 323-89 won-lost record with three state titles, one at Peabody High School (Petersburg, Virginia) and two consecutive titles at Petersburg High School (Petersburg, Virginia). Carl has run off 42- and 50-game winning streaks during his career and was the high school coach of Moses Malone.

We had believed in a man-for-man defense for years—until we weren't getting personnel fast enough to play it. So we started experimenting with zones and ended up with the 1-3-1.

NOTE: We have been playing it now for three years and we like it. And we're getting progressively better. The first year out we were 10-10; the second year, 17-3; this past year, 25-0.

We put a lot of emphasis on our defense and work hard at it. In fact, at the beginning of each season, we practice nothing but defense for the first two weeks.

Our 1-3-1 zone defense has worked successfully against the following offenses: man-for-man, 1-3-1, 2-1-2, 1-4, 1-2-2, 2-3. And it does a fair job against the "North Carolina Four Corners."

NOTE: It appears that many coaches do not like the 1-3-1 because the corners are the most vulnerable spots. But we make this play our strongest point and we have a drill for it, which will be discussed and illustrated later in this article.

Alignment and Responsibilities

Proper alignment of the players, and especially the base man, is necessary for the 1-3-1 zone defense to function properly. The players are point man, left wing, middle man, right wing or strong side, and base man. All men are free to steal long passes, regardless of where the ball is in play.

Point Man

1. Force the offensive guard to one side (if we are going to trap at mid-court).
2. Front the center when at high post, when the ball is onside.

3. On any pass to center or wing, hustle back to foul lane.
4. Must always be in position for long rebound when shot from corner, and ready for our fast break.
5. Overplay pass back to other guard.

Left Wing

1. Never go beyond the head of the circle (except on half-court press).
2. Rebound and screen off side corner man from the boards.
3. Must be able to play base man position when he pulls out to cover corner.
4. Front center man in some cases.
5. Help trap in corner.

Middle Man

1. Follow the ball. Must stay between the ball and the basket at all times.
2. Front center man when at low post.
3. Be able to exchange with base man.
4. Must stop penetration by dribbler (block shots).
5. Help other players to stay in position and tell them when being blocked or screened.

Right Wing (Strong Side)

1. Responsibilities are the same as the left wing.
2. The right wing should be the stronger player of the two.

Base Man

1. Keep the lanes blocked to baseline runners. Fight through blocks and screens.

2. Must help with wing man and sometimes with middle man.
3. Play about two to three feet in front of the basket and cover the appropriate corners.
4. Follow the ball and stay in line with it.
5. Must help stop all penetration along baseline.

NOTE: We ask our players to talk on defense and to help out wherever possible without hurting our zone. When we trap and the ball escapes the trap, we immediately go to our match-up defense, which is our 1-3-1. If a guard cuts through and goes away from the ball, we let him go. But if he goes to the ball side, we send our guard with him. The same holds true if they send both guards. We always line up in a straight 1-3-1 zone first and move with the ball. As long as the ball is in the front court, we stay. But when the ball is in back court, we jump into passing lanes, trapping, and sometimes we double-team a man (the best scorer).

Lineup Against Various Offenses

Before each game, we plan our defense against the opponent. It is based on the offense used and the opponent's personnel. In all cases, X1 plays the ball regardless of where it is.

- **Diagram 1** (vs. 2-3 offense): X5 will handle either 02's or 03's man when the ball moves from guard to guard.
- **Diagram 2** (vs. 1-4 offense): X5 will take anyone who comes to the back court.
- **Diagram 3** (vs. 1-3-1 offense): Here, we line up as they do but adjust with ball movement.
- **Diagram 4** (vs. 2-1-2 offense): X1 plays the ball. X2 or X3 will be responsible for the other guard. X5 takes the corner man where the ball will be. X2 or X3 (depending on where the ball will be) takes weakside forward.

- **Diagram 5** (vs. 1-2-2 offense): X4 takes ballside forward and X5 takes weak side.

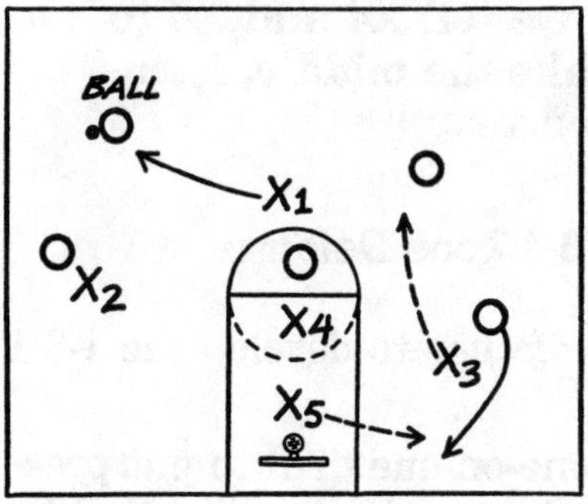

Diagram 1

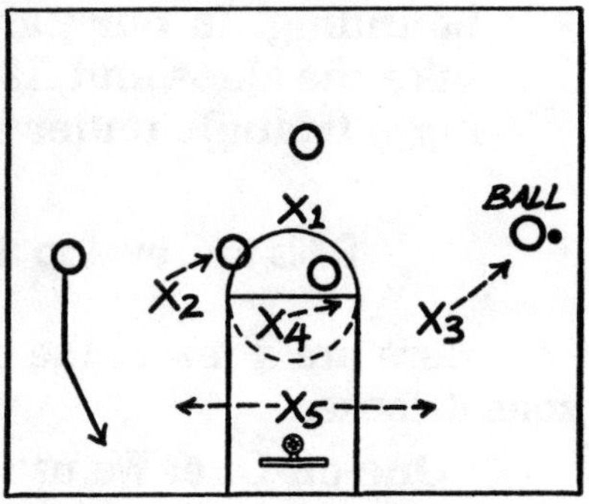

Diagram 2

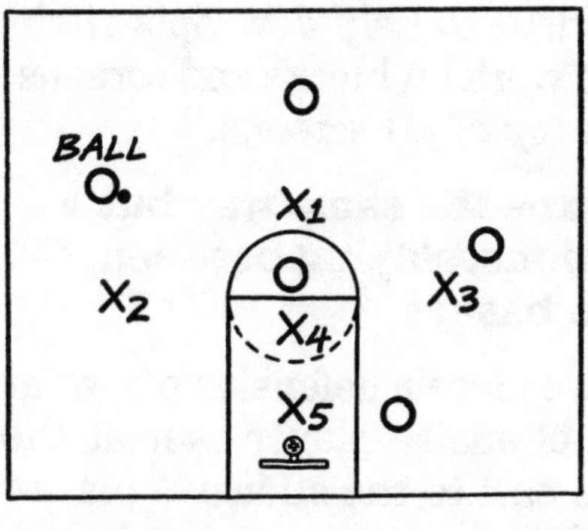

Diagram 3

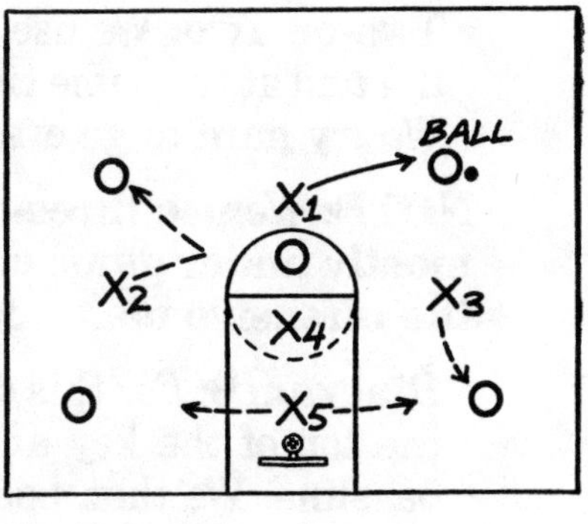

Diagram 4

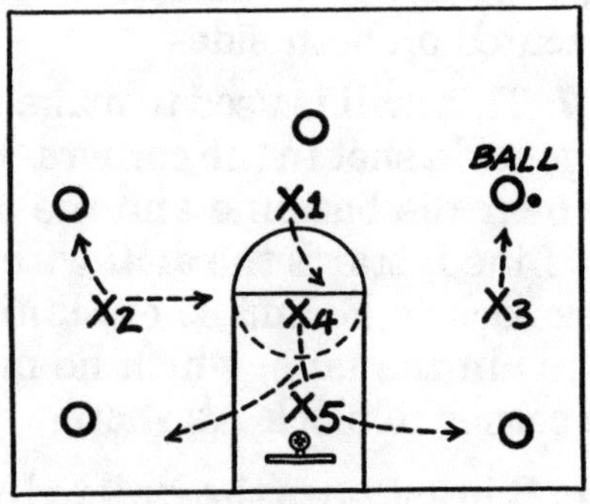

Diagram 5

NOTE: The other players should be assigned according to their abilities to play defense. In this defense we are in good position for rebounding. In our pattern we tell X4 and X5 to take the sides and X3 to take the middle, forming a triangle under the basket.

Drills to Develop the 1-3-1 Zone Defense

Here are a few of the drills we use to develop the 1-3-1 zone defense.

- **One-on-One:** We use the one-on-one drill to put pressure on the man physically, for turnovers and so that he cannot use the baseline. This is a must drill for all positions.
- **Two-on-Two:** We use this drill to help develop switching and at the same time to work on blocks and screens. We try hard to go over the top of all screens.

NOTE: We use three-on-three the same way but mostly under game conditions, staying between the offensive man and the basket.

- **Diagram 6:** For this drill we place a defensive player at the top of the key and an offensive player over at the baseline. We then pass the ball to the offensive player. As the ball is passed, the defensive player must hustle over to stop the offensive player from using the baseline, and bring him down the middle or stop him entirely. This is executed on both sides.
- **Diagram 7:** This drill is used to make it difficult for the offense to get off a shot in the corners. We start with two lines, one near the baseline and the other going down the center. Line B starts the drill with a pass to line A, who passes back to B, and so on, until B comes to the object (chair) in the lane, which he must go around to get to the corner to block A's shot.

NOTE: Line B must pass the ball to line A before he goes around the chair. Line A must dribble

to the corner for a shot with no fakes or double pumps—just a straight shot.

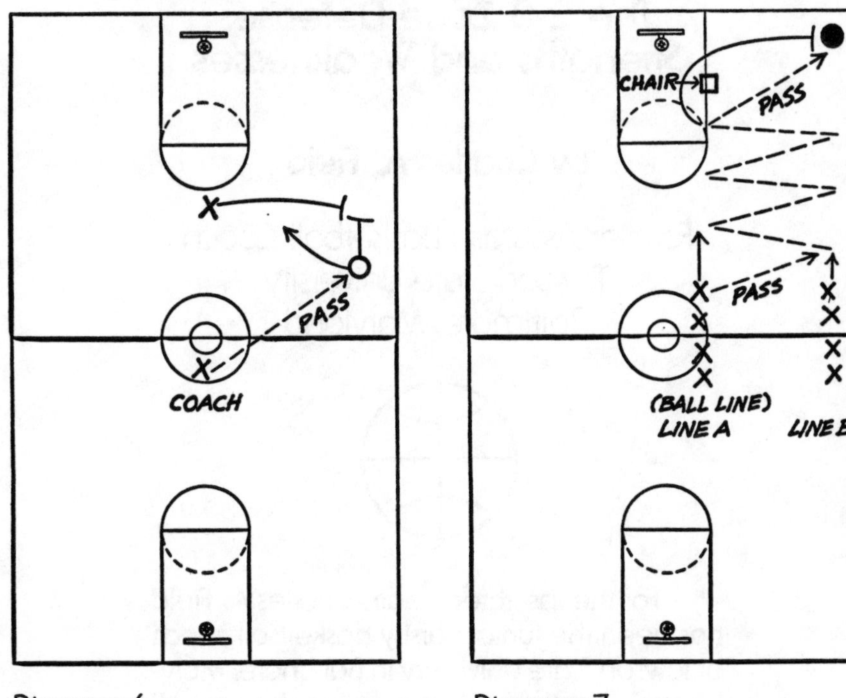

Diagram 6

Diagram 7

This is done to cut down on possible injuries. As you can imagine, this drill brings out game situations, ball handling, passing, one-on-one work, and shooting under pressure.

3

The 2-3 Zone Defense: Strengths and Weaknesses

by Charles A. Field

Former Assistant Basketball Coach
Towson State University
Baltimore, Maryland

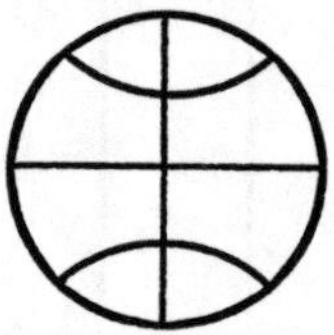

For the last three years, Charles A. Field has been the junior varsity basketball coach at Towson State University in Baltimore, Maryland. Currently, he is the college's baseball recruiter. Coach Field has coached football, basketball, and baseball during his career and has been the director of intramurals at Towson.

As we all know, basketball is one of those games where the team that scores the most points before the time runs out wins. And, as with all other games of total points, the players who score those points receive the most rewards and hero worship.

NOTE: But the players who stop the other team from scoring, and the methods they use, are in this writer's view more important. Defense, then, is surely one of the most important and constant parts of the game.

Look at the records of the champions in any league and you will see that they have a fine defensive team (the Boston Celtics and UCLA, for example).

Thoughts on Defense

Compared with offense, defense takes more effort, time, practice, and dedication. Naturally, there are many types of defenses, so it is most important for the coach to select the type that fits the needs of his players and team—and not the other way around.

NOTE: To illustrate my point, I'll touch briefly on the 2-3 defense. To be sure, it has its weaknesses as well as its strengths. But if a team with average ability masters the fundamentals of sound defensive play, it can be an effective weapon.

Strengths of the 2-3 Zone Defense

The 2-3 zone defense (Diagram 1) places two men at about the foul line, one man in the middle of the lane, and one man on each side of the lane.

The 2-3 provides good rebounding position and good basic position for the fast break.

But when a coach is considering what defense to use in a certain game, he should give thought to the following aspects:

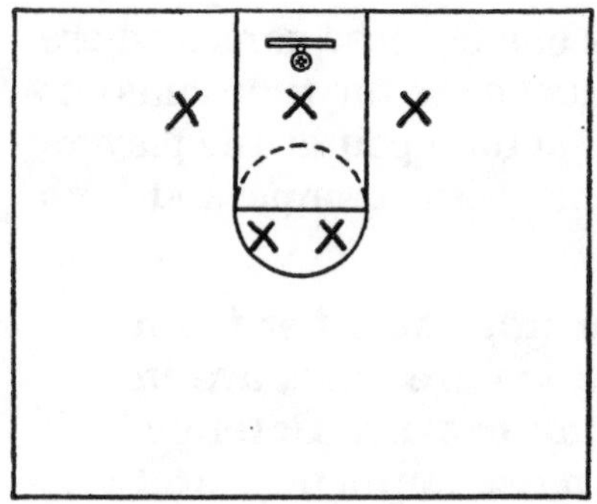

Diagram 1

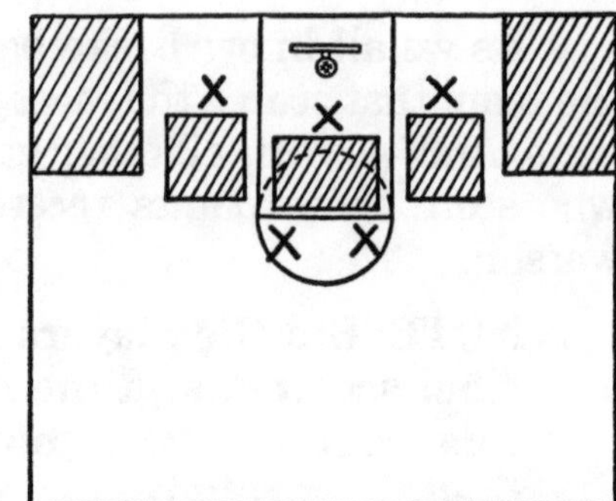

Diagram 2

1. First of all, he must have players who are capable of playing the defense. They must be quick and well-schooled in tough defensive play.
2. He should not dismiss the man-to-man defense—the basics of all defensive play.
3. If his players are poor man-to-man players for any length of time, he should stick to the 2-3 defense and save the man-to-man defense until it is absolutely necessary.
4. Once again, the players must be quick enough to overcome the weaknesses of the 2-3 zone, of which there are a few.

Weaknesses of the 2-3 Zone Defense

The main weakness is the 10- to 15-foot jump shot. The diagonally shaded areas (Diagram 2) are inherent weaknesses of this defense. These areas can, of course, be covered with good, aggressive defensive principles. The horizontal areas are weaknesses *only* if the defense is not executing fundamentally.

NOTE: If the offense continues to exploit these areas, it is a sign that the defense should either be shaken or changed completely. It should also be noted here that the deeper areas of the corners should not be considered a weakness

and no attempt to defense them should be made unless the offense continues to score from these areas.

When the ball is in the corner (Diagram 3) another weakness is noted. When 03 has the ball, X3 is forced out away from the basket. This ruins the rebounding triangle of the defense's best rebounders. It also opens a free rebounding zone (shaded area) for the offense (considering that X5 must go in for the rebound, allowing 01 the free area).

Another area of weakness in the 2-3 zone is the middle. If 02 or 03 breaks into the middle, X3 would have to move up to take away his short jump shot. By doing so, X3 opens up the back door pass to either 04 or 05. If either man is closed off, 02 or 03 would be open for another short jump shot.

NOTE: Still, with good, quick execution of zone defensive principles, the offense can be closed off. (See Diagram 4.)

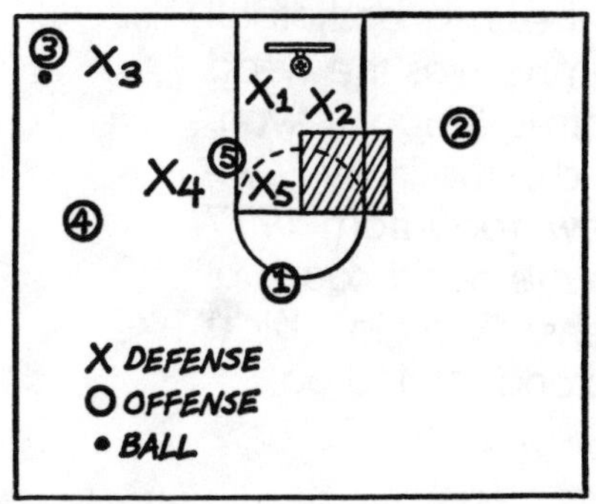

Diagram 3

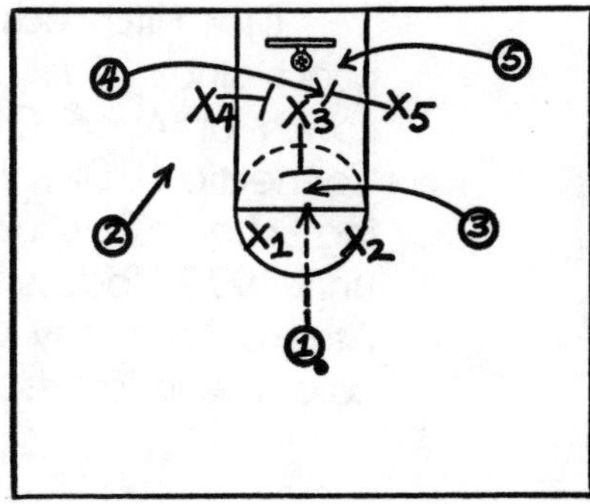

Diagram 4

Conclusion

The 2-3 zone defense, like all defenses, has its strengths and weaknesses. But if it fits the personnel on hand and if they are drilled to execute the defense correctly, it will be as effective a weapon as any defense. As previously stated, good defense takes effort, time, practice, and dedication to make it work.

4

2-3 Zone Variations

by Dick Hitchcock

Head Basketball Coach
Athens Academy
Athens, Georgia

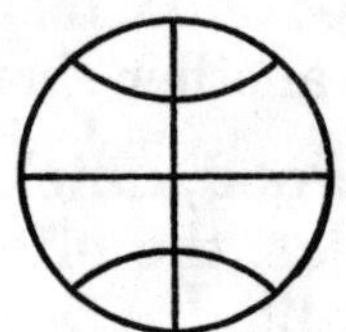

Dick Hitchcock has been a basketball coach since 1972, when he was the head coach at Avon Old Farms School (Avon, Connecticut). Dick worked at the Trinity-Pawling School (Pawling, New York) from 1977 until 1979. Today, he is the head coach at Athens Academy (Athens, Georgia). Dick's career won-lost record stands at 110-65.

The 2-3 zone—used by some coaches as a variant of the 2-1-2—is a defense that must be used with caution. The increasing expertise of high school shooters, the inherent weaknesses on the wing, and the overuse of this zone, can cause a passive 2-3 to be a frustrating and ineffective defense.

However, with aggressiveness and proper slides, we believe that the 2-3 can be a satisfactory zone. It does solve many of the high school coach's problems, providing good rebounding, little inside penetration, and simplicity of defensive assignments.

The Standard 2-3

To apply some zone pressure and to avoid sluggishness, we have rules for each position in the zone. The basic alignment is shown in Diagram 1. The guards are at the lane and foul-line intersection, the forwards are one step outside the black block, and the center is near the dotted half of the jump circle. As the ball nears the offensive area, the following rule goes into effect.

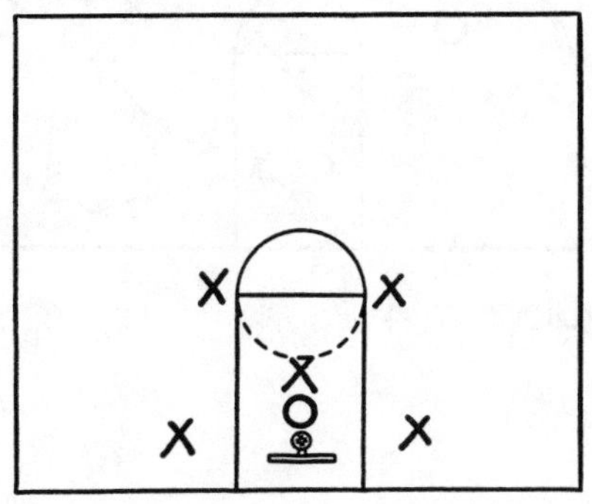

Diagram 1

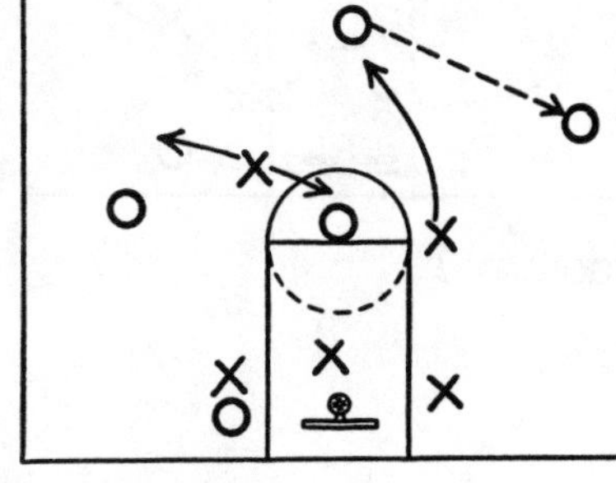

Diagram 2

RULE ONE: One of the guards must pressure the ball, forcing the initial pass over his head to his side (Diagram 2).

The remaining guard bisects the passing lanes to the foul line and his wing, assuring the first pass to the pressure guard's side. We have thus dictated on which side the offense will operate.

As the ball reaches the vulnerable wing position, the next rule prevents the easy 15- to 20-footer.

RULE TWO: The ballside forward must pressure the wing on the *baseline* shoulder (Diagram 3).

The pressure guard is retreating and can soon take over primary responsibility. The forward can then cover the baseline or low post. Should the ball be passed quickly by the forward to the baseline, the final rule is in force.

RULE THREE: The center must cover a shooter *within range* on the baseline, hollering "Switch!" to the pressure forward, who will sink and cover the low post (Diagram 4).

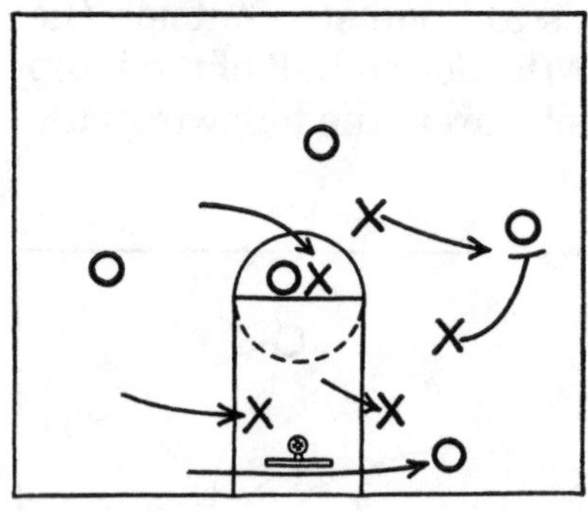

Diagram 3

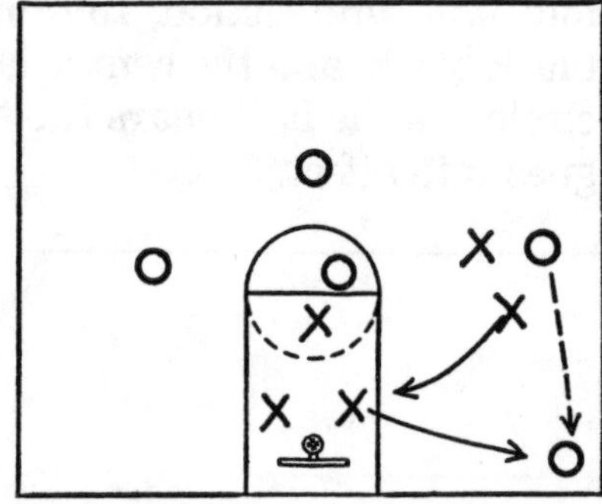

Diagram 4

The opposing center, deep in the corner, is generally not considered "within range." The high post is fronted by the opposite guard. The low post and weak side are always covered. Thus, this version of the 2-3 offers good inside coverage and moderate pressure of the ball. Double teams may be effected on the wing (pressure guard and ballside forward) or on the baseline (forward and center).

The Pressure 2-3

If a team is trailing, or if the ball is being moved effectively around the standard 2-3, a pressure or "laning" zone may be used, in which the passing lanes are blocked and the ball is stopped.

The basic alignment is identical to the standard, as is the initial move of the pressure guard (although abbreviated). When the ball goes over his head to the wing, the lanes are blocked (Diagram 5). The pressure guard must retreat quickly and apply extreme pressure *by himself* to the wing man. The off guard, instead of sinking to the high post, shuts off the return lane to the point. The ballside forward "lanes" the baseline, and the center slides quickly to the high post. The only possible pass is cross-court to the other wing. With a quick, anticipatory slide of the guard, similar pressure can be applied to this wing man.

The keys to this laning zone are the technique of the pressure guard (he *cannot* allow the wing man free movement, but he doesn't have to steal the ball himself) and anticipation by the laners (especially the center).

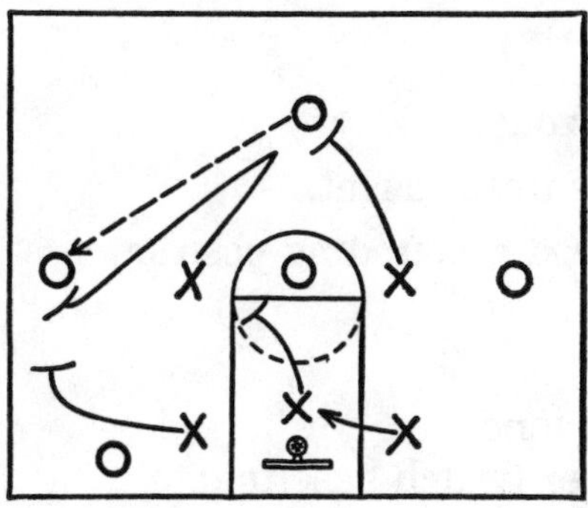

Diagram 5

The Combination 2-3

As the season progresses and a more sophisticated defense is sought, the 2-3 combination or match-up zone might be the answer. The essential concept is playing man-to-man within a given zone, giving man pressure and zone balance.

We align the zone as always and label the zones as shown in Diagram 6. We also indicate four "key spots"—black blocks and lane and foul-line intersections. We then present a careful set of rules for each zone and drill them extensively in a half-court area.

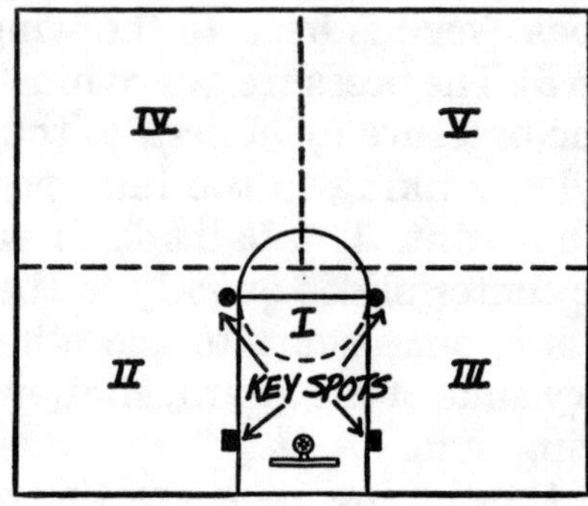

Diagram 6

Combination Zone Rules

Zone 1

Never leave zone.

Play man nearest basket.

Establish good rebounding position.

Zones II and III

1. Play near lane.
2. Play corner (watch baseline).
3. Play sideline.

If your zone is empty, move to "key spot." Watch Zones I, II, III.

Screen out.

Zones IV and V

1. Play near lane.

2. Play top of key.
3. Play sideline.

If zone is empty, move to "key spot." Watch Zone I, then II, III.

General Zone Rules

Prevent dribbling.
When playing a man without the ball:

a. Contest passes.

b. Watch for other drivers.

When zone has two men in it, play outside man.
Key spot man will cover near man.
When zone is vacant:

a. Move to "key spot."

b. Watch Zone I.

c. Find ball.

d. Stop drivers.

This combination zone is not a cure-all. There are problems, such as dribbling through zones, overloading corner zones, making a big center in Zone I cover a quick forward. But it can cause confusion to the opponent's offense (they can't cut through or pass around it); and with players of equal (if average) talent, it can be the ultimate in 2-3 zone coverages.

5

The 1-3-1 Match Zone

by Jerry Dugan

Head Basketball Coach
Lee High School
Huntsville, Alabama

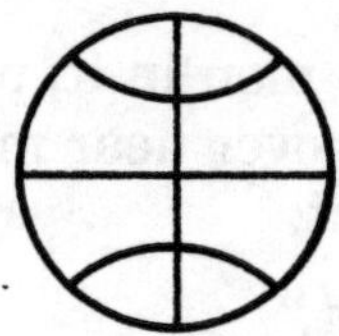

Jerry Dugan has been the head coach at Lee High School (Huntsville, Alabama) since 1968. He has a career mark of 328-154, and has won two back-to-back state titles.

Lee High School has the reputation of playing a tough 1-3-1 match zone. Many of the teams in our area began playing this zone after we were successful with it. It is not a "cure-all" defense, but it does enable us to teach only one zone defense to go along with our man-to-man defense.

We line up in our zone just as everyone else does in the 1-3-1 zone. The alignment is shown in Diagram 1. We do believe that some of our ideas make our 1-3-1 zone different.

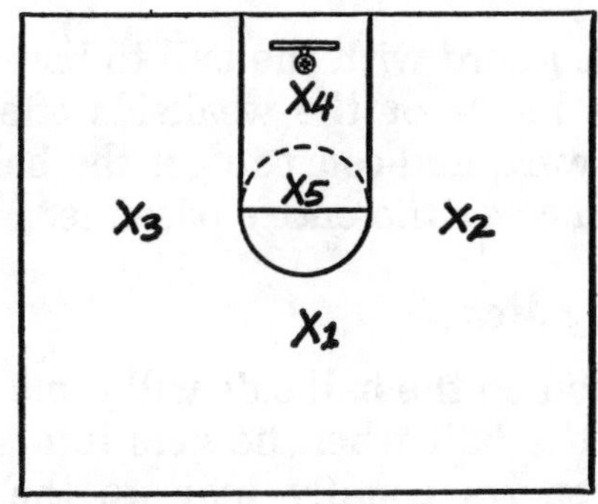

Diagram 1

Personnel Placement

The placement of personnel in this zone is very important. We have had success playing our biggest guard on the baseline. Our baseline man has to cover from corner to corner, so we have to have a quick man on the baseline. We play our other guard at the point position.

Our two forwards play the wing positions, with the best rebounder playing the left wing or X3. The reason for this is that most teams play right-handed, and the left wing will have more rebound chances. If we have a right-handed and left-handed forward, we play the left-hander at the right wing because of the outlet pass possibility.

Our center plays the middle position and has the opposing center man-to-man in most cases. He must be a big, tough kid who will do a good job of blocking out.

Responsibilities for Each Position

X1—Point Man

The point man, X1, is to take the man with the ball as he crosses the half line and influence him toward the weakest side. (We try to run the man away from the best shooter.) After the point man runs the guard to our wing man, there are two things that he can do. He may double-team with our wing man, or he may drop back and try to cut off the pass to the weakside guard.

We want the guard with the ball to have to lob the ball over our guard's head—or the weakside offensive guard to have to break toward mid-court to get the ball. This will let our baseline man cover the entire baseline.

X2 and X3—Wing Men

The wing men on the ball side will come up and pick up the guard with the ball when he gets into shooting range. (Our scouting reports usually indicate the distance from which this guard can shoot accurately.) The wing man should get his hands up and make it difficult for the guard to get the ball inside. If the point man has dropped off, the wing man plays the man with the ball, just like man-to-man. If the guard dribbles the ball, the wing man goes with him until he stops his dribble, or he can release him to someone else.

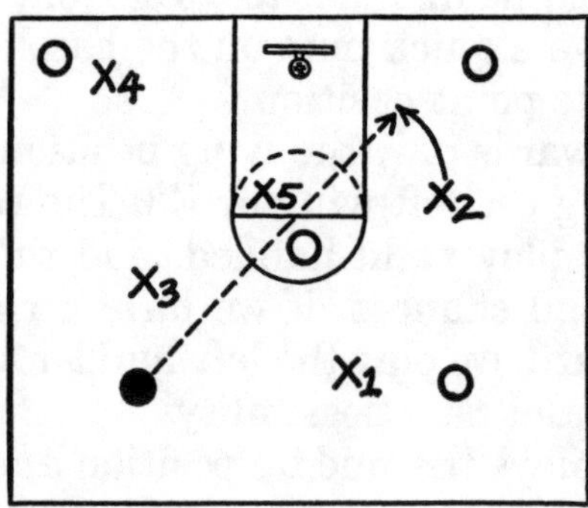

Diagram 2

The weakside wing man must drop back under the goal to protect that area. This drop is shown in Diagram 2. He must not let the ball be thrown from the strong side to the weak side for an easy shot. He must be conscious of an overload and be ready to cover it as well as to call out "Overload" to warn his teammates. This wing man must also be ready to come up and cover the weakside guard if the ball is passed over the point man's head.

X5—Center or Middle Man

The center will play the opponent's man in the middle, man-to-man most of the time. If it is a high-post offense, he will play behind or to the side of their post man. He will try to discourage the ball from being passed to the middle. If the point man is trapping with the wing man, he will move in front of the high-post man.

If the opponent is in a low-post offense, or a 1-2-2 type of offense, the center will drop back a bit and cheat toward the biggest man when the ball is in the middle of the floor. Otherwise, he will cheat toward the ball side and be especially conscious of the pivot man flashing in.

X4—Baseline Man

The baseline man's primary rule is to stay parallel with the ball. He must be quick and ready to really hustle to do this. He must be able to cover the entire baseline. The point man can help him with this by making the guards out front lob the ball. He cannot cover the baseline if the opponents are able to throw straight, quick passes to get the ball back to the weak side.

If the ball is passed to the corner man, the baseline man plays him man-to-man. He must protect the baseline and still get pressure on a corner shot.

Matching the 2-1-2 or the 1-2-2

Most teams will attack a 1-3-1 zone with either a 2-1-2 or a 1-2-2 offensive formation. The 1-3-1 zone can be flexed to match these offensive threats. We will adjust to the 1-2-2 a little differently from the way we adjust the 2-1-2 formation.

To cope with the threat of the 2-1-2 offensive formation, the wing man will pick up the man with the ball. With each man flexing to cover the offensive threats in different areas, the defense now resembles a 2-1-2 zone (Diagram 3).

When the ball is in the right corner, X4 takes the corner, X5 takes the second position, and X3 takes the goal, thus keeping three men in line between the ball and the basket (Diagram 4). X1 pinches toward the middle to protect this vital area with X5. X2 has three alternatives. He may double-team the ball in the corner, overplay the receiver in the area of the free-throw line extended, or pinch to the middle and help out with a dangerous pivot man. X3 has the same alternatives when the ball is in the left corner. In our pre-game preparation, we determine exactly how the wing men will slide.

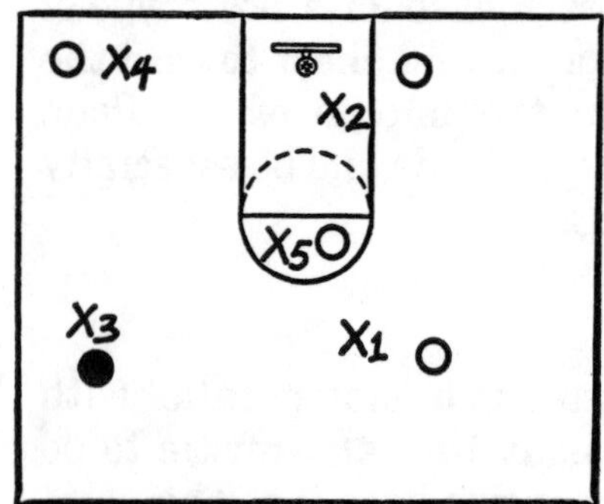

Diagram 3

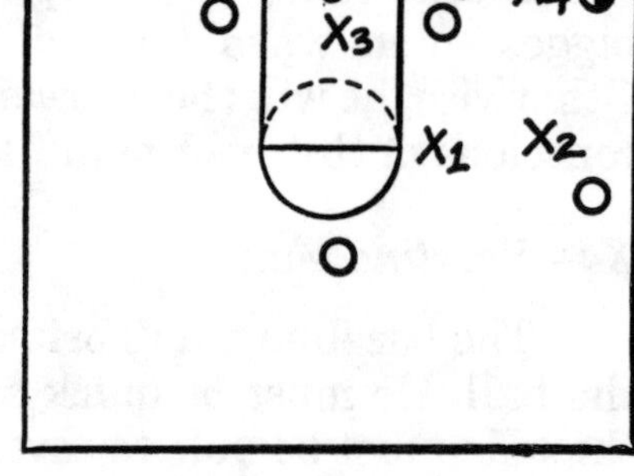

Diagram 4

When the wing man decides to double-team in the corner, our center, X5, will front the opposing center. Our point man, X1, will come over to the wing position to overplay the pass out of the corner. Our offside wing man will split the difference between the offside forward and the weakside guard. He is ready for the interception if the corner man tries to pass all the way across to the weakside guard (Diagram 5).

When the offensive team chooses to employ a 1-2-2 formation, the middle man, X5, drops back to the dotted line and cheats toward the bigger post man (Diagram 6). The baseline man, X4, and the middle man must communicate with each other to cover both low-post men. This can be a dangerous situation if the baseline man and middle man do not communicate. The other defensive players keep their same positions. As the ball moves around the perimeter of the defense, the players take the same slides they took in the basic 1-3-1 zone.

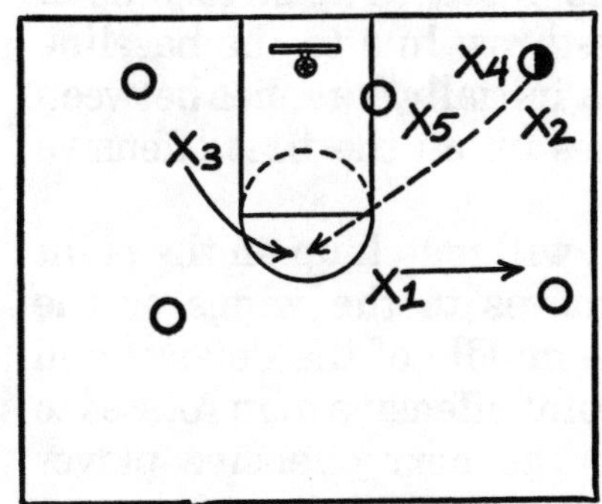

Diagram 5

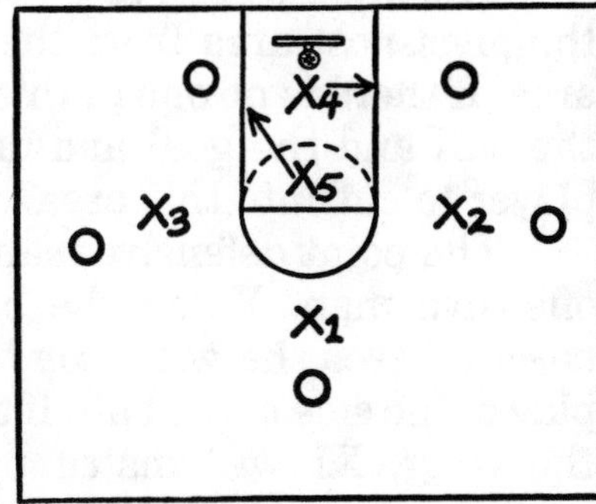

Diagram 6

One of the most common offensive techniques against the zone is to pass to the baseline man from the wing and send the wing man through the defense to the weak side. Our "match-up" against this technique is illustrated in Diagram 7.

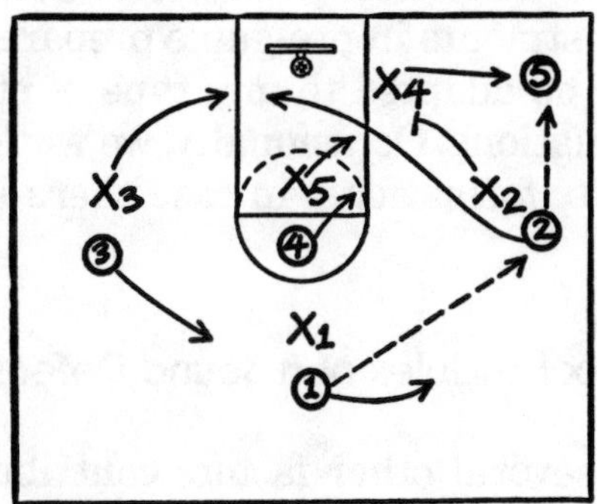

Diagram 7

The defensive wing man, X2, plays the offensive man aggressively and attempts to cut off his cut through the defense as much as possible. He will cover the wing man for two or three steps into the defense, then release him and match up on the next offensive player moving into this area.

The baseline defensive man, X4, matches up on the offensive baseline man as soon as the pass is made. He plays the man aggressively and protects against the baseline drive.

The middle defensive man, X5, matches up on anyone in the pivot-post area from the free-throw line to the baseline area. If there is no one in this area initially, he zones between the ball and the goal and matches up on the first offensive player to cut into this area.

The point defensive man, X1, will match up on the point offensive man. When the ball moves to the wings or the baseline area, he will drop to the middle of the defense and play to the side of the ball. If the point offensive man rotates to the wing, X1 will match up on the next offensive player coming into his zone area.

The weakside wing, X3, matches up on the offensive wing man initially. When the ball penetrates the defense opposite his position, he drops to the weakside goal area, where he has the assignment of covering the important weakside rebounding area. He will pick up the offensive wing man, who has rotated through to the weak side.

We feel that if we can successfully defend against the 1-3-1, the 2-1-2, and the 1-2-2 offensive formations, we are prepared to cope with almost any situation that will arise. With slight adjustments in pre-game preparations, the match zone can easily be adapted to any type of offense, including unorthodox formations. Occasionally, we work against some of these unorthodox formations, in case there is ever a need to defense one.

Six Principles of a Sound Defense

There are several other factors contributing to the success of the match zone. These six principles will help to establish a sound defense.

1. Beat the offense down the floor.
2. Keep the hands and arms extended at all times. This will discourage shots and passes, especially long passes that will shatter a zone.
3. Recognize the offense and flex to match it before the ball penetrates. Each man should guard the man in his area man-to-man.
4. Do not allow the ball to be passed into the middle. Overplay offensive players stationed on or near the free-throw line so that they cannot receive the ball.
5. Do not give teams a good outside shot. Always put a hand in the shooter's face.
6. After a shot is taken, block out for the rebound.

6

Making the 2-1-2 Zone Defense Work

by Donald "Swede" Quam

Head Basketball Coach
Fort Washakie School
Fort Washakie, Wyoming

Donald "Swede" Quam has been coaching for 16 years. The past 12 years have been spent at Fort Washakie (Wyoming) School, on the Wind River Indian Reservation. His junior high boys have compiled a 123-76 record, have won the WRCCA tournament three times, and have finished second for five years.

Our school is a member of the Wind River Conference Athletic Association, which determines the length of our basketball season. We cannot begin practice until the first of November and we can play up to a 16-game schedule, which includes tournaments.

Because we have three different teams participating in the basketball program (fifth and sixth grade boys, junior high girls, and junior high boys), we can practice only twice a week with any team. This also means practicing with two teams on the same night on the same floor.

Because of the number of teams practicing on our floor and the shortage of practice time, I stress fundamentals and aim at winning the tournament at the end of the basketball season.

The 2-1-2 Zone Defense

Defense is stressed, ranging from a full-court zone press, to a full-court man-to-man, to my own revised 2-1-2 zone defense. I consider the 2-1-2 zone an excellent defense. The teams always start out in the 2-1-2 zone alignment, but we very seldom look as if we're in this particular zone defense.

I use the 2-1-2 to key on certain individuals or plays that the offense may use. On *most* teams there will be one or two players who are outstanding ball players and who control the ball, set up plays, or really control the tempo of the team's offense. In these cases, the revised 2-1-2 zone defense excels.

If a high- or low-post man is to get the ball, I'll put our center on him, man-to-man, when he is in the key area. All four of the remaining defensive players are to sag and help out whenever the center is in their assigned area (Diagram 1).

If a pass comes in from G1 to his center, two men, our center and sagging guard, are put on the center (Diagram 2). If there is no offensive man in the corner or beneath the basket, the forward can come up and triple-team—but this is risky.

Let's say we've double-teamed the high-post man who has the ball. The remaining three defensive players must be alert for cutters. G1 may break for the basket. It is possible that G2

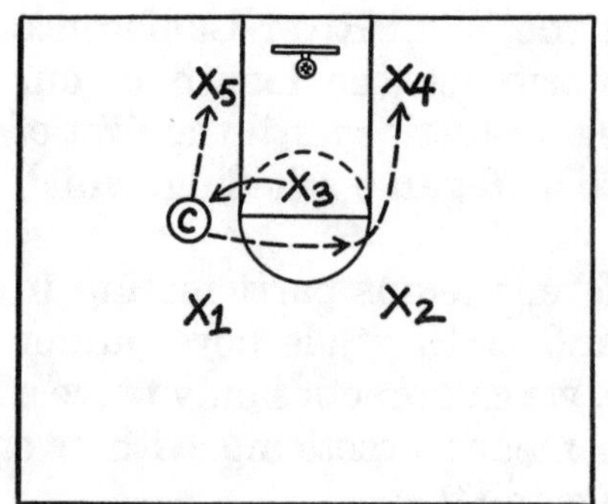

Diagram 1

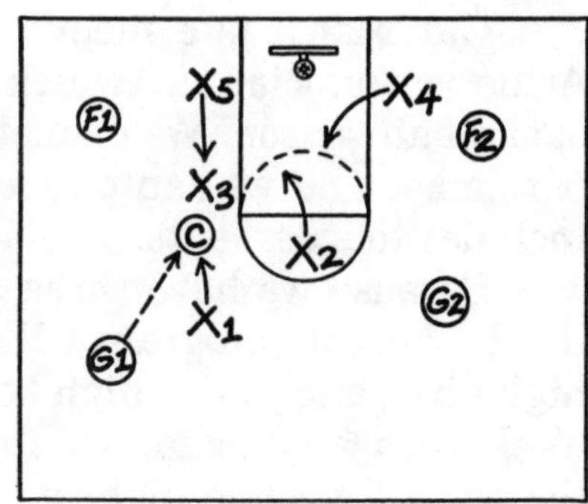

Diagram 2

or the two forwards might try this, too. We must try to block all cutting alleys with our remaining three defensive players.

Basically, what we will strive to do in this case is to harass the center where he may make a violation, or we may tie him up for a jump ball. If we can't do any of these things, we want him to have to pass the ball back out to G1 or another player who has taken his position.

REMEMBER: Hands are always up and active on defense. Any try for the basketball should be made with an upward motion.

On a play to a corner offensive forward, we will place our defensive forward on that side all the way out to the ball (Diagram 3). Everybody moves with the ball, actually going out of position, but the driving or cutting lanes are blocked so that the opponent must either pass over our zone, pass around it, or try a shot.

Under no circumstances should the defense allow a man to drive the baseline. The only man to stop him would be the center, and at his angle he would probably foul. Worse, the center could open up the middle area or the area beneath the basket for a quick pass and an easy goal.

The offense should be made to bring the ball to the defense. If, for example, the offense sees the 2-1-2 zone weaknesses in the oval areas (Diagram 4), attacks them, and proceeds to get good open shots before your guards can slide

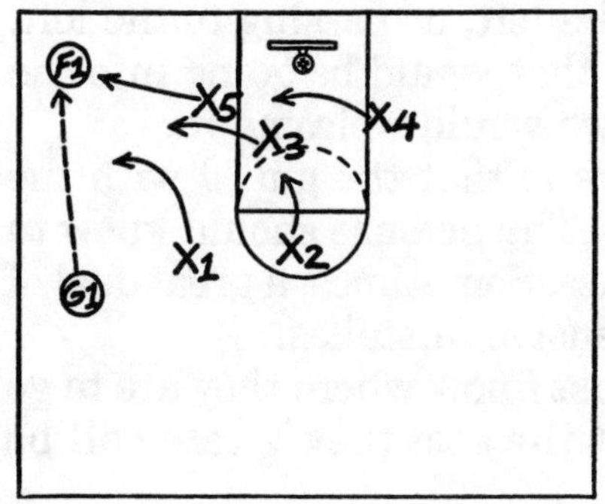

Diagram 3

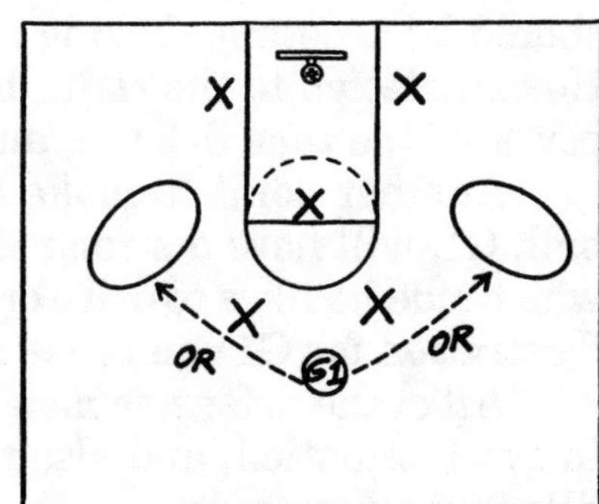

Diagram 4

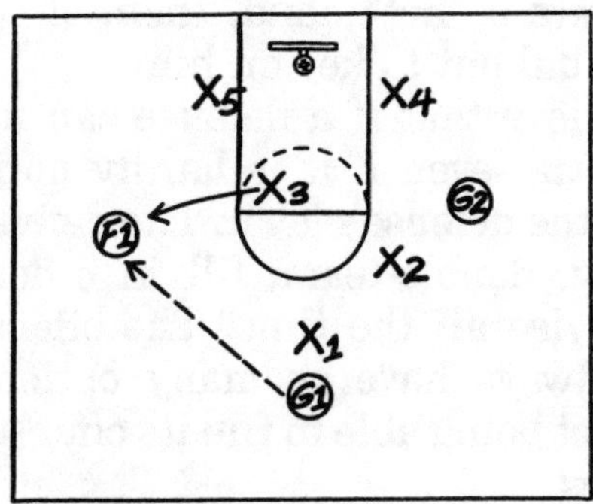

Diagram 5

over to cover, allow the offensive guard to pass to only one side. And, of course, the side left open should be the side with the weakest player in it. For example, the left side might be left open because of a player who has trouble driving to his left.

Slide X1 up to almost a point guard position. X2 will fall back and prevent a pass on that side to G2. The center, X3, will slide over and pick up F1 on the opposite side if he gets a pass (Diagram 5).

> **CAUTION: The point guard on defense *must not* let the guard with the ball drive around him and into the free-throw line area.**

The guard with the ball, G1, should be left with three choices, choices that the defense is waiting for. The options should be shooting, driving to the left, or passing to the left. He can also go to the right, but that would be going into the power of the zone defense, and we would welcome it.

Another point to make here is that the guard with the ball, G1, will have a strong side. The defense should know to which side he likes to drive or pass. Sometimes, a great deal of frustration for G1 can cause offensive mistakes.

All of the defensive men must know where they are to go in every situation, and also that the spot they vacate will be filled by a teammate.

Give the offensive man a shot from around 20 feet out with nothing more than a holler or a hand swung up. If the offensive man gets a "hot" hand, then, of course, you must send one individual out to key on him.

I firmly believe that if a defense can make the offense change its pattern—even if it is hardly noticeable—it's certainly a plus in the defense's favor. The defense knows that it will have to sag, double-team, fill in other positions, and generally improvise all the time. The offense, on the other hand, doesn't always have as many options and may get discouraged at not being able to run its offense. Then come the careless mistakes.

Of course, to have a good defense, goals must be set—not necessarily season goals but game goals, such as keeping the other team's high scorer under ten points for the game, not allowing more than ten field goals in a half, and making less than five fouls in a half.

Any goal is a good goal if it isn't out of your team's range. I prefer game goals instead of season goals for defense because a season goal would be based on past teams, and teams tend to have different personnel from one year to the next.

Heap praise on your ball players and you'll be surprised at how much they will do for you, or at least try to do.

7

The Rolling Zone

by Tom Dickman

Head Basketball Coach
Governor Thomas Johnson High School
Frederick, Maryland

In Tom Dickman's five years at the helm of Governor Thomas Johnson High School (Frederick, Maryland), the team has compiled a won-lost record of 107-42, with one state title (1975), one state runner-up (1978), and the Tri-State League Championships (1975, 1979).

Different basketball defenses have different primary objectives. Some are meant to cause turnovers, some to control tempo, and others are designed to confuse the offense. The *rolling zone* has one and only one purpose; to limit the points scored by our opponents by forcing bad shots, eliminating easy shots, limiting the number of shots, and reducing fouls.

Zone Responsibilities

In designing the rolling zone, I wanted to include player responsibilities that are not always included in the "standard" zones. These responsibilities, when accomplished, should prevent the ball from penetrating within ten feet of the basket. By performing these duties, we achieve two very important things that reduce the number of points scored against us:

1. We force the offense to shoot the low-percentage shot.
2. We keep out of shooting foul situations.

Moving with Purpose

One of the players' responsibilities is to move with purpose. The downfall of many zones is the assumption made by players that by merely being in their proper positions they are playing good defense. To overcome this "standing" zone, the rolling zone gives each player specific duties. Players must anticipate and move quickly to execute their duties. This anticipation prevents offenses from crushing our defense.

Contesting Shots

Another responsibility is to contest every shot from the five critical shooting points around the perimeter of the zone (Diagram 1). We take pride in getting a hand in the shooter's face in these critical areas. This distraction adds to the poor shooting percentage and low scoring of our opponents.

Knowing the Matching Principles

The final, general responsibility of the players is to know the matching principles of "blocking off." Many coaches believe that by playing a zone defense and forming the rebounding triangle, their teams will be able to defeat opponents on the board. I have found that this rebounding method is not always successful because defenders do not know exactly which offensive players they should be blocking off the boards. The rolling zone includes simple match-up rules that make the block-off puzzle easy to figure out. These matching principles allow us to initiate our fast break, with our players in their specific positions on every shot.

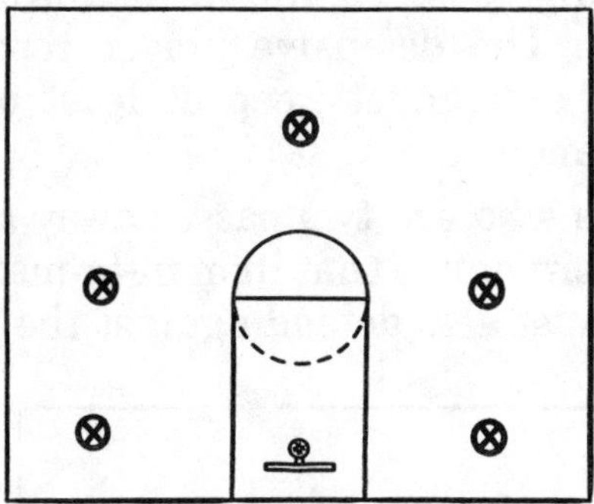

Diagram 1

Personnel

The personnel needed to play this zone are basically divided into two groups. Players 1 and 2 are the guards. They are interchangeable. Players 3, 4, and 5 are the forwards and center, also interchangeable. Quickness is a more important requisite than height in all aspects of the zone. A dominant, big player is therefore not a necessity.

Basic Rules

1. The defensive player guarding the man with the ball uses the traditional boxer stance. When they are in this particular defensive position, we make our players yell "Ball." If everyone knows who has the man with

the ball, we can match up more easily. The defender guarding the ball encourages the outside shot and discourages penetration.

2. *Front* all offensive players who take a low-post position. Deny this pass by playing directly between the ball and the low post. The defensive player must work constantly to stay in this fronting position. Fronting is the key to shutting off the inside game. It is the responsibility of 3, 4, and 5.
3. *Side* the high post. Again, we discourage any passes to this area. The defensive player responsible for the high-post area must keep at least one hand in the passing lane.
4. Defenders who are two passes away are in the "help" position, similar to that in man-to-man defense. These players must also defend against the lob pass.

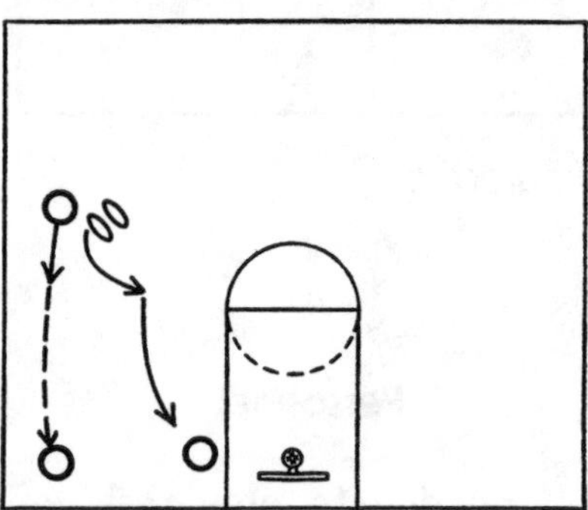

Diagram 2

5. The *roll* move is performed by 3, 4, and 5. This is the radical maneuver of the rolling zone. When either of the inside players must leave this position to cover a wing, this move is used on the resulting pass to the corner. This move is nothing more than a front pivot toward the ball, continuing on to front the low post (Diagram 2). Although this move seems risky, we have found that our players can roll to front the low post

quicker than they can coming from the lane. We also intercept many passes because we are coming right into the passing lane untouched.

6. Never give the baseline.
7. To prevent the penetrating pass, the four players who are not guarding the ball handler play with their hands up. This not only prevents passes, but it also discourages attempted passes.

The Defense

The original set of the rolling zone is a 23. We split the court in half by drawing an imaginary line from basket to basket (Diagram 3). The "regular side" is the side on which players 1 and 2 can defense the wing. The side on which the back line must defend the wing is the "roll side."

Player 1 takes the ball at the point. On the pass to the regular-side wing, player 2 plays the ball, 1 drops to side the high post, and 4 fronts the low post (Diagram 4).

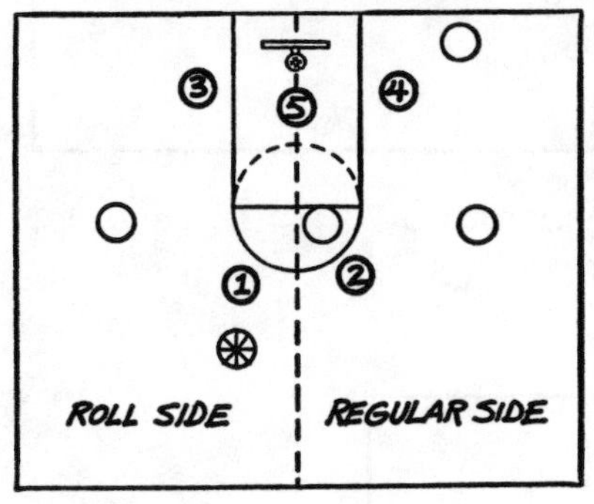

Diagram 3

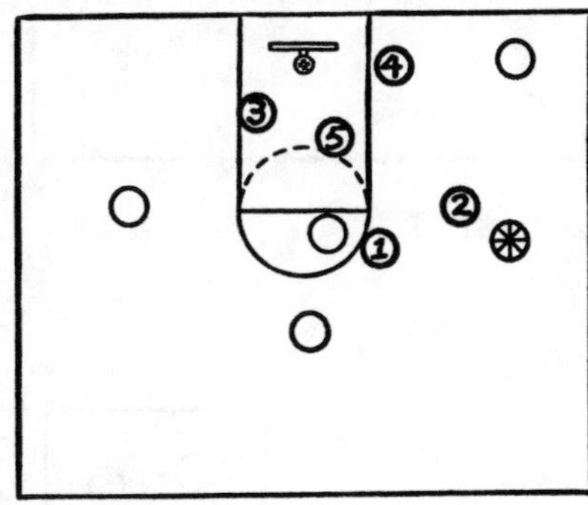

Diagram 4

On the subsequent pass to the regular-side corner, 4 plays the ball, 5 fronts the low post, and 2 drops to side the high-post area (Diagram 5).

On the pass to the wing from the regular-side corner, the defensive alignment is exactly the same as in Diagram 4.

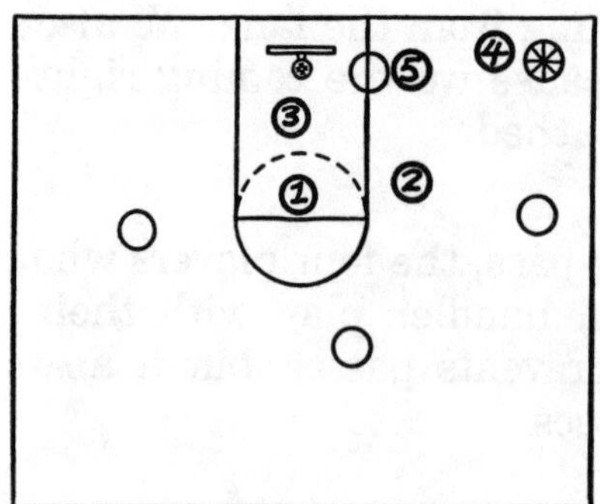
Diagram 5

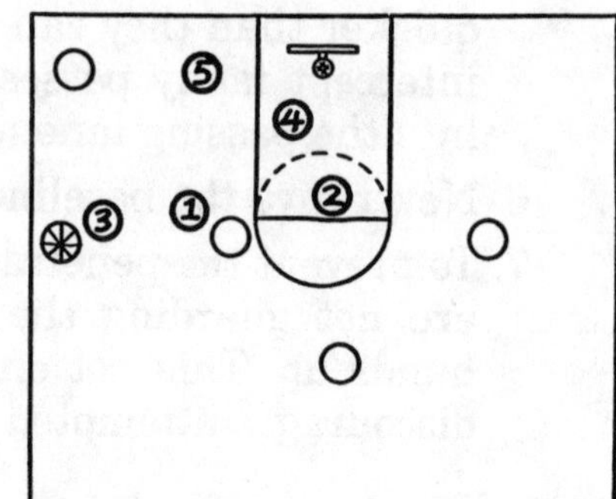
Diagram 6

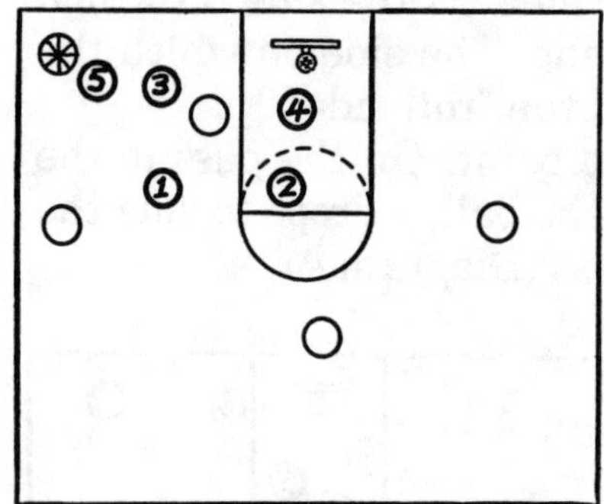
Diagram 7

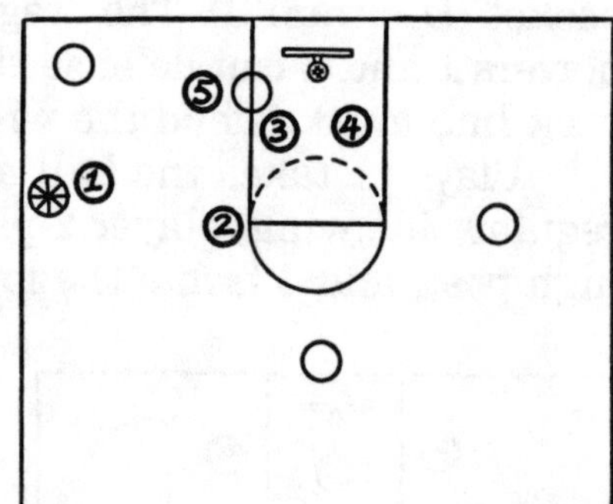
Diagram 8

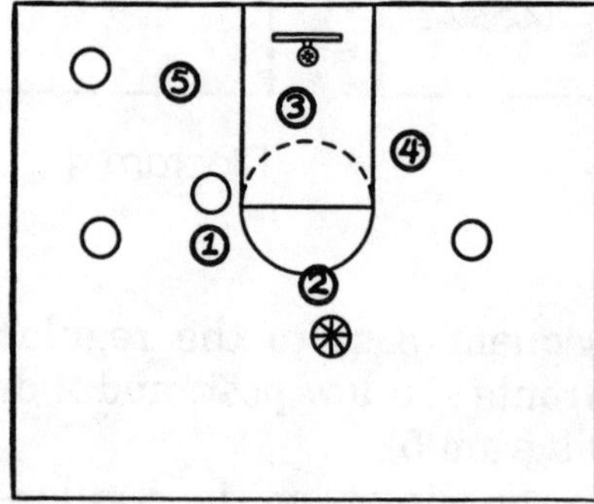
Diagram 9

On the pass from the regular-side wing to the point, the defense is exactly the same as in Diagram 3.

On the pass to the roll-side wing, 3 plays the ball, 5 fronts the low post, and 1 drops to side the high-post area (Diagram 6).

On the pass to the roll-side corner, the roll move becomes important (Diagram 7). Player 5 defenses the ball, 3 *rolls* to front the low post, and 1 drops lower to side the high-post area.

On the pass out of the roll-side corner, 1 plays the ball, 5 drops back to front the low post, and 2 sides the high-post area (Diagram 8).

On the next pass to the point, the sides reverse themselves (Diagram 9). Player 2 takes the ball, 1 anticipates a pass to the new regular-side wing, and 4 anticipates a pass to the roll-side wing.

8

Techniques for the 2-2-1 or "Y" Zone Press

by John Dougherty

Head Basketball Coach
St. Thomas Aquinas High School
Fort Lauderdale, Florida

John Dougherty is the head basketball coach at St. Thomas Aquinas High School (Fort Lauderdale, Florida). He has compiled a 120-70 won-lost record and during his career he has been named Coach-of-the-Year six times, and has won six district titles, three regional titles, and three state runners-up.

The full-court zone press is one of the most effective weapons in basketball today. At St. Thomas, and before that at Mary Immaculate, we used the "Y" press as our basic defense 32 minutes per game for the last six years.

If a coach decides to use a zone press, he must thoroughly study and understand two very simple zone press principles:

1. Court division
2. Areas of coverage

Court Division

In court division, divide the length of the court into five sections (Diagram 1). Allow a pass forward into the middle divisions of the court. We allow teams to pass the ball backward, but the ball must be kept out of the middle.

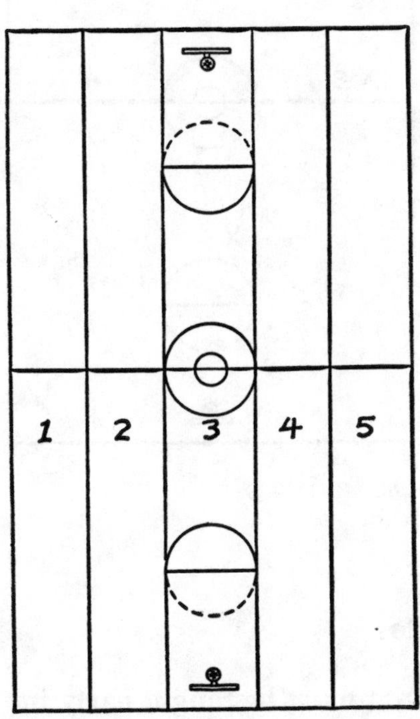

Diagram 1

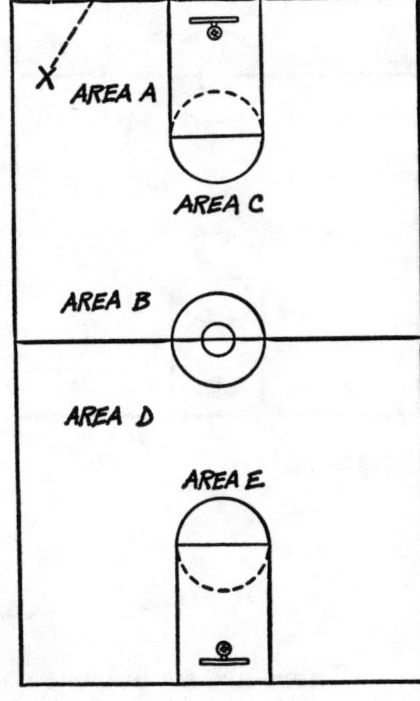

Diagram 2

Areas of Coverage

There are five basic areas of coverage (Diagram 2):

- The player with the ball after the inbounds pass has been made
- The trap area on the sideline where the ball is guided
- The area in the middle, forward of the ball
- The sideline area in front of the trap
- The basket area

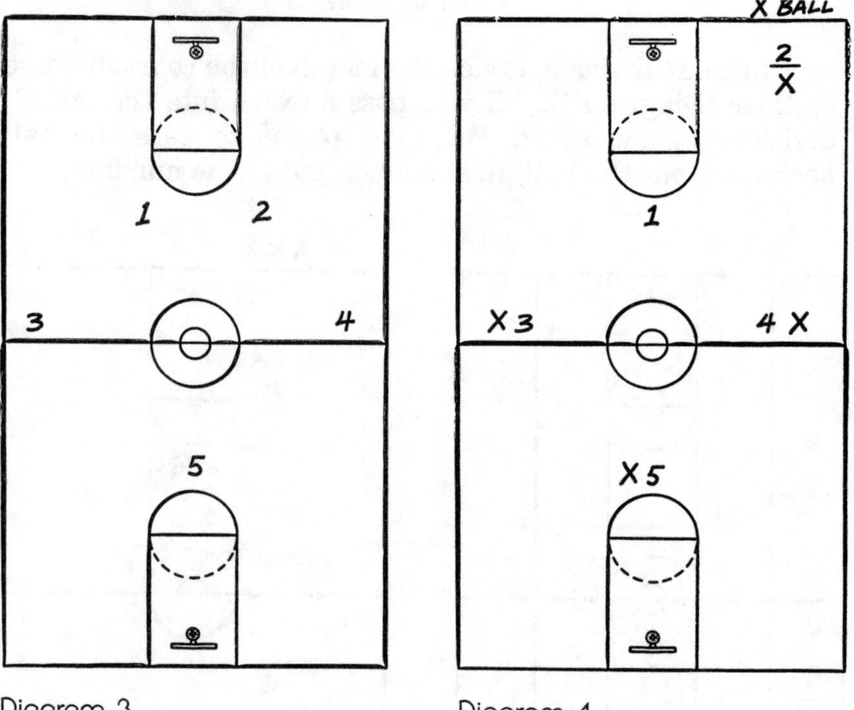

Diagram 3

Diagram 4

Basic Rules

There are some basic rules that must be taught early in the season if the press is to be effective:

1. Never allow the first inbounds pass with guards to go lower than the foul line and pinch to the middle. This does not apply if we are in our "up" position.
2. Never try to steal the ball. The press is designed for the opponents to make mistakes. Attempting to steal often results in fouls which negate the effectiveness of the press.
3. The rotation has to be followed. Regardless of the position of the ball, the areas of coverage must be filled.
4. The ball must always be pushed to the sidelines. Never allow it to go to the middle. (If the middle is penetrated, the effectiveness of the press is greatly reduced.)
5. The basket must be protected at all times.
6. When the ball is in front court, players drop back into their normal defense.

Basic Start of the Press

Our press is started in one of two ways. If we have just scored on any type of lay-up, fast break or otherwise, we call the "up" press (Diagram 3). Basically, this means a man-to-man press where we contest the first pass inbounds.

NOTE: Each player plays a man until the first pass is inbounds. Once the ball is in play, we revert back to our zone rotation.

If we score from a set pattern, our press is started as a zone immediately and we allow the first pass to come in uncontested (Diagram 4). The guards line up behind the foul line.

Start with Fundamentals

We teach our press initially by stressing the importance of excellent physical condition. We spend much of our practice time on physical conditioning and we have our players run sprints or line touches.

In regular practice, our players run from 20 to 40 line touches each day. Throughout the season, our players are kept in condition by this type of running. We have found our press to be especially effective at the end of the game when our opponents are tired. We then start teaching the fundamentals of man-to-man defense.

In our press there are many instances when our players find themselves in some type of man-to-man coverage. We immediately stress that the ball must be kept out of the middle, and start our players forcing the dribbler to the sideline immediately, without allowing him back into the middle. Also, we never allow our players to reach in for the ball or, when the ball is stopped, never to grab for it. The technique is to play tough defense, not to try to steal the ball.

Individual Responsibility

Guards

The two men who play guard positions must be in excellent physical condition with excellent speed. We use the guards to force the ball to one side or the other into the trap in or around the half-court area (Diagram 5). The off-guard has to fall back into the middle to cut off any passes to that area.

If the ball is passed backward to the other side, the off-guard becomes the forcer and moves over to keep the ball in the sideline (Diagram 6). The other guard rotates into the middle as a floater to play the next logical pass receiver in the middle.

NOTE: The most important thing for the guards to remember is that the ball must be kept out of the middle and the dribbler must be forced up the sideline into the trap.

Forwards

The two men who play forward positions must also be in good physical condition. They must be relatively quick and tough enough to stand and take a charge. We use the forwards to trap the ball on one side of the court or on the other.

Before the inbounds pass, the forwards have to pick up anyone breaking into the middle. Once the ball is passed inbounds, they revert to zone responsibilities. The forward on the ball side sets up the trap while the other forward initially covers the middle until the off-guard gets there and then drops back to protect the basket area (Diagram 7).

If the ball shifts and goes the other way, the basket-protecting forward comes back up to trap the ball and the former trapping forward rotates back to protect the basket.

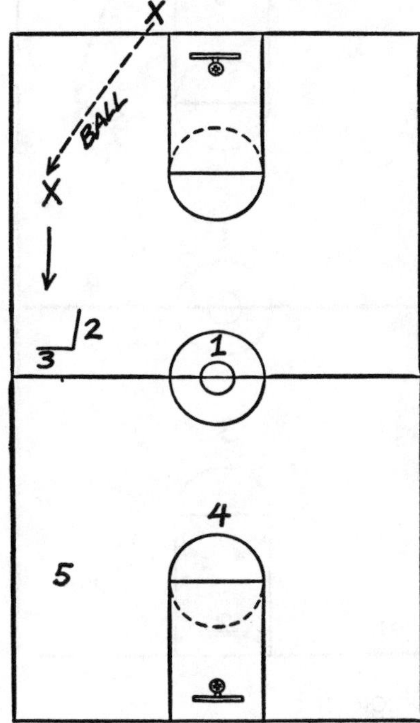

Diagram 5

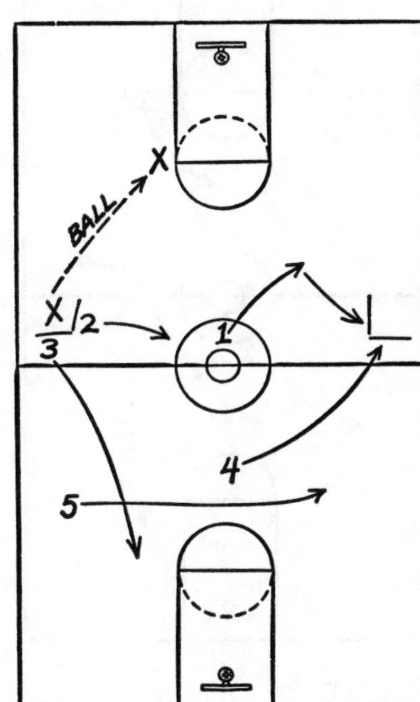

Diagram 6

The Rover

We call the back man in our press the "rover" because that's exactly what he must be. He must be your best athlete, extremely fast, have good lateral movement, and possess good basketball instincts. The rover has to cover the whole back half of the court. He rotates to the side to which the ball is passed in Diagram 8.

His responsibility is to take away the first long pass from the trapping area to the next man on the side on which the ball is moved. He does not have to worry about what is behind him—that is the off-forward's responsibility since he (the off-forward) has dropped back to protect the basket.

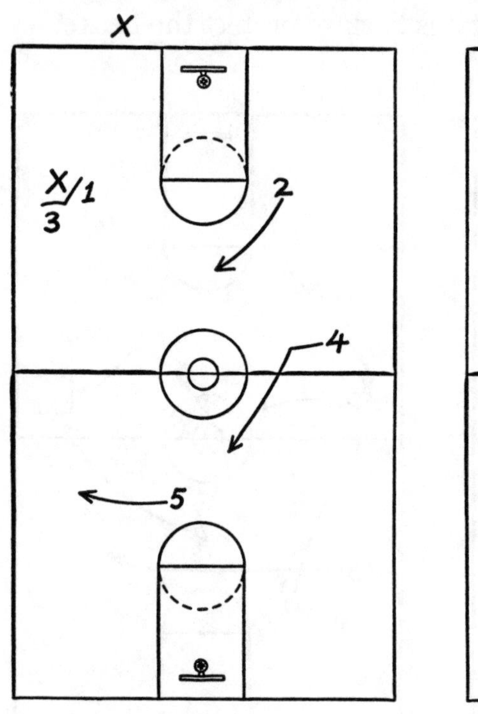

Diagram 7

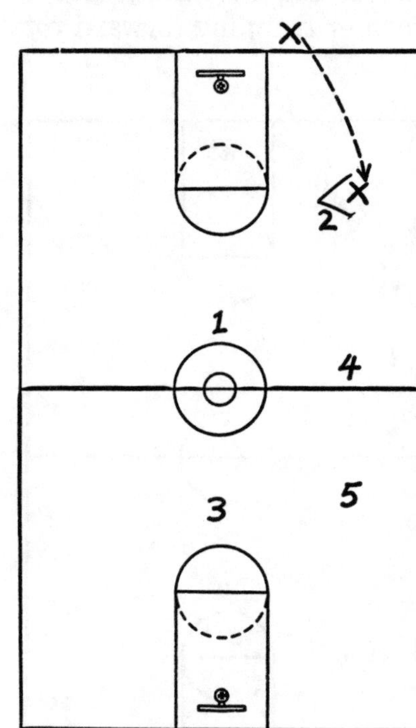

Diagram 8

Conclusion

The "Y" press is a devastating weapon. When used correctly, it can win many games for your team. You must remember that the press is not going to prevent the opposition from breaking it occasionally and scoring the easy lay-up from setting up their offense.

It has been our experience that when the team gets down on the floor and sets up, they are forced to set up near half-court, far away from where they would like to be. In this instance, we feel that the press has accomplished our goals. It has been our experience that even when our press does not seem to be effective, we may suddenly cause five or six straight turnovers.

Both coaches and players must have confidence in the press and must stick with it throughout the game. Patience is the key to the successful press. Eventually, your opponent will make the mistake you're hoping for, and we have found with pressing that mistakes—the other team's—come in large doses.

Again, caution your players to use discipline. Don't try to steal the ball. Needless fouls might result, demoralizing your team. The purpose of the press is to force the other team to make mistakes—and with patience this will happen.

9

The 1-1-2-1 Half-Court Zone Trap

by O. G. (Bid) Sanders

Head Basketball Coach
Santiam High School
Mill City, Oregon

In seven years as the head coach at Santiam High School (Mill City, Oregon), O. G. (Bid) Sanders has compiled a 114-27 record, with three conference championships, a conference co-championship, and the state title (Class A).

Our most effective pressure defense in the past has been the 1-1-2-1 half-court zone trap. At first, the trap confuses the offense and panic usually sets in. But if it is used too often, or for an extended period of time in one game, the offense will learn how to beat it.

The trap is best used in spurts with an alternate defense to keep the opponent off-balance. We might open with a man-to-man defense and allow the opponent to get used to putting the ball on the floor. Then we switch to the trap, possibly at the quarter. We make our opponent pass the ball while double-teaming the ball handler, and try to cut off his passing lanes.

NOTE: The trap is an exciting defense to watch if a coach has the personnel to run it properly. Both the players and the fans get excited when we are executing the trap properly. It can completely demoralize the opposing team, cause numerous turnovers, and create many fast break opportunities.

Description of Players

Guard X1 serves as the point man or chaser for the defense. He is the smaller of the two guards, has good lateral movement, is quick, and has lots of stamina.

His job is to force the offensive ball handler into the trap areas (as shown in Diagram 2). He attempts to force the ball to the sidelines, making the opponent dribble with his off hand. X1 will then team up with X3 or X4, depending on which side of the floor the ball is on. In this manner, they form a trap for the ball handler.

Guard X2 should be tall in order to front any high-post offensive center. He should possess the same qualities as X1, with the exception of height. X2 also teams with either X3 or X4 to form a trap on the ball.

Forwards X3 and X4 are the wing men for the trap. Their responsibility is to double-team with either X1 or X2 to form the trap on the sidelines. They also double-team with X5 to trap along the baseline or in the corners. Either X3 or X4 will cover the middle of the key area if X5 has pulled out to trap in the corner.

The center, X5, is usually the tallest and least mobile of the players in the trap defense. His area of coverage extends from the foul line to traps in either corner.

Executing the Trap

The basic set for the 1-1-2-1 half-court zone trap is shown in Diagram 1. X1 plays at the center of the half-court line. X2 is stationed at the top of the foul circle. X3 and X4 position themselves about five feet from the foul line extended. X5 shades just behind and in the center of the key, close under the basket.

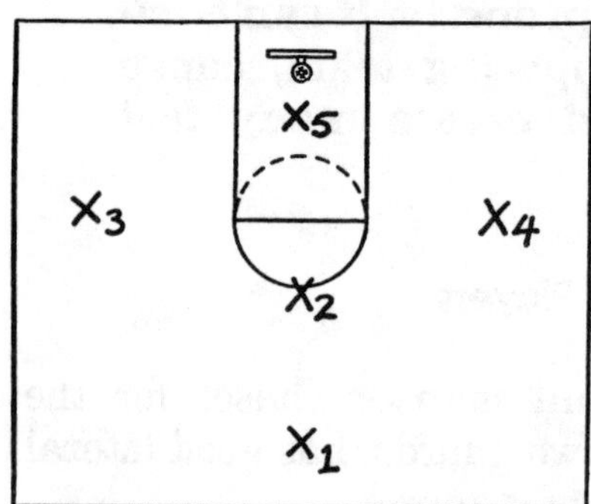

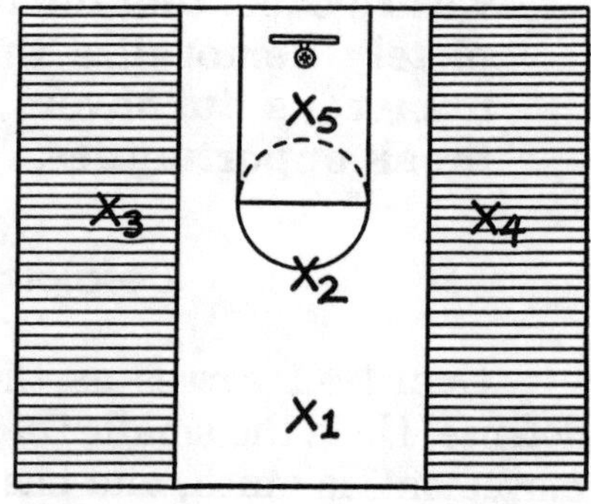

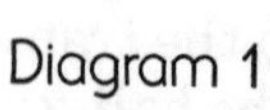
Diagram 1

Diagram 2

Diagram 2 depicts the main areas where the trap most frequently occurs. Diagram 3 shows the various directions of movement each man in the trap must follow. The trap is based on zone principles.

As the offense moves the ball just over half-court, X2 tries to force the ball handler in a certain direction toward the sidelines. If the ball handler passes to a wing position, X2 immediately comes out to help X4 trap, while X1 hustles to cover the top of the key. X5 moves in the direction of the ball, and X3 moves to cover under the basket (Diagram 4).

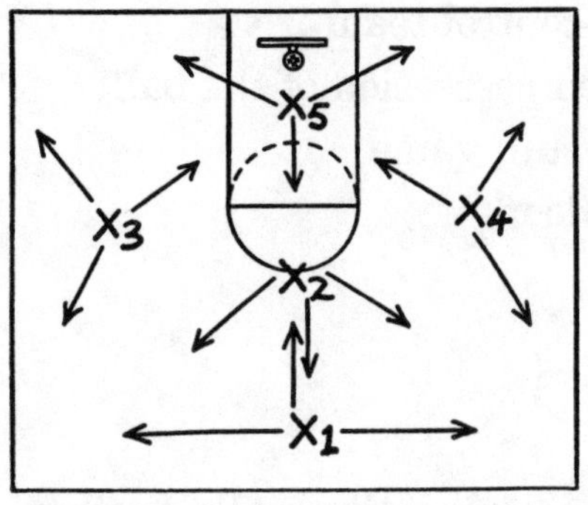

Diagram 3

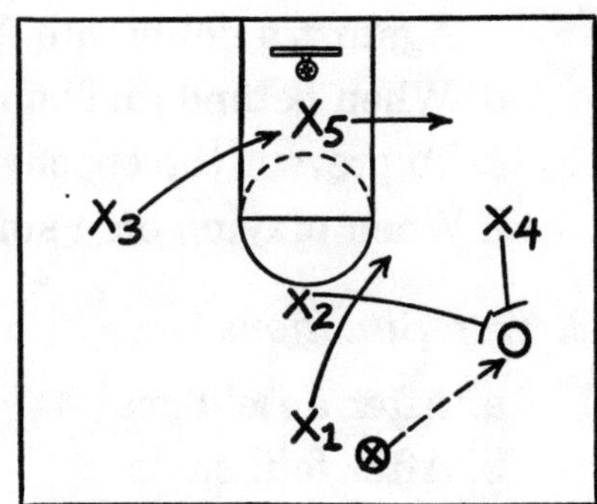

Diagram 4

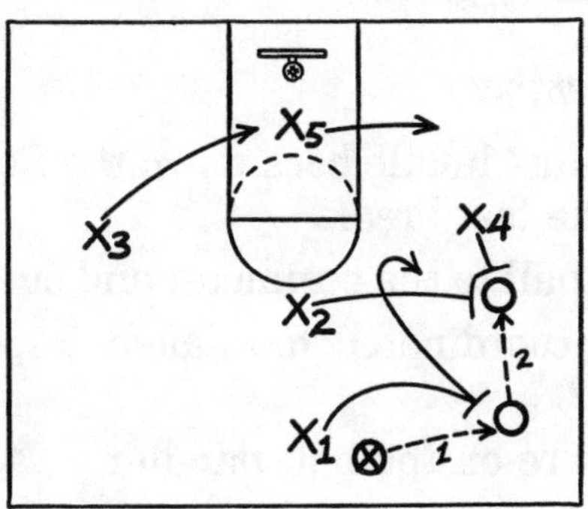

Diagram 5

If the ball is moved laterally by a pass just after passing half-court, X1 will follow and put pressure on the ball in that area. When the ball is then passed to a wing position, X2 comes out in a hurry to form a trap with X4. X1 moves rapidly to cover X2's vacated position. X5 and X3 move to the ball side to protect the key area (Diagram 5).

GUIDELINES

A. Use of the Trap

a. Against poor ball-handling teams
b. Against a tall, slow team

c. Against a deliberate, ball-control team
d. When behind and you need possession of the ball
e. To prevent the opponent's stall game
f. When playing on a small floor

B. Trap Situations

a. After a field goal
b. After foul shots
c. For short intervals of time alternating with another defense
d. For the entire game

C. Points to Remember

a. Defense must hustle back down the floor to set up and prevent the fast break.
b. Force the ball to the perimeter and out of the key area.
c. Use good coordinated movement, especially between X1 and X2.
d. Put pressure on the ball handler.
e. Don't reach and grab—steals will come automatically.
f. The trap is used mainly to keep the offense from running their own offensive game.
g. Players not pressuring the ball must stay alert and protect the passing lanes.
h. Players must be in excellent condition.
i. Players must have faith in the defense and in each other.

If the ball is advanced to the corner, X4 continues down the sideline and traps with X5 in the corner. X3 moves all the way over to protect the basket in the low-post area. X2 moves to a position halfway along the key area. X1 still covers the top of the key but shades to the ball side (Diagram 6).

NOTE: All of the defensive players face toward the ball side and put pressure on the ball handler and his passing lanes.

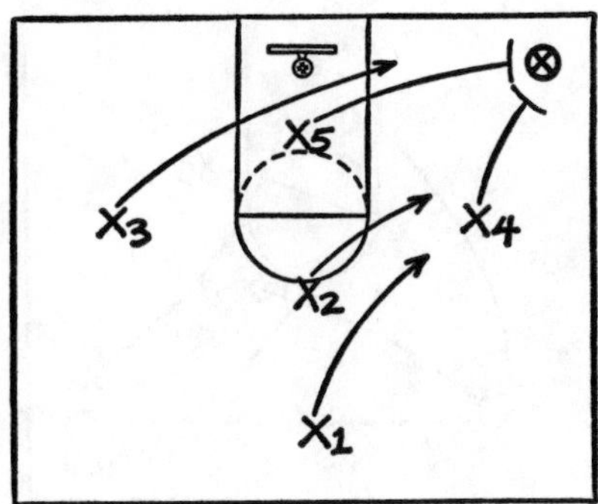

Diagram 6

Special Situations

Sometimes, after the ball has been advanced just beyond half-court, a pass is made to a wing position and then thrown cross-court to the opposite wing man. If this happens, X2 and X4 trap while X1 guards the top of the key. If the cross-court is not intercepted, X1 then moves out to the opposite wing and traps with X3. X2 again protects the top of the key. X5 and X4 shift to the ball side to protect the key (Diagram 7).

The point guard, X1, always follows the dribbler by forcing in a certain direction. As the dribbler gets deeper, X4 comes up to trap with X1. X2, X5, and X3 all shift to the ball side (Diagram 8).

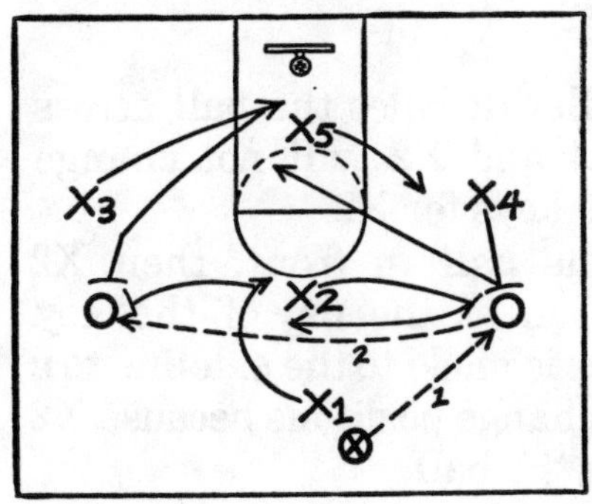

Diagram 7

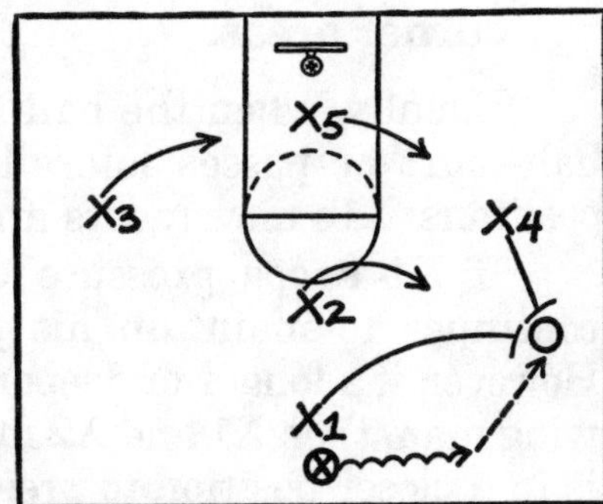

Diagram 8

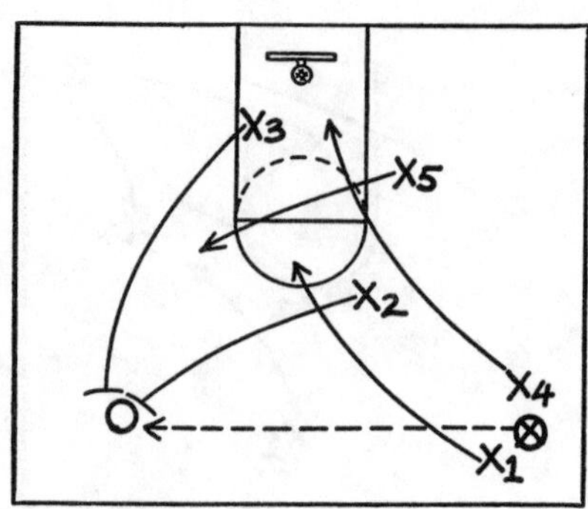

Diagram 9

If the dribbler stops and fires a cross-court pass, X2 rushes out to help trap on the sideline with X3. X1 moves to cover the top of the key. X4 and X5 move to guard the key and shade to the ball side (Diagram 9).

The Two Guards

The real key in running the trap effectively is the movement of X1 and X2. They are constantly shifting positions to trap and to cover the top of the key respectively.

IMPORTANT: The top of the key area must be guarded at all times in order to force the offense away from the middle and into the side or corner areas.

Usually, when the ball handler dribbles the ball across half-court or passes laterally, X1 and X2 will not change positions. X1's movements are the keys for X2.

If X1 keeps pressure on the ball in front, then X2 continues to maintain his position at the top of the key. However, if a longer or deeper pass is made to the sideline to a wing man, then X1 and X2 must change positions because X2 is in a closer position to pressure the ball.

Other Considerations

In addition to the effective movements of the two point guards, the defense must really hustle down the court to set up the trap against a fast-breaking ball club. Any loafing by any one player against a fast-moving opponent will spell disaster for the trap.

The trap also becomes more effective on a small floor or against a poor ball-handling team. In these two instances, we have used the trap to our advantage in numerous games.

A weakness of the trap, even though at first it may not be apparent, is the middle of the key from the foul line to the basket. For this reason, the trap should always try to keep the offense from penetrating the key area and to force the opponent to pass the ball around the perimeter of the court.

Part Two

PRESSES

10

The Adjustable Area Man-to-Man Press

by Burrall Paye

Head Basketball Coach
William Fleming High School
Roanoke, Virginia

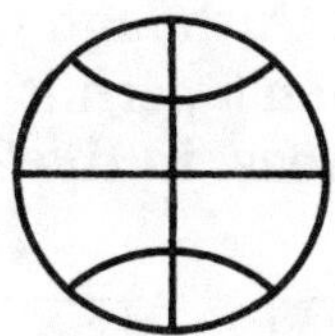

In Burrall Paye's 21 years of coaching, he has built up an impressive won-lost record of 327-72. He has been the head coach at William Fleming High School (Roanoke, Virginia) for the past three years. Coach Paye has won six of eight city championships, 12 district, and four regional titles. He has won one state title (1974), and has been named Coach-of-the-Year 22 times. Coach Paye has authored four books for the Parker Publishing Company: *Winning Power of Pressure Defense in Basketball, Secrets of the Passing-Dribbling Game Offense, Coaching the Full-Court Man-to-Man Defense, Complete Coaching Guide to Basketball's Match-Up Zone Defense.*

My philosophy of defensive basketball may be summed up in one word: *pressure*. We begin everything off a man-to-man pressure base, and we devise defensive stunts for every team we face. I'll now discuss one of the stunts that we use frequently during the season, the adjustable man-to-man press. This press is unique because our opponents determine what our press will be like.

This press is man-to-man unless the offense isolates to let their best dribbler attack it; then it becomes a zone press. The zone press is a 2-2-1 or 3-1-1, depending on the original backcourt alignment of the attackers. Diagrams 1 and 2 show the basic defense from the 2-2-1 zone press. Diagram 3 shows the basic 3-1-1 zone press. Although our press is primarily a man-to-man press that won't permit the isolation move, we assign our players zone areas, in the 2-2-1 press (Diagram 1).

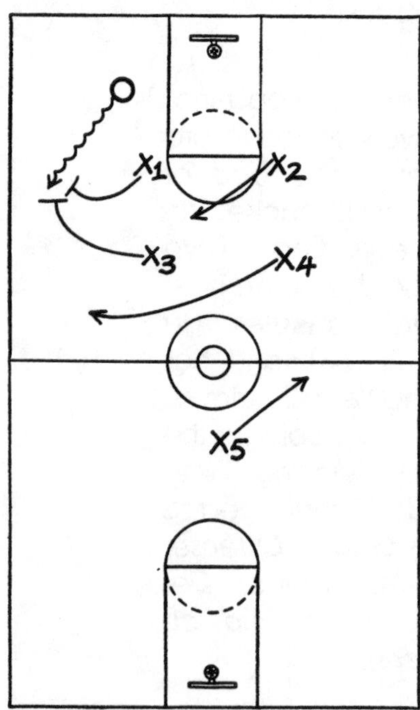

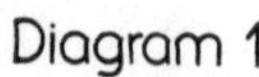
Diagram 1

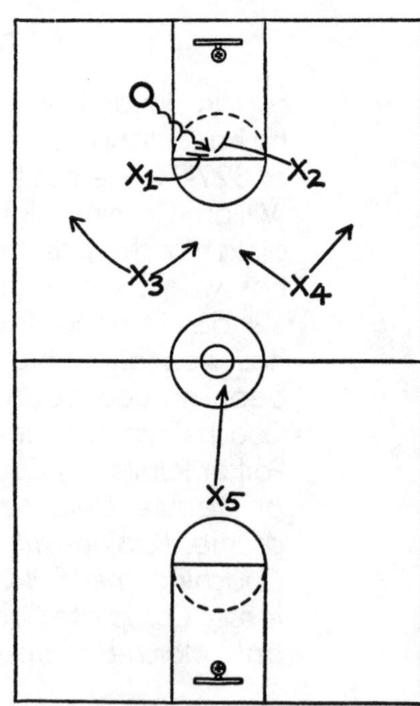

Diagram 2

From the 2-2-1 zone position, we initiate our press, with X1 covering the first man on the left side of the court and X2

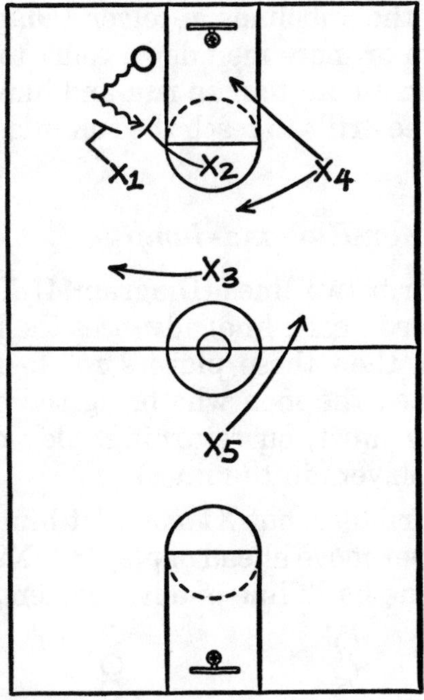

Diagram 3

guarding the man who throws the ball inbounds (Diagram 2). Should the ball be thrown in on the right side of the court, X2 would get the receiver and X1 would get the out-of-bounds passer.

> **NOTE: If there is a third man in the back court, the forward opposite the throw-in receiver would pick up this third man, and X1 and X2 would still perform the same tasks. In this case, the defensive forward on the side of the throw-in would become the short safety in the 3-1-1 zone press.**

Offense Determines Press

Once the ball is passed inbounds, the offense tells us which press to run. If the attackers start clearing out, we immediately run the 2-2-1 or 3-1-1 zone press, with a quick double-team on the inbounds receiver (Diagram 3). If the offense keeps two or more men down court to help bring the ball up, we stay in a man-to-man run-and-jump press. We use the following three drills to teach the run-and-jump press and shooting the gap.

Drill One: Two-Man Run-and-Jump

1. Players form two lines (Diagram 4). The offense (the first player in each line) advances the ball down court and back; then these players rotate from offense to defense (i.e., the men who bring the ball down court offensively must, on returning, play defense against the next players in the lines).
2. Player 1 dribbles, but X1 won't let him outside. Player 2 may never move ahead of player 1. X2 may never fall beneath the ball's line of advancement.

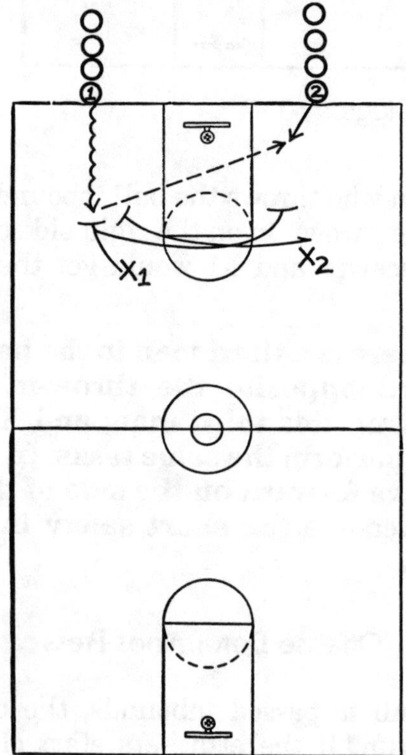

Diagram 4

3. Whenever he desires, X2 may run directly at 1, while X1 forces 1 inside. If 1 continues his dribble, he must charge X2 or veer outside. If he veers outside, X1 continues his pressure and X2 helps. If 1 picks up the ball to pass to 2, X2 tries to deflect it, while X1 races to cover 2. We continue this run-and-jump the length of the court and back. If X1 and X2 steal the ball, they fast break. If 1 and 2 cross, X1 and X2 switch, giving the impression of a zone press.

Drill Two: Three-Man Run-and-Jump

1. Players form three lines (Diagram 5). The offense advances the ball down court and back; then the players rotate from offense to defense.
2. If 2 (the player in the center) is dribbling, he must be going toward 1 or 3. In either case, it's a two-man run-and-jump (Drill 1). However, if 1 or 3 is dribbling, we force him to the inside, and run our three-man run-and-jump.
3. For purpose of discussion, let's say that 1 drives to the inside. As 1 drives inside, X2 races toward 1, double-teaming with X1 until 1 puts both hands on the ball. This is X1's cue to race hard to cover 3. Meanwhile, X3 has shot the gap between 1 and 2 for the interception. Even if the pass is completed, we are still in a man-to-man press: X1 on 3, X2 on 1, and X3 on 2. If the offense should start clearing out, we would still be in a position to run the 3-1-1 zone press. When using this drill, the coach should require that the two offensive men without the ball stay behind the ball's line of advancement. That not only expedites teaching—it permits more running and jumping per possession. This is important because time is of utmost value for a coach.

Drill Three: Three Defenders/Two Attackers

1. Players form two lines (Diagram 6). The offense advances the ball down court and back. X3 starts at safety on the way down court, and X1 starts at safety

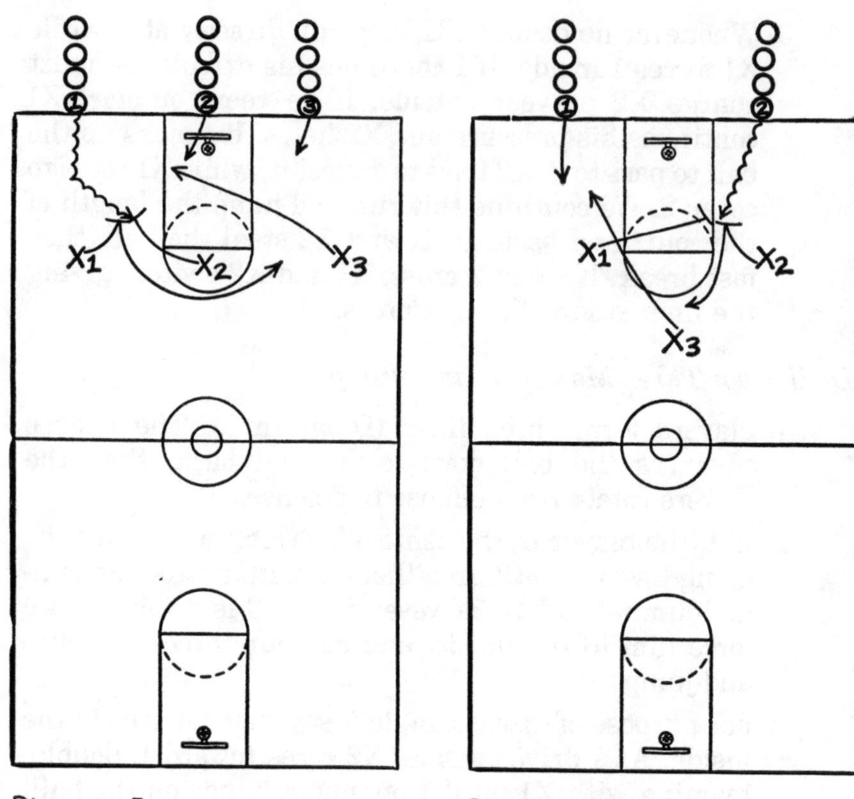

Diagram 5

Diagram 6

on the way back. X2 is the first safety when the players rotate, after returning from down court.

2. X1 and X2 run and jump, while X3 shoots the gap. After X1 and X2 stop 2's dribble, X2 drops and becomes the new short safety. He waits to shoot the gap on the next run-and-jump.

Rotation

If the defense is to be a zone press, the front four rotate as shown in Diagrams 1 and 3. This leaves the deep safety, X5, to concentrate on stealing errant, long lob passes, while the front four concentrate on pressing.

The front four's rotation can create the illusion of a man-to-man press. Couple this with the rotation on a cutter, and the defense can even confuse offenses that run the most sophisticated attacks.

The rotation on a give-and-go cutter is shown in Diagram 7. X2 covers the ball handler (2) while 1 tries a give-and-go cut. X1, who sagged toward the ball, goes with 1, preventing a return pass that would break the press. X3 rotates to the area vacated by X1, and X1 covers the area left open by X3.

If it was a clear out by 1 for 2, X3 and X2 would double-team the ball. If 2 began dribbling, X3 would run at him, activating the three-man run-and-jump between X1, X2, and X3. X4 would prevent any penetrating downcourt pass.

If 1 runs a backdoor cut, breaking far behind X1, then X1 would release him to X3 and return to his original area, ready to run and jump or zone press, whichever is applicable.

A coach could activate drill three above during a game to prevent an opponent from attacking with two offensive men. The defense can easily bring down a forward, the one opposite

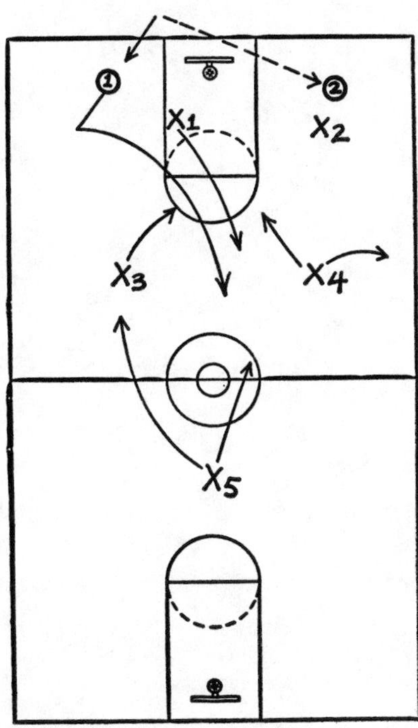

Diagram 7

the throw-in receiver, and run a three-man run-and-jump against two attackers, with a two-man tandem on their defensive end of the floor.

To vary the effective use of the press, a coach could have X1 and X2 front the first two receivers to delay the inbounds pass (five seconds violation) or to steal it. The passer cannot throw a lob over X1 or X2 without X3 or X4 intercepting. The defense could permit X3 or X4 to face-guard the third potential receiver and have tight pressure on all potential receivers; or if the offense chooses to attack with only two guards, X1 and X2 could double-team the single inbounds receiver. The defense could, if it was strategically beneficial, allow X1 to pressure the passer, bring up X3 as a wing defender, and create the impression of a 1-2-1-1 zone press.

The coach could also drop this defense to three-quarter or half-court and be equally effective. The defenders can alter the amount of pressure applied on the ball handler, thereby either speeding up the game or slowing it down offensively.

11

The Half-Court Zone Press Defense

by Ed Beyer

Head Basketball Coach
Hillsboro High School
Hillsboro, North Dakota

Ed Beyer has been the head basketball coach at Hillsboro High School (Hillsboro, North Dakota) for 20 years, with a 340-113 won-lost record. Coach Beyer has taken his squad to the state tournament eight times and won the Class B championship in 1973, 1974, and 1977.

The half-court zone press is a defense that every good basketball team should be able to play effectively. There are many different types of half-court zone presses, including a 1-3-1, a 1-2-2, and a 3-2 zone press. The basic alignment of the players in each of these formations is not as important as the shifts that they make with the ball in different positions on the court.

I feel that too many coaches use the half-court zone press only as a last-ditch attempt to catch up at the end of a ball game. Actually, there are many other situations when this defense can be an asset to your team.

Half-Court Situations

Some of the situations in which the half-court zone press can be effective are the following:

1. As a surprise defense whenever you want to change the momentum of the other team or need a few quick baskets to get back into a game.
2. At the end of a game, when your team is trailing, you will have to apply some pressure to get the ball back and make points. Too many times, teams stick to the basic man-to-man press when they do not have players who can press man-to-man effectively. It is a lot easier to use the zone press if you have slower ball players.
3. At the beginning of a game, or at any time during the game, when you are facing a team with guards who like to dribble the ball a lot. It is a very effective defense against a team with one really good shooter who likes to handle the ball a lot and takes many of his team's shots.

NOTE: I am going to cover one type of half-court zone defense that may be a little different from the one most coaches are using.

Personnel

Diagram 1

Diagram 1 shows the basic alignment of the players

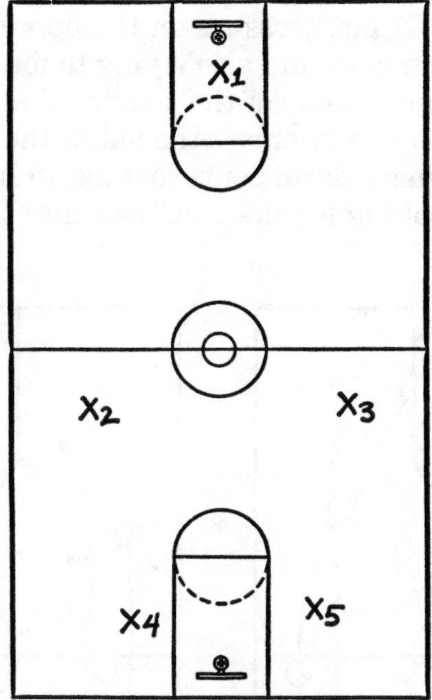

Diagram 1

before the ball is thrown inbounds by the opposition. X1 should be your quickest guard, and he should be released to bother the opposition guards when they are trying to get the ball inbounds. X2 and X3 should be your other guard and your shortest, quickest forward. They should line up about six feet on the other side of the ten-second line. X4 and X5 should be your pivot man and your largest forward. They should line up about even with the free-throw line, or closer to the basket.

Bothering the Opposition

Diagram 2

In Diagram 2, we see that X1 should bother the opposition's guards as much as possible as they bring the ball down the court. Too many teams who use the half-court press do not put enough pressure on the opposing guards. Many times they come down, stop their dribble, and just wait for their teammates to get set up in the proper positions to attack the press.

By letting X1 put pressure on the opposing guards, you are keeping them busy and also trying to force them to bring the ball down the outside of the court. X2 and X3 should be ready to move up and intercept the ball if the forwards on the opposing team move down court looking to help out. X4 and X5 should be looking for the long pass into the basket area.

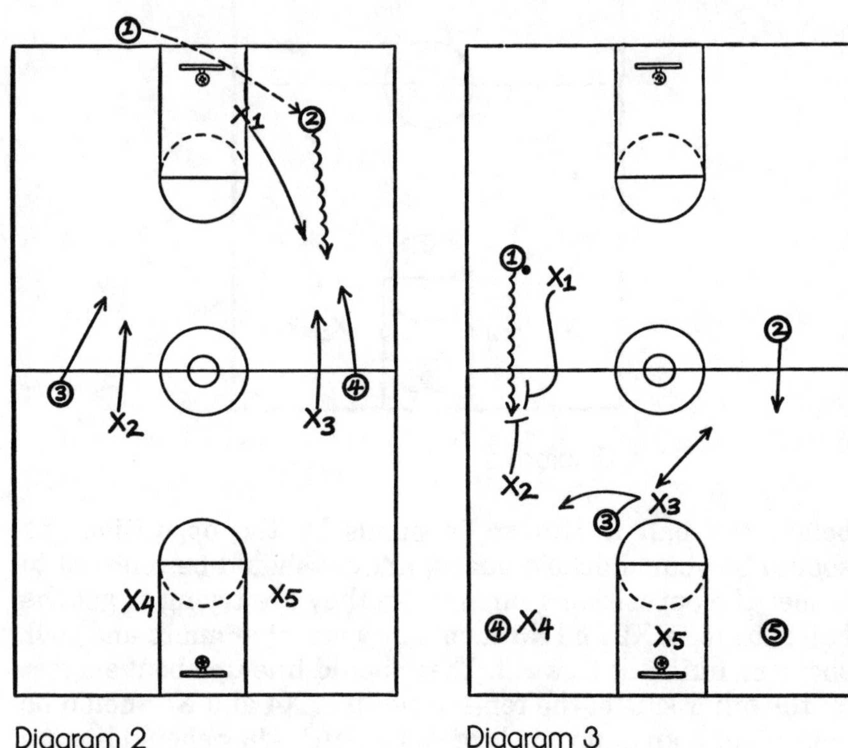

Diagram 2

Diagram 3

Defensive Positioning

Diagram 3

Diagram 3 shows the positioning of the defensive players when one of the guards is being trapped out by the ten-second line. X1 and X2 are putting the trap on 01. X3 should move over into the middle of the court and look for anybody in this area. This is one of the main areas used most frequently by the attacking team.

X3 should also look for the steal on a return pass to 02, but it is more important that he try and plug up the middle area. If he sees that 01 is in trouble in the trap, he should look for the steal of the pass back to 02. X4 should move over and look for the pass to 04, but it is not too important for him to always go for the steal in that situation. If 04 gets the ball out by the sideline, he's not going to hurt you from that position.

X5 should move over into the center of the lane but not come too far across, because, if he does, the attacking team can throw the ball cross-court and get a cripple lay-up on the weak side. This is one area where many teams get hurt when they run a half-court zone press.

Diagram 4

If the pass goes from 01 into the middle to 03, X4 and X5 should remain back on both sides of the lane and not get too far from the basket. X3 or the weakside wing man should try to come up from behind and slap the ball away from 03 if he gets the ball in the middle. Overcommitment by X4 and X5 will many times give the attacking team an easy lay-up.

Shifting Positions

Diagram 5

Diagram 5 shows the movement of the ball players as the ball is reversed to the opposite guard on the other side of the

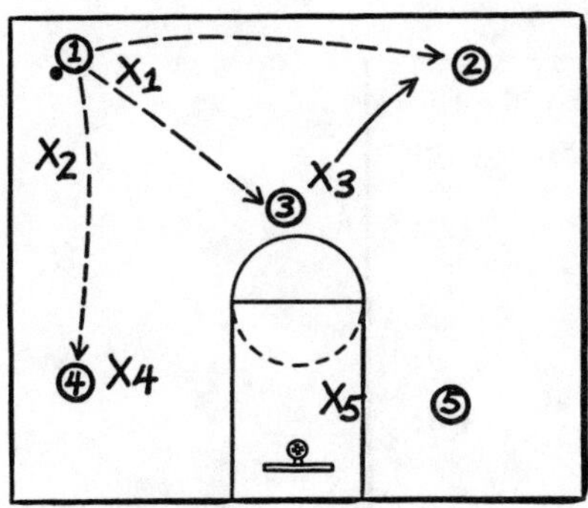

Diagram 4

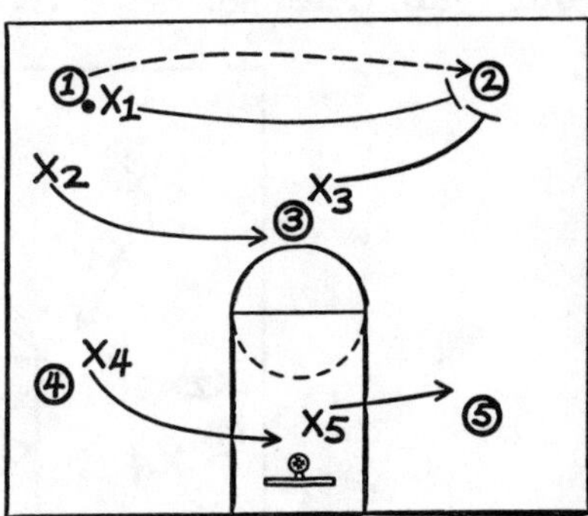

Diagram 5

court. X1 leaves his position, guarding 01. He moves over and sets the trap on 02. X3 leaves the middle area and goes out and sets the trap on 02. X2 then moves from his position to the middle area, where he tries to plug up any pass attempted there. X5 moves from the middle of the lane out toward the sideline, looking for the easy interception, but he should not be too eager to overcommit himself. X4 moves into the middle of the lane.

Diagram 6

Diagram 6 shows the positioning of the ball players when the ball is advanced to one of the opposing forwards on the side of the court. X1 moves down into the middle area, where he looks for the pass either to 03 or back to 01. X2 double-teams the ball in the corner with X4. X4 must make sure that he doesn't give 04 the baseline on defense.

X5 moves far across the lane and plays anybody in that area man-to-man. X3, the weakside wing man, moves all the way down to the weak side of the lane, where it is his responsibility to rebound any shots on the weak side.

NOTE: We continue to chase the ball until the other team takes a shot or we make a steal.

This is one method of playing a half-court zone press defense that is not the all-out gambling type played by some teams, which may often get beaten on the weak side and give up easy lay-ups. If used properly, it can add a great deal to your team defense.

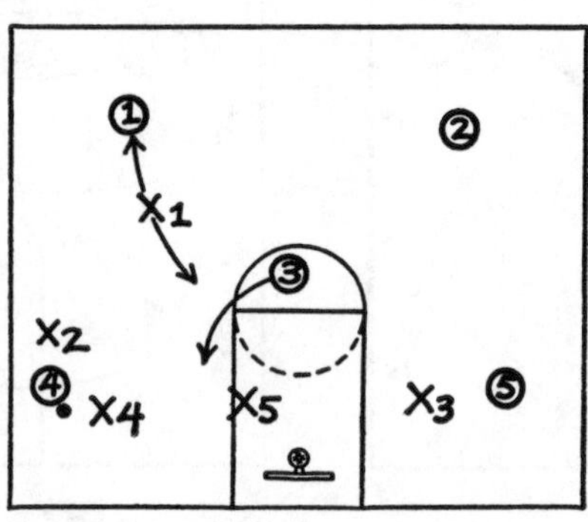

Diagram 6

12

Developing the Full-Court Pressing Game

by Jerry LaRoque

Former Head Basketball Coach
Three Forks High School
Three Forks, Montana

Jerry LaRoque retired from his head coaching position at Three Forks High School (Three Forks, Montana) in 1978. In his last five years of coaching, Jerry compiled a 102-31 record, with four trips to the state tournament and one state title.

Every coach must have a defensive system that he believes in, that is successful for him, and that he can sell to his players. For me this system is a full-court zone press and a half-court zone.

In order to develop the correct techniques to press at the varsity level, the groundwork to build upon is laid at the freshmen and junior varsity levels. Both of these teams press man-to-man for the entire season. They use a free-lance man-to-man offense depending upon the fast break and baskets after turnovers created by the press for the major part of the offense.

We teach only one very simple offense to be used against all half-court zones. This enables us to spend the major portion of practice time on our full-court press and on teaching the basics of the half-court, man-to-man "help" defense. The purpose of these two teams is to prepare the players for eventual varsity play. It appears to be wasted time and energy to teach these teams an offensive pattern that they may never use again as they move up. Even the varsity may change parts of its offense from year to year depending on personnel. It is better, therefore, to concentrate on phases of the game that will never change: defense, rebounding, and the other fundamentals. This article deals primarily with the drills that are used to teach the man-to-man pressing techniques that we desire at the freshmen and junior varsity levels.

Wave Drill

Our first drill is the wave drill. Its purpose is to teach the correct defensive body position. The players form four lines at one end of the court (Diagram 1). The coach stands at the same end of the court, with the first four players out front facing him.

On a given signal, these players slide diagonally down the court to the opposite end, changing directions on the coach's arm signal. Each time the players change directions, they must come to a momentary stop and bend their legs to touch their hands to the floor. They must keep their backs straight and heads up looking at the coach. Touching the floor is intended to force the players into a good defensive crouch.

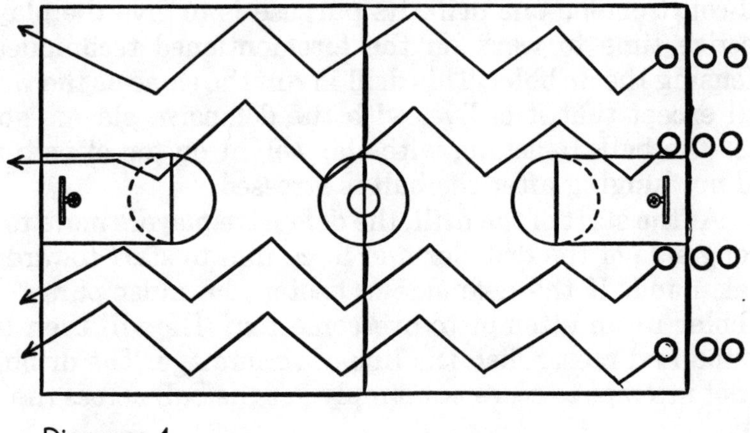

Diagram 1

Weave Drill

The next progressive drill is the traditional weave drill. The purpose of the drill is to teach defensive body position in relation to the dribbler. The court is divided into three lanes and the players are divided into three groups. The players pair up, with one player dribbling the ball and the other playing defense.

The dribbler does not try to beat his man but simply dribbles down the floor, weaving from one side of his lane to the other side. The defensive player must get out in front and turn the dribbler, stepping out-of-bounds if necessary to cut him off. It is stressed that the hand closer to the dribbler is kept out in front to prevent the dribbler from crossing over with the ball in front of the defensive player. We are hoping to get the dribbler to reverse pivot so that later on in games we can double-team as he comes around. The defensive player is not to attempt stealing the ball, but should concentrate on moving his feet and maintaining body position.

Full-Court One-on-One Drill

After the basics are sufficiently mastered, we move to the full-court one-on-one drill. Its purpose is to give the players practice time to work on the forementioned techniques of defensing the dribbler. This drill is run the same as the weave drill except that it is live, with the defensive players going after the ball. Reaching with the weight on top of both feet and not lunging after the ball is stressed.

At the start of the drill, the defensive players move to the strong side of the dribbler and force him to start toward his weak hand. If the defender is beaten, he must pursue the dribbler in an attempt to overcome him. He will then turn around and reestablish the line of scrimmage. The dribblers do not attempt to score but simply get the ball across the end line.

Three-on-Three Drill

From learning to play the dribbler one-on-one, we move next to pressuring the inbounds pass. As shown in Diagram 2, this is a three-on-three drill. The defender covering the man who is passing the ball inbounds will drop off to play on the free-throw line or deeper, depending on where other offensive players are located. The two defenders guarding the two inbounds players front their men and mid-point with their eyes, seeing both their man and the ball. They use a normal forcing stance. The defender on the free-throw line must read the throw-in and intercept any pass that goes over the heads of his two teammates. If he cannot intercept and the pass is completed, then he must automatically switch and take the man with the ball while his teammate takes the player passing the ball inbounds.

Each trio of defenders goes five times in a row on defense to see how many turnovers they can cause. The offense will attempt to get the ball across the half-court line. If they succeed, the defenders will hurry back and defend against the next three in line.

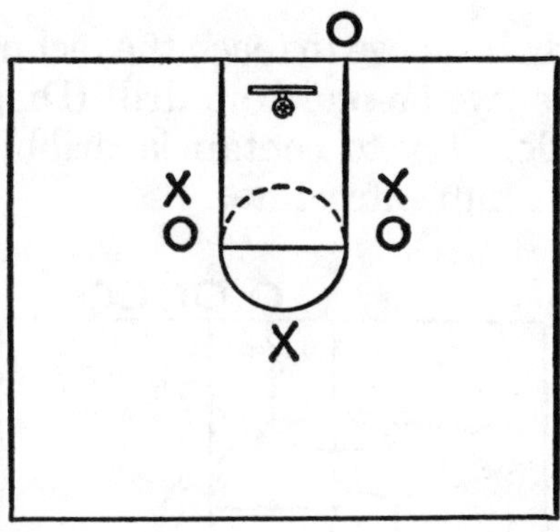

Diagram 2

55 Full-Court Hatchet

The final drill used is the 55 full-court "hatchet." Its purpose is to practice all of the techniques in the man-to-man full-court press and half-court "help" defenses. This is a five-on-five drill where each team is given the ball five times in a row. The defenders will pressure the inbounds pass and then attempt to keep the offensive team from scoring.

The objective for the players is to see which team can keep the other from scoring the most times out of five tries. If the defenders intercept or get a defensive rebound, they will fast break to their own end and try to score quickly. If the defensive team scores or the offensive team gets the ball back, it counts as one turn and the offensive team will take the ball out-of-bounds again. After five turns with the ball, the two teams will switch around. The players are stopped at any time to point out a good defensive play or an error. Early in the season, when the offensive team takes the ball out-of-bounds, we have them hold the ball until the coach's signal. We want to check the defenders' positions and stance before the ball is put in play.

Two-on-One Trap Drill

During the last month of the season, we teach the 2-2-1 zone press to the junior varsity. They will also drop into a 2-3 zone. The main drill we use to teach the techniques of the zone press is a simple two-on-one trap drill (Diagram 3). In this drill, two defenders try to contain a dribbler, keeping him from crossing the half-court line.

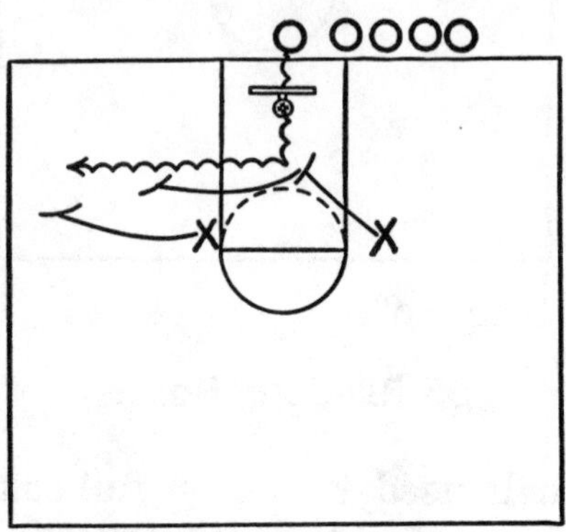

Diagram 3

The defender on the strong-hand side of the dribbler should move up to try to force the dribbler to his weak side. Once the dribbler has committed himself to going in one direction, it becomes the responsibility of the defender on that side of the court to keep him from progressing up the court. The other defender must close in from the side and prevent the dribbler from progressing back across the court.

We hope to force the dribbler to reverse pivot. If this happens, then the defender coming in from the side will try to steal the ball, tie up the dribbler, or at least get the dribbler to pick up the ball with his back to the rest of the floor. Aggressiveness is encouraged by the defenders.

Each pair of defenders will go either three or five times in a row. After the basics of the two-on-one trap are learned, the players can be broken up into smaller groups so that more opportunities can be provided to practice the techniques in a shorter amount of time. The major part of our time in teaching the zone press is spent in a full-court hatchet drill.

With this background of man-to-man and zone pressing for two years, the players have the basics necessary to become a good varsity pressing team. At the varsity level, however, the objective is to win. We view the season as a preparation for tournaments that come at the end of the season. With this in mind, a man-to-man press is emphasized at the beginning of the season and zone presses after the holiday break. Both the 2-2-1 and 1-2-1-1 zone presses are used.

In the 2-2-1, we do not pressure the inbounds pass and we do not pressure it in the 1-2-1-1 either. This forces the opposing team to adjust to different situations. As shown in Diagram 4, the different presses are geared by one of our front men. If he stays back, we will be in a 2-2-1. If he moves up to pressure the inbounder, then the player behind him will move up and front anyone in his area, as will the other wing, and we will be in the 1-2-1-1.

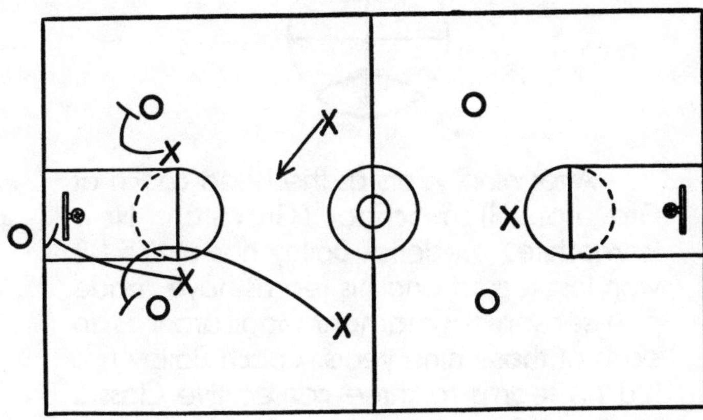

Diagram 4

13

The 1-3-1 Half-Court Press

by Frederick Bailey

Varsity Basketball Coach
Groveton High School
Groveton, New Hampshire

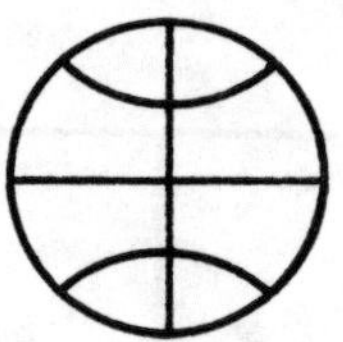

After nine years as the head coach at Groveton High School (Groveton, New Hampshire), Frederick Bailey has a 175-33 won-lost record and his teams have made post-season tournament appearances in each of those nine years. Coach Bailey has led his teams to three consecutive Class S titles, a 53-game winning streak, and an unbeaten at-home record since 1975.

My basic philosophy of basketball has been to put pressure on the opposition, both offensively with the fast break and defensively with pressing defenses. Therefore, I have spent a great deal of time attempting to find a defense that would put sufficient pressure on the opposition while at the same time providing ample rebounding to start the fast break.

With these two factors in mind, I finally settled on a 1-3-1 half-court trapping defense, and over the last two years I have had great success with it. I have found that this defense accomplishes three purposes:

1. It forces turnovers by creating pressure on the opposition.
2. It forces the opposing team out of its pattern of play, especially if the opponent uses a deliberate offense.
3. It forces the opponent to play our game, which is to run.

Basic Alignment

X1—the chaser. Must be quick, possess good defensive sense, and be in good physical condition.

X2—left wing. Put your best rebounding and quickest forward on this side.

X3—right wing. Put your slower or weaker rebounder on this side.

X4—middle man. Usually your center. I like to have my best rebounder here, but if you have a slow big man, put him here as this position requires less movement.

X5—back man. Must be able to anticipate passes, must be quick and defensively smart. I prefer to place my best ball-handling guard in this spot. Rebounding ability is not essential because this man is not usually called upon to rebound. (X2, X3, and X4 are designated as rebounders.)

Players line up as shown in Diagram 1, with X1 pressuring the dribbler. X2 and X3 are lined up along the foul line extended and are ready either to rush the ball or rebound. X4 fronts the opponent's post man—or if there is no post man, plays at the head of the circle. X5 is stationed behind X4, sizing up the opponent's offense by checking the position of the ball and the likely passing lanes of the ball handler.

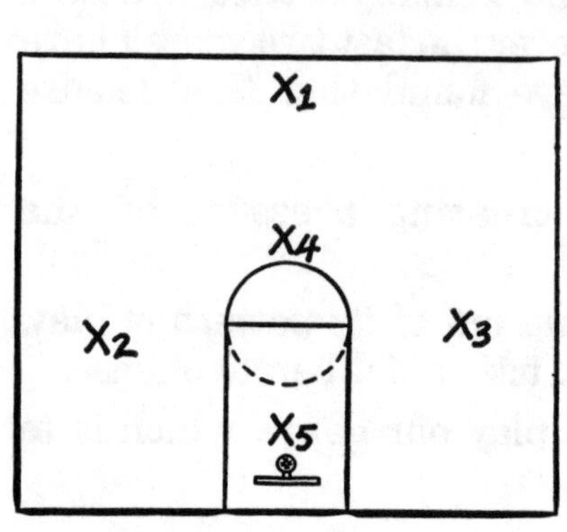

Diagram 1

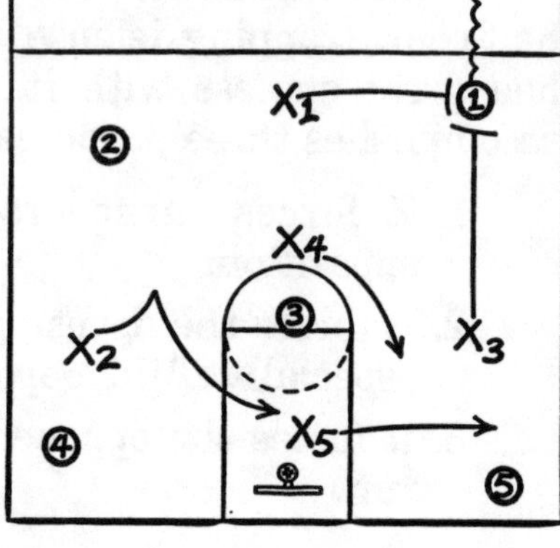

Diagram 2

The Operation

The chaser, X1, is instructed to drive the ball to X3 on the left side of the court. I do this because I have found that most offenses seem to prefer operating on the right, probably due to the fact that most guards we face are right-handed. By forcing the ball to the left, we often disrupt the opponent's offense and create additional pressure on their guards by forcing them to use their left hands. Experience has also shown that our chaser should not play the ball handler tightly at first, but slowly force him to the left and near the sideline.

As our chaser and the ball reach the mid-court line, I have the wing man, X3, rush the ball (with hands up) for a trap. Timing here is vital. X1 and X3 must arrive on the trap at the same time. This prevents the dribbler from slipping between them. I hope to have the ball (01) trapped just across the ten-second line and near the sideline. 01 is now cornered on four sides by X1, X3, the sideline, and the mid-court line (Diagram 2).

With the ball now trapped at mid-court, I play to intercept 01's pass by cutting the passing lanes. Again, experience has shown that a ball handler being pressured by X1 and heading toward the sideline will usually pass straight ahead into the corner area—if not there, then probably across the court into the X2 area.

It becomes X5's job to try to intercept the pass to the corner to 05 (Diagram 2). X4 still fronts the post man and rolls with 04 if he cuts down the lane. X2 now has two responsibilities: 1) to cover the weak side and prevent a pass to 04, or 2) to rebound any shot taken from the corner and start the fast break.

If the ball is successfully passed to 05, the back man (X5) must seal off the baseline and hold 05 until X3 can recover and form a trap in the corner (Diagram 3). X4 now must prevent a pass from 05 into the post area; or if 05 slips the trap, he must pick him up. X1 must now quickly size up the situation. If the offensive post man (03) has rolled low, X1 must cut the foul line area to prevent a pass from 05 to 02. At the same time, X1 should be anticipating the possibility of a pass back to 01.

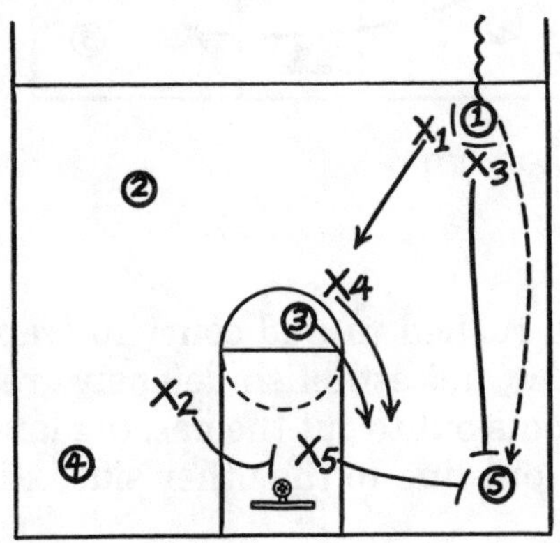

Diagram 3

NOTE: With a good trap in the corner on 05 by X3 and X5, X1 can usually intercept a pass into the foul line area or back to 02. By a good trap, I

mean one in which both trappers have their hands up, making it difficult for the. offensive man to make a good pass. Many times I have found that trapped offensive men will lob the ball out of a trap.

I have now covered the defense as it plays for the pass into the corner. But let's suppose the offensive man, 01, decides not to pass into the corner. In this case, his pass can be made to go to 02 by having X4 front 03, with X2 cutting the passing lane to 04. Once the pass is made to 02, X2 must rush the ball, preventing its penetration and holding the offensive man until X1 can reverse and trap with him on the other side (Diagram 4).

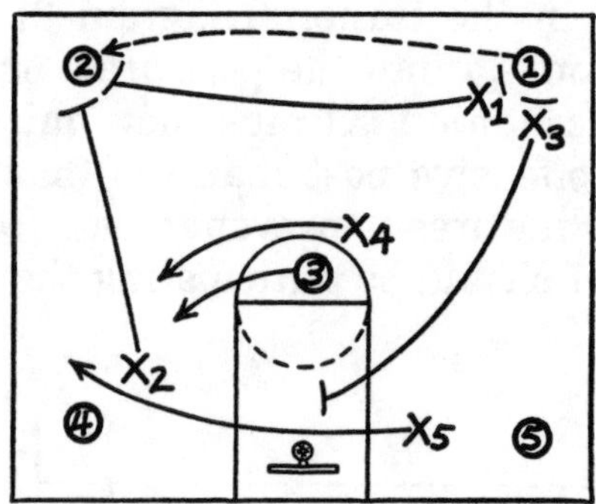

Diagram 4

X3, who has rushed to mid-court to trap 01, must now quickly slide under and establish defensive rebounding position on 05. X5 shoots out to cut the passing lane to 04, and X4 shifts across the foul line to the other side, still fronting 03.

Dangers of the 1-3-1

Three things must be avoided when using this defense:

1. Do not allow the offensive man to dribble through a trap.

2. Do not allow the ball into the middle of the court. Keep it along the sidelines.
3. Do not allow the man bringing the ball down the floor to pass to the opposite corner, such as a pass from 01 to 04. (I use drills teaching our wings to anticipate and prevent this pass from being completed. I also instruct the middle man, X4, to always play with his hands up, hoping that this will discourage or possibly knock down the pass through the post area.)

One final word about this defense: *There is always a man open!* But I emphasize that this unguarded man is the farthest away from the ball and the farthest away from the basket. Thus, if the pass is successfully completed to the open man, he will be too far away to score, and by the time the ball reaches this man, the defense can shift and trap.

14

1-3-1 Three-Quarter-Court Press

by Dale E. Klay

Assistant Basketball Coach
Florida College
Temple Terrace, Florida

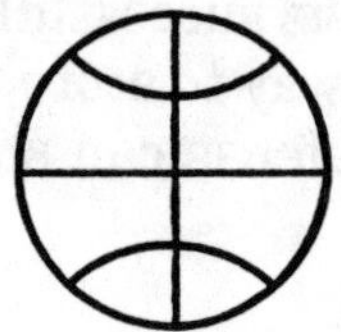

Dale E. Klay is the assistant basketball coach at Florida College (Temple Terrace, Florida). Before joining the Florida College staff, Dale was head basketball coach at Jefferson High School (Tampa, Florida), where he compiled a 61-40 record. Coach Klay was named Coach-of-the-Year for the 1973-74 season.

When faced with the problem of training their teams to encounter defensive presses, many coaches prepare for either a full-court or half-court press. Often, they overlook the possibility of confronting a three-quarter-court press. Thus, their teams are not able to handle this type of press and fall victim to its unusual pressures.

Generally, coaches teach their players not to advance the ball across the ten-second line for fear of being trapped. Instead, they tell them to hesitate a few feet from the ten-second line, look for an open man to pass to or a clear opportunity to advance the ball on the dribble. The three-quarter-court press eliminates this situation.

Disguised as a full-court press, the three-quarter press is not concerned with the ten-second line. Our players are told to trap whenever they feel they can successfully contain the dribbler. In Diagram 1, the basic alignment of the players is shown.

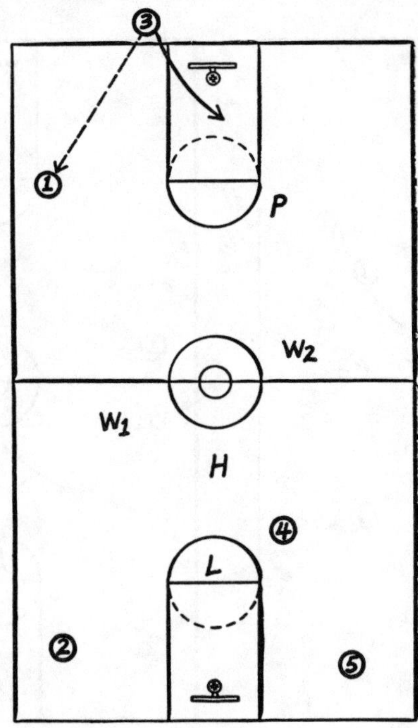

Diagram 1

Basic Alignment of the Players

Notice that the point guard, P, is positioned on the side of the floor opposite the player bringing the ball in. P, your quickest guard, is responsible for channeling the ball down a specific side of the court. It's very important for wing 1 and wing 2 to know which side of the court the ball is coming down. Keying off the point guard, they will be "cheating" to either the trap side or the interceptor side of the court.

Meanwhile, P is applying no pressure to the dribbler. However, he is preventing a cross-court pass from 01 to 03. P slides with the dribbler, giving 01 plenty of room to advance the ball down the court. The trap can come at one of several places. The point guard keys the trap. As P starts toward the dribbler to make the trap, W1 releases and moves toward the dribbler, being careful to stay in the passing lane from 01 to 02. W1 is coached to prevent bounce or chest passes, allowing only a lob pass, which H should easily pick off (Diagram 2).

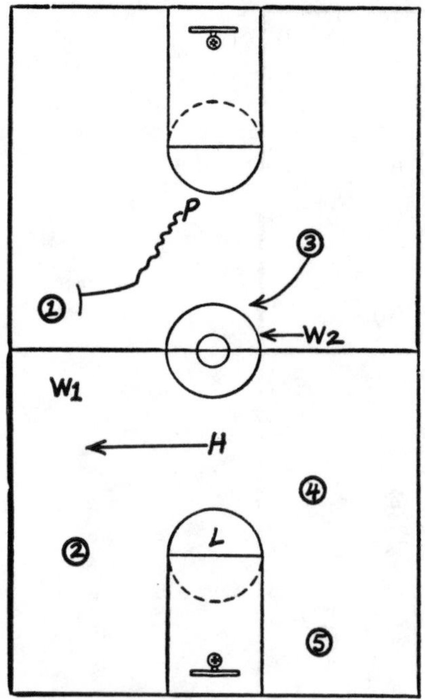

Diagram 2

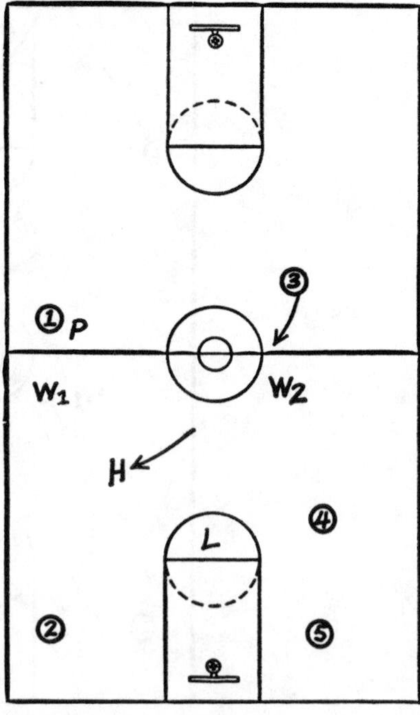

Diagram 3

At the moment when the trap is set, H releases to the side to intercept any lob passes from 01 to 02. W2 is moving to the middle, splitting the gap between 03 and 04 (Diagram 3). L moves up to relieve some of the pressure from W2, also aware of his responsibilities. We tell our players to watch the passer's eyes. A man in trouble will look when he is going to pass the ball. This enables our players to anticipate the pass, an important factor in a gambling-type press.

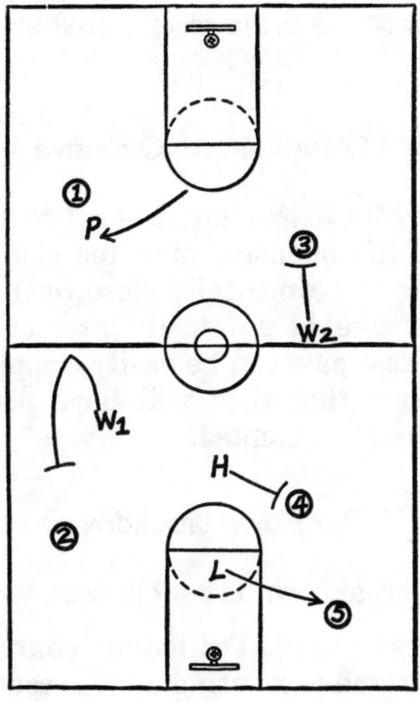

Diagram 4

Other Options

This is the basic movement of our three-quarter-court press. However, we run other options from this alignment. One of these is the fake trap. This is when W moves toward the dribbler, forcing him to pick up the ball. He then backtracks and covers 02 (Diagram 4) while his teammates, reading the key, go to a man-to-man coverage and we force a ten-second or a five-second violation. This movement keeps the offensive team guessing about what type of defensive pressure they will be facing. They will be unable to set up in a specific offensive pattern to attack the pressure.

If the offense is able to swing the ball around the point guard, wing 2 picks up 03 in a man-to-man coverage. This matches our best defensive man with their second-best ball handler. Also, whenever the offense is able to penetrate the press, we retreat to the three-second area and build out from the basket.

Don't Overguard an Offensive Man

One major point to emphasize is not to allow a defensive player to guard his offensive man too closely. We tell our defensive players to be mentally close to the offensive man and at the same time, be physically far enough away so that the offense thinks a pass can be easily completed. We assure our defensive men that they will have plenty of time to intercept if a pass is attempted.

The Player Breakdown

Our player breakdown is as follows:

P. Quickest guard. Drilled in channeling the ball handler and preventing a cross-court pass.

W1. Quickest forward. Drilled in trapping and preventing lob passes.

W2. Guard drilled to anticipate passes and to play man-to-man defense.

H. Quickest big man. Must cover a lot of area. Must anticipate passes to wings.

L. Must not allow a lay-up. Must force a 15-foot jump shot. Should be best defensive post man.

15

1-2-1-1 Full-Court and Half-Court Presses

by Mark Reiner

Head Basketball Coach
Brooklyn College
Brooklyn, New York

Mark Reiner is the head basketball coach at Brooklyn (New York) College. After coaching Canarsie High School (Brooklyn) to two New York City championships, he moved to Kansas State University (Manhattan, Kansas) as an assistant coach. He then went to Abraham Lincoln High School (Brooklyn) where he has been for the last two years prior to accepting the Brooklyn College position. Coach Reiner's overall coaching record stands at 161-49.

The full-court and half-court presses have been called gambling defenses. There are many variations of these defenses. Before a coach chooses any defense, he must decide what effect he desires and what the purpose of the defense is.

Our coaching staff decided a few years ago that we wanted to give zone pressure all over the court, but not the kind of zone pressure that tries to steal continually. We hoped to "grind it out" from the beginning to the end, playing it conservatively most of the time while leaving room for gambling when the offense dictated that to us.

NOTE: This defense is tough and can be played only by well-conditioned, aggressive players who believe in it and understand its strengths and weaknesses.

As a long-term policy, this type of defense gives the team something to rally around. In our case it has given us the kind of reputation that is very often an advantage before the game starts. Many coaches have told me that before playing us they must work against our zone defense for so long that they cannot prepare as strongly as they would like in other areas.

Full-Court Duties

We start our defense with a 1-2-1-1 full-court press (Diagram 1). The defense is played conservatively unless a gamble is called or unless we find that we are behind and want to try to make a move. The only player on the defense who is gambling full-court all the time is the point guard.

Point Guard

The point guard plays on or about the foul line and tries to disrupt the offense if he can. He lets the first pass in if it is in front of him, but he tries to keep the ball from getting behind him, leading to breaks.

The point guard's duties include the following:

1. To keep the ball in front
2. To try to get the guards dribbling

3. To force the dribbler to use opposite or weak hand if he has one
4. Not to let the dribbler penetrate
5. To stay on his feet
6. To force the dribbler to the wings if possible
7. To swipe from behind and take off down court

He is also telling himself that he will try to pick up and bother the offense without losing position and letting offense get behind him. Sometimes the offensive team sets up incorrectly and the point guard has a field day. More often than not, the well-coached teams set up correctly and he has to play intelligently.

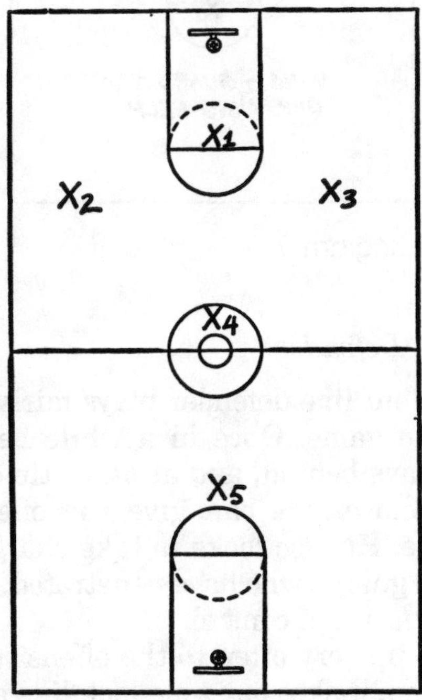

Diagram 1

Wings 2 and 3

The wings' specific duties are as follows:

1. Not to let anyone dribble their sideline

2. To try to keep the dribbler in front and double-team on sidelines
3. To move to the middle to steal when opposite side wing and point guard are doubling
4. To protect the opposite side low against the long pass on the opposite side

The wings must box out well (Diagram 2). They often have bigger men to handle.

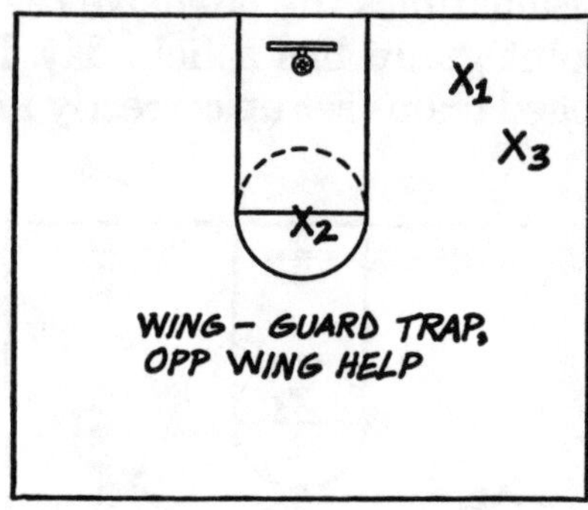

Diagram 2

Center Foul Line Defender

The center foul line defender plays fairly conservatively during the whole game. Once in a while he fronts a man, sometimes he plays behind, and at other times he drops. By mixing up his moves, he can give the offense trouble in reading his game. He also looks to take charges continually, especially on the guards who have penetrated, hoping to catch them in the air or out of control.

He matches up very often to the offensive forwards and, with the back man, makes our zone look like a 1-2-2 at times. He also drops to help pick up charges or block shots or forwards coming to the basket.

Forward Back Man

Our last man back is quick and can leap. His duties include the following:

1. Not to let the ball get behind him
2. To play together with our foul-line defender
3. To go to block all corner jump shots in an attempt to force forwards to drive to the middle where the foul line defender is waiting for change
4. To protect the end line
5. To look for long passes and steals

NOTE: We practice this defense for at least one hour each day and use all types of offenses against it, patterned or wild. We keep telling ourselves that the only way to beat our press is to score against it.

Half-Court Press

Some teams take the ball up over the half-court line with relative ease, but we then trap them with a hard half-court or keyhole press.

Some teams' full-court offenses have no relationship to this half-court offenses, and often we catch one or two players going to a new position. Our defense reacts well to that.

Other teams against whom we have had success beat us down court, but their forwards, or men who end up with the ball over our half of the court, cannot dribble well enough or do not have the confidence to take it to the basket. They have a tendency to look back and give the ball to the guards.

Once the offense comes over half-court, we go into a 1-2-1-1 zone press. It very often turns into a 1-3-1. We trap them at half-court if we can, but we usually have more success at the keyhole (Diagram 3).

If we are trapping in the half-court, we may give them the guard-to-guard pass (Diagram 4) with the opposite side falling back to either stay foul line extended or to help out. Or we play in front of the foul line man if he is there, and let number 4 play behind (Diagram 5).

In Diagram 6, we see the ultimate press where we have moved in front of our men strongly because we are sure that the offense is trapped.

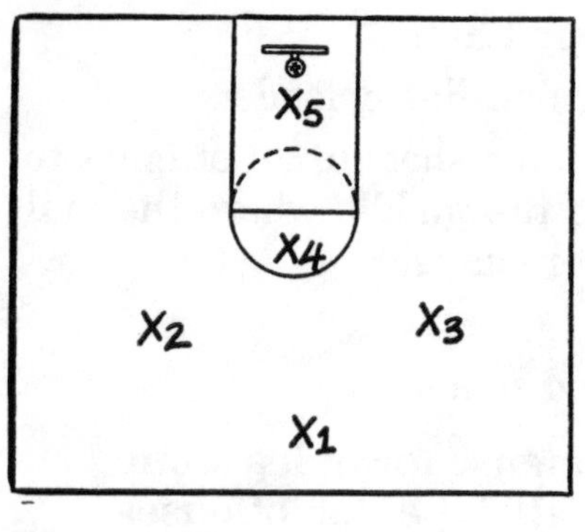

Diagram 3

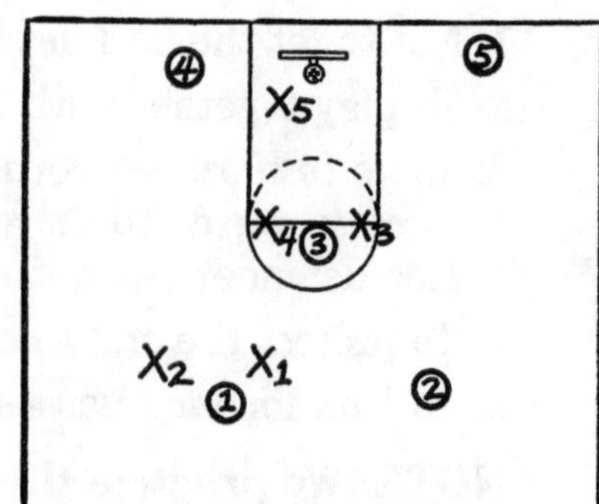

Diagram 4

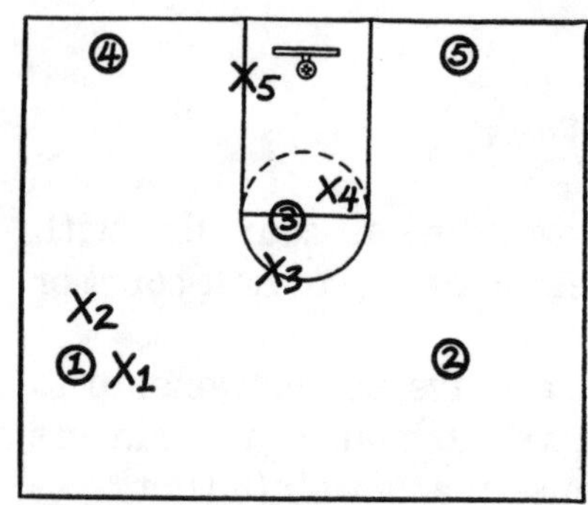

Diagram 5

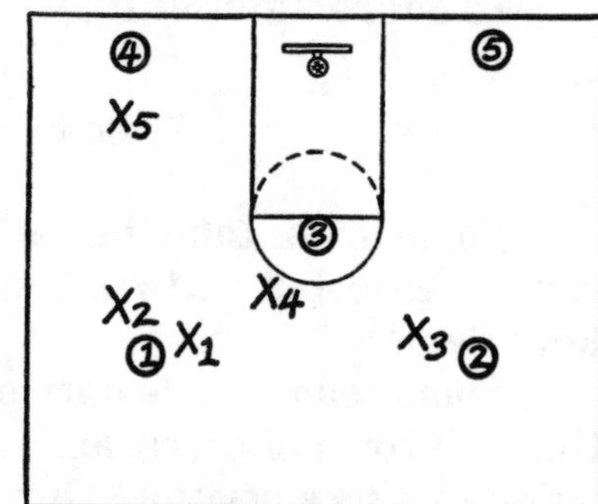

Diagram 6

Half-Court Duties

Guard

The point guard's duties are the same as in the full-court press except that when the ball is in the corner he must help protect the foul line (Diagram 7). He is always running toward the two guards when the ball is high. If the ball is passed out to the guard from the forward, the defensive point guard helps by trying to double up with a wing.

Wings

The wings are to double up on top with the point guard or the man running side-to-side under number 5. When the ball is on the opposite side, the high wing protects the foul line and then slides under (see number 3 in Diagram 5). Number 3 has moved under (Diagram 7) and is boxing on the opposite side forward. When the ball gets to the foul line, both wings should know to drop back quickly to protect the inside game.

Center

The center's duties in the half-court defense are the same as in the full-court defense, but he must drop down and front any man coming low when the ball goes to the corner. His responsibility of covering the foul line ends and the point guard covers that area (Diagram 7).

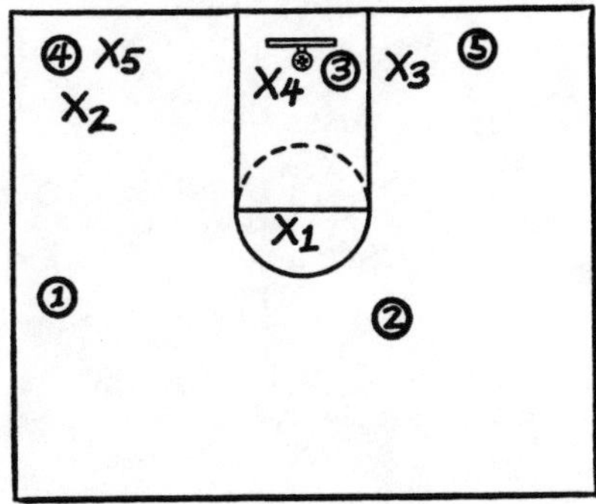

Diagram 7

Forward

This jumping jack protects the end line, doubles up on everything in corners, forces drives, and backs up the foul line defender on lob passes. He blocks a lot of shots and steals a lot. He leaves rebounding to the center and wings when a shot is taken from the corner (Diagram 7).

NOTE: If running ceases, this zone can be taken apart. Only with continual pressure can it work successfully.

Part Three

MULTIPLE AND CHANGING DEFENSES

16

A System of Multiple Defense

by Frank Pasqua

Former Head Basketball Coach
Catholic High School
Baton Rouge, Louisiana

Frank Pasqua is the former head coach at Catholic High School (Baton Rouge, Louisiana). Coach Pasqua's career won-lost record stands at 160-75.

We at Catholic High School believe that defense is the key to whether we win or lose. Furthermore, we know that because there is so much emphasis on other phases of the game, our defensive thinking must be simple, but also sound.

NOTE: Some coaches believe that one defense is sufficient, and if it's applied correctly that defense can be played throughout a game or a season. We do not discount this belief, but we do feel that in today's game of specialization, which requires increased scouting and study of films, it is highly possible for a good offensive team to adjust very easily to a stereotyped defensive team.

For this reason, we think it is necessary to be ready to play multiple defenses and adjust on any given situation. The defense that we use allows us to be diversified, to adjust, and to spring the element of surprise on our opponents.

Multiple Defenses

We feel that it is necessary to play man-to-man, zones, and pressing defenses to win. However, our man-to-man defense is the key to all the others. That is why, during our spring workouts and in our summer league play, we do not allow any other defense except man-to-man.

NOTE: Good man-to-man technique must be taught first. Thus, we designate our man-to-man defense as our number one defense.

Identification

Most zone offenses plan their attack by recognizing the defensive front of the opponent, whether it is odd or even. We play 2-1-2 zone (even front) and 1-3-1 zone (odd front). Thus, we designate our 2-1-2 zone as our number two defense and our 1-3-1 zone as our number three defense. Any special defenses, like combination or box (or diamond) and one, are called numbers four and five. It is then easy to identify each defense by its number (Chart I).

> **NOTE: Integrating the numbering system with the divisions of the court makes it easy for us to call a defense, change from one to another quickly, and play defense all over the court.**

"Pickup" Points

We divide the court into "pickup" points numbered 10, 20, 30, and 40 (Diagram 1). The 10 pickup point is five feet from the top of the key that we are defending. The 20 pickup point is three feet into the back court. The 30 pickup point is at the free-throw line extended. The 40 pickup point is at the end line of the back court of the offensive team.

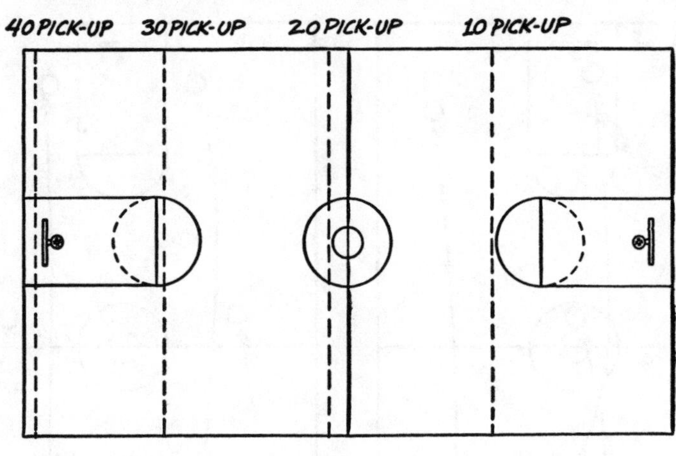

Diagram 1

Calling Defenses

Now that we have a numbering system for our defenses and for our pickup points, we put them together. A call of 130 would mean that we pick up man-to-man (#1) at the free-throw line extended in the back court (30), or a three-quarter-court pickup. This makes it very easy to change defenses during time-outs, free throws, out-of-bounds, and so on.

> **NOTE: We have also noticed that our opponents have had to regroup to the changing of the defense. This cuts down on movement of the offensive team and takes away a great deal of the offensive concentration.**

We integrate our presses into our defense with the last of the three digits. We use the digit "5" instead of "0" as the last digit as our code to press.

To press, we must make some alterations in our zone defenses. We utilize two zone presses, the 1-2-1-1 zone press and the 2-2-1 zone press. The alterations come with the 1-2-1-1 press from the 1-3-1 defense, and the 2-2-1 press from the 2-1-2 zone. These alterations are illustrated in Diagrams 2 and 3.

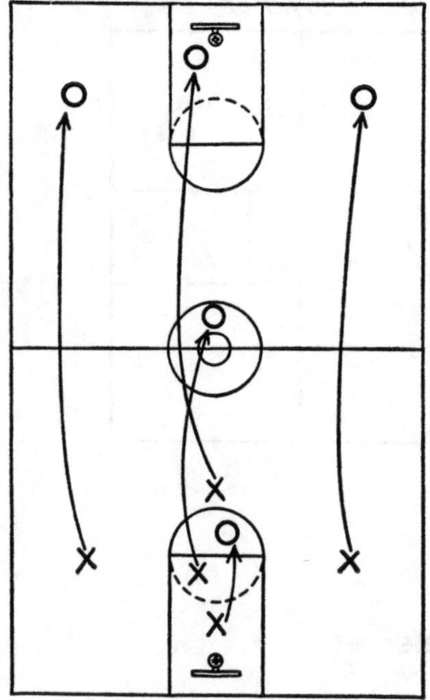

Diagram 2

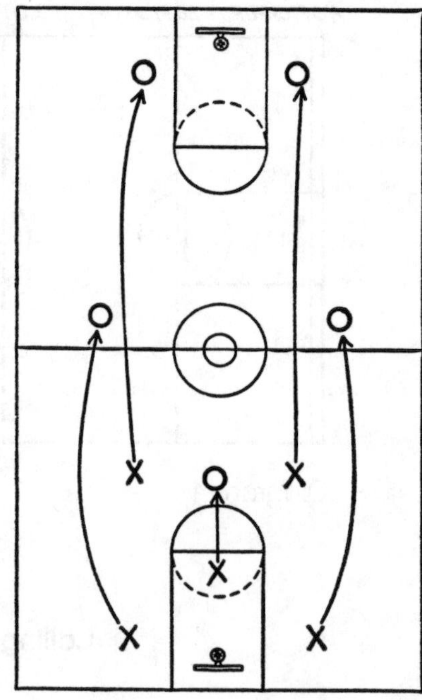

Diagram 3

Knowing how to make the switch from zone pickup to zone press makes the defense very easy to call. For example, a 235 call means a 2-2-1 press at three-quarter court. This differs from a 230 call. A 230 call means only a three-quarter-court pickup without traps.

NOTE: Thus, we are able to confuse the opponent into thinking that we are pressing when we are only extending our zone. This makes it possible to detect the opponent's press offense.

Conclusion

Our defensive system may seem a bit confusing on the surface, but we have found it to be very easy to execute. We are able to put it into our program at the junior high level, and it is grasped very quickly by these young players.

The system gives players defensive responsibilities that in turn require alert thinking. Thus, it makes playing defense an integral part of the makeup of the basketball player.

In short, it emphasizes defense. And defense, we believe, determines whether we are winners or losers.

Chart I

Defense Identification

Number	*Defense*
1	Man-to-man
2	2-1-2 zone
3	1-3-1 zone
4	Combination
5	Box (or diamond) and one

17

Pointers on Coaching the Combination Defense

by Myron S. Huckle, Jr.

Head Basketball Coach
Hazen High School
Renton, Washington

Myron S. Huckle, Jr., is the head coach at Hazen High School (Renton, Washington). He has compiled a 130-129 won-lost record with one league championship and a second place. In three trips to the state tournament, Coach Huckle's squads have placed second, tenth, and eighth.

There seem to be two basic theories concerning high school basketball defense:

1. You have so much to teach high school players in so short a time that teaching one defense and teaching it well is the most you can do with the available time and talent.
2. You should teach as many defenses as possible so that your opponents have a myriad of defenses with which to contend.

NOTE: The argument is one of basic strength in one area of defense versus a combination of defenses (of which none will be as strong as one basic defense).

Of the two theories, I prefer the latter. Here's how we employ a combination of defenses as part of our overall attack.

The Basic Defense—Man-to-Man (Blue)

You must spend 60 percent of your time teaching defense. We start the season with individual defense and pick our teams according to the individuals' defensive hustle and desire, if the individuals' offensive skills are equal. One-on-one, two-on-two and three-on-three work are part of every practice, and all half-court and full-court scrimmages early in the season are devoted to man-to-man defensive skills.

NOTE: We stress that man-to-man is the best way to go if you have one way to go. We mix defenses, but if players get confused or lost, we tell them to go man-to-man.

After the individual skills are covered, we spend whole evenings on team defense, half-court and full-court. We always rebound four defensively. We pick our rebounding guard (foul line) and our defensive guard (mid-court line) and stay with them throughout the season. Offensive rebounding is part of our team defense. We work on the "hustle back," the "look back," the "talk," and each man's defensive position.

The Man-to-Man Press (Dark Blue)

The next step is the press. We work on it out of all situations: loose ball, foul shot (both good and missed), normal rebound, steals, interceptions, and when we scrimmage we press. This does many things:

1. It provides good conditioning.
2. It is excellent practice for us to learn the press as well as how to break it.
3. It is good practice to work under the pressure of a press, physically as well as mentally.
4. It provides practice in reacting to pressure quickly.

NOTE: We use a basic 1-2-2 set to break the press, and we work on it a lot while learning the press defensively.

The 3-2 Zone Defense (Gold)

We start working the zone defense in front court. We believe in the 3-2 because it allows the perimeter shot like other zones but affords us good rebounding placement. At first we work on this half-court, and then go to full-court and try to beat it with a break. Then we go to scrimmage sessions using the zone only. We still rebound the guards as described in man-to-man and insist that the players race back on defense. We insist upon hands up and feet and mouth working hard.

The 1-2-1-1 Zone Press (Dark Gold)

When the players have learned the fundamentals of the front-court zone and the ways to try to attack it, we have them work against a full-court zone. We use the 1-2-1-1 and slide back into a 3-2 if we are beaten down court. This zone press has given us more success than any of the others.

NOTE: Offensively, we stress ball movement, body movement, and overload just as in front court. Defensively, we stress upsetting the other team's deliberate style, conditioning, teamwork, hustle, and hard work. Again, we find ourselves killing two birds with one stone. We work as hard on the defense as we do trying to defeat it. We run a 1-3-1 vs. the 3-2 in front court and our old reliable 1-2-1-1 vs. the full-court zone press. The players have a lot of fun with this defense.

Combining the Defenses (Green)

Up to this point, we have talked about the defenses as they are run or practiced as separate defenses. We follow the same pattern with the players. Finally, with but a few days to go before the first game, we allow them a peek at the Hazen High School defense, which is a combination of all of the defenses they have been learning separately.

NOTE: We code our defenses with our school colors: gold, blue, green. When we teach this, it takes a period on the blackboard. The code is as follows: blue—regular man-to-man (pick them up at half-court); gold—regular front-court 3-2 zone defense; dark blue—full-court man-to-man defense; dark gold—full-court zone press (1-2-1-1); green—combination of blue, gold, and dark gold.

The green defense is our defense. We start with it and we stay with it unless extreme measures must be taken to 1) get back in the game (dark blue), 2) speed up a team's super-deliberate play (dark gold), 3) preserve a lead late in the game with players in foul trouble (gold).

Our green defense is put into effect in the following way. We play all of our opponents the same way to start the game:

1. If you make the field goal, hustle back in gold.
2. If you miss the field goal, hustle back in blue.
3. If you miss the free throw, hustle back in blue (just like a missed field goal).
4. If you make the free throw, attack with dark gold (zone press back into 3-2).

NOTE: We have done this for four years now and have at times given in to various pressures to abandon the green for pure blue or gold. But statistics show that we do better in the long run to stay with the green except in those situations outlined above.

Teaching the Combination (Green)

To teach the combination you must start out as outlined above. First, get a good man-to-man base. Then add the press. Then comes the zone, and the full-court zone is added last.

NOTE: When you describe the combination, do it in detail verbally and with lots of chalk and blackboard. Practice in scrimmage with just the zone when you make, and man-to-man when you miss, at first. Have all of the players yell "blue" or "gold" depending on the situation when they come down court.

In other words, when you start don't put in the zone press after a good free throw. Let this go for a while until the players understand the changes in defense according to what happens with a field goal. After you have spent a day or two with this, add the zone press. The players must learn to yell out the defenses, and the more experienced players can help here.

Combination Defense for the Entire Program

We teach this program to freshmen and by the time the players are seniors they know what we want. Being a four-year school has certain advantages and this is one of them. Each year the players become more and more experienced and better at changing defenses. They must learn to do it without thinking.

NOTE: Basically, the big advantage of the combination defense is twofold: The kids learn both offensively and defensively how to react to various defenses and our opponents must prepare to meet several defenses. The only disadvantage is time. But somehow, one manages and profits accordingly.

18

Change Up on Defense

by Charles B. Sullivan

Junior Varsity Basketball Coach
Baltimore Polytechnic Institute
Baltimore, Maryland

Charles B. Sullivan has been coaching basketball since 1963. Currently the head coach at Polytechnic Institute (Baltimore, Maryland), Coach Sullivan has a 171-95 won-lost record with two Maryland Scholastic Association championships. In football, he has won two championships and he has also won a baseball championship.

As a coach at the undersquad level, I believe that you must change up on defense throughout the game if you want to be successful. We have been using four basic defenses, with some variations, to cover all aspects of the game.

NOTE: In some years a particular defense may be used 75 percent of the time. But in another year, that defense may be used only 25 percent of the time. Much depends on your personnel in any given year, and how well they execute the defense.

The point is that your players must be able to execute several defenses well. We use the following four basic defenses:

1. Man-to-man
2. 3-2 zone
3. Half-court zone press
4. Full-court zone press

Coaching Points

Usually, the half-court zone press and the full-court zone press are used only after a made field goal or free throw, when the opponents get the ball out-of-bounds under their defensive basket. It is also very important to be able to go back into your half-court defense from the pressure defenses.

Normally, we go back into our 3-2 zone from the half-court pressure defense and into our man-to-man from the full-court pressure. The following are several items to be extremely careful of in this regard.

1. When dropping into your man-to-man, tell your players to pick up the men nearest the basket first. Other than the man with the ball, who will be covered, these men are the most dangerous. Too often, especially early in the season, you will find a player looking for his man and leaving a man wide open under the basket.

NOTE: As always, in any defense, impress upon your players the necessity for talking on defense.

2. When he is heading back down the court, especially when he is opposite the ball, the player should keep his head up and eyes open. Quite often a cross-court pass will be picked off or deflected.

3. When dropping back into a zone the player should fill the nearest spot in the zone where he plays. In other words, it is not necessary for the right front wing man always to play the right front position. We would like the deep men always to be deep and the front men to be out front—but other than that, when setting up quickly, we take what we can get.

NOTE: From time to time, we also vary the positions where we pick up our men on the man-to-man defense (i.e., at full-court, double-team the inbounds pass; at half-court, overplay the forwards to deny them a pass, or sag back and help out inside). I believe this gives you the effectiveness of having three different man-to-man defenses with very little extra effort.

Man-to-Man Defense

Naturally, if your players do not know how to play man-to-man, no other defense will be successful. There is no reason to discuss stance, positioning, or the techniques of the man-to-man in this article. Many articles and books have been written solely on this subject. However, we do use several very effective drills to begin our practices.

- **One-on-one full-court.** Divide the squad into two equal groups, preferably in different-colored shirts. Then divide each group in half again. One color will be offensive in one direction and the other color will be offensive coming back down the court. See Diagram 1.

  We first go up and down twice without the ball. Each group uses the area from the center of the court to the sideline. The first time, at half speed, has the defender working on good position; for the second time, at full speed, we work on all phases of defense.

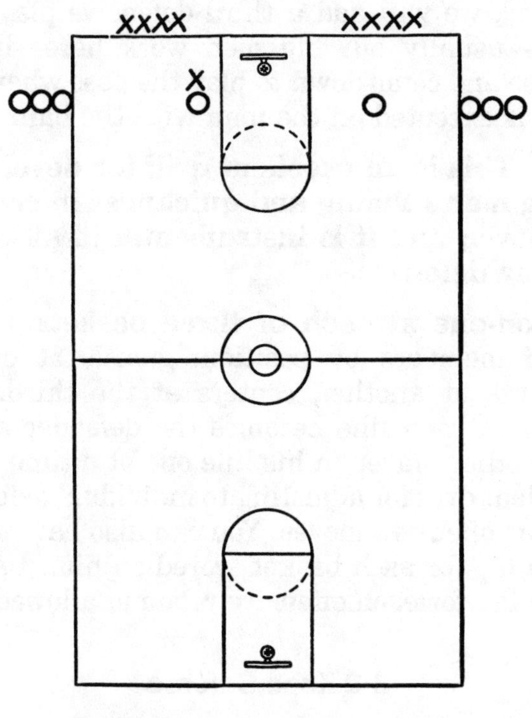

Diagram 1

NOTE: The offensive player must change direction and stimulate an aggressive action toward the offensive basket. Now, with a ball, we go up and back again, this time attempting to score.

- **Two-on-two full-court:** Again, to simplify the changeover we use different-colored shirts. We work this two ways: a) Allowing the inbounds pass, we work on forcing the dribbler to turn his back and reverse dribble to the other defender, who will come over and try to double-team without fouling. b) We double-team the inbounds pass to deny the pass from out-of-bounds.

The key here is to make certain that the defensive player responsible for the man inbounds plays *behind* him and the defensive player on the man throwing the ball in is fronting the man inbounds. As this drill is learned, we will add a third defensive player at mid-court—usually our big men work here—in order to release and come down to play the pass when a double-team is executed on the man with the ball.

NOTE: This is an excellent drill for developing the big man's timing and quickness in creating a turnover, and it is instrumental in all of our pressing defenses.

- **One-on-one at each of three baskets:** Line up all squad members by position: guards at one basket, forwards at another, centers at the third. The first player in each line becomes the defender and guards every other player in his line one at a time. This is an excellent drill for adjusting to individual defense versus various offensive moves. You can also have each player run a lap for each basket scored on him. I also like to add a lap for each offensive rebound allowed.

3-2 Zone Defense

About the only thing we do differently from a normal 3-2 alignment is to double-team the corners and drop our opposite wing man deep into the rebounding position. See Diagrams 2 and 3. The point man is responsible for the middle of the defense. He plays in front of the offensive middle man, about halfway down the lane where he can be picked up by the opposite deep man.

NOTE: If your point man is alert, he will get several steals off the double-teaming efforts in the corner by intercepting the lob pass outside to an offensive player beyond the key. Also, a wing man can fake the double-team and sometimes force a bad pass. Encourage your players to be very aggressive in this defense.

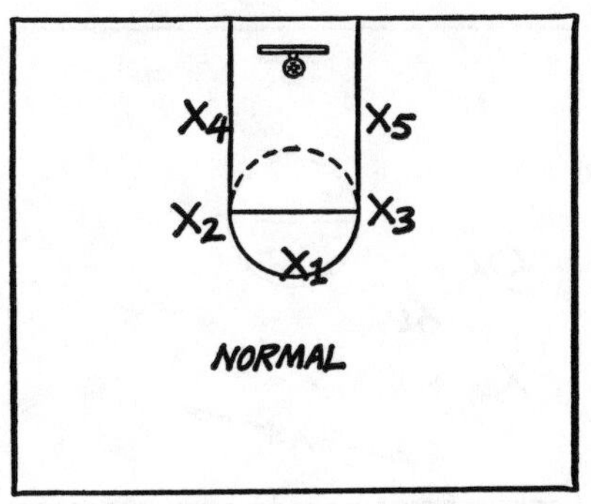

Diagram 2

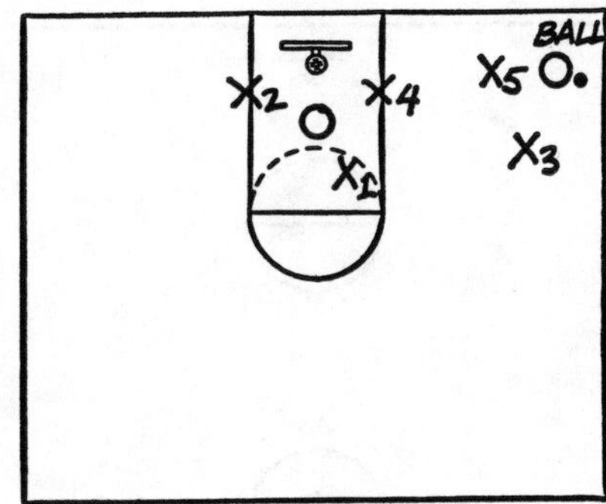

Diagram 3

Half-Court Zone Press

From the basic alignment shown in Diagram 4, the key man is our point man, X1. His job is to force the ball to one side or the other—it makes no difference to us which side. Make certain that he does not attempt to steal the ball because more often than not, he will be out of position.

If the dribbler stops deeper than the top of the foul circle (approximately three-quarter court), X1 simply drops back and waits for the pass before looking for the double-team. If the dribbler is closer to the center line than the top of the key, the double-team is put on by X1 and either X2 or X3. Hence, our half-court press may become a three-quarter-court press.

NOTE: Ideally, we would like our opponents to bring the ball across half-court, but the teams are generally too well-coached for this to happen with any degree of regularity, so again we take what we can get.

When the ball is forced to a double-team, the opposite wing man, say X3, is responsible for the steal. He should play the man closest to the ball, either a man in the middle or in the back court. X4 moves in front of the nearest man on the side of the ball as soon as X1 forces the ball to one side. See Diagram 5.

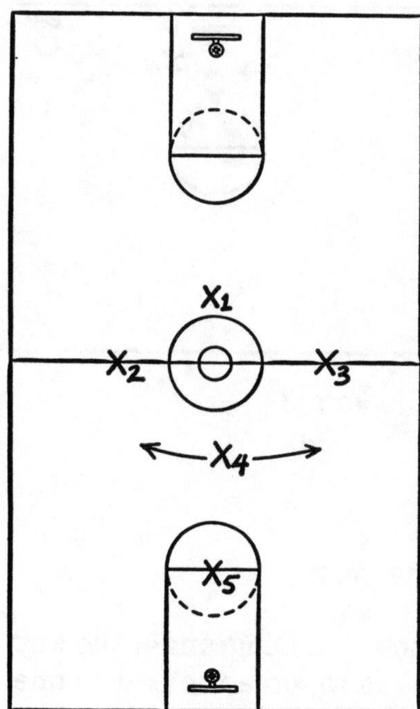

Diagram 4

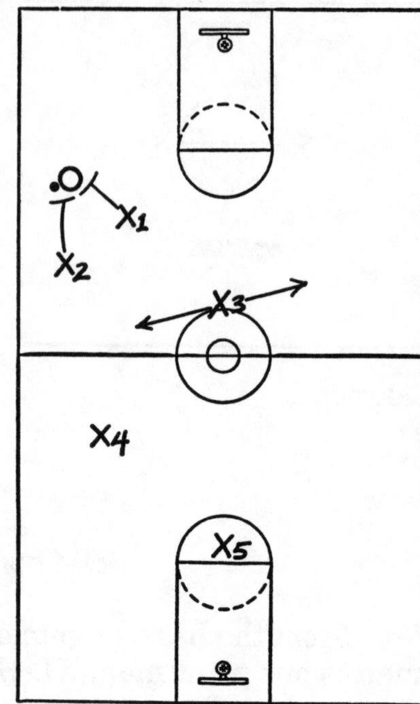

Diagram 5

NOTE: X4 should not wait for the double-team but should move as soon as the ball is on one side. This is the reason why X1 must force the ball to one side and keep it there. X5 must be the safety man and not give up a lay-up. If the offense is successful in reversing the ball in the back court, after X4 has committed himself to a side, instead of giving up on the press simply change the responsibilities of X4 and X5 as quickly as possible. This must be called by X5, who will say, "X4, get back, get back."

Also, if a team is able to throw a pass from near mid-court or deeper into their deep offensive end, the opposite mid-court defender (X2 or X3) must hustle back under the basket to help X5, who can then release to play the man in the corner with the ball. Quite often, the man hustling back will pick off a pass thrown into the center.

- **Team drill:** This is an excellent team drill for working on the press and all of its aspects. Divide the squad into three teams, all with different-colored shirts (such as orange, blue, and white).

  First, orange is on defense and sets up in the half-court press, with blue on offense at one end and white at the other end ready to go on offense from out-of-bounds. Blue attacks orange; if orange steals, they try to score; if blue gets the ball up court, they try to score quickly without setting up in offense.

  All shots are considered good and orange immediately returns to defense as if they had scored. The third team, white, then attacks from out-of-bounds while orange is setting up the half-court press. After five minutes of continuous action, the teams change positions and another team becomes defensive and orange becomes one of the offensive teams.

NOTE: This teaches setting up quickly on defense after scoring, adjusting to different personnel and techniques, and is also a good conditioning drill.

Full-Court Zone Press

We use the 2-2-1 setup (Diagram 6) and apply pressure two ways: either "weak" just to let the other team know that we're around, or "strong" in order to try to get the ball.

If "weak," our players just drop back as the ball is advanced up court, looking to force as many passes as possible, perhaps to have one thrown away, or hoping to intercept a lob pass. If we are "strong," X1 or X2 forces the dribbler to stop and turn back for the other to double-team. X3 (or X4, whoever is opposite from the ball) is then alert to intercept any pass. The other mid-court man moves to play in front of the nearest man in his area. Again, X5 is the safety. As a variation, X1 or X2 can harass the inbounds pass.

> **NOTE: We often use this defense after a free throw. If we have a good foul shooter, we will take our big men off the lane and put our guards up to press quickly. Even though what we will do is obvious, this does get results often.**

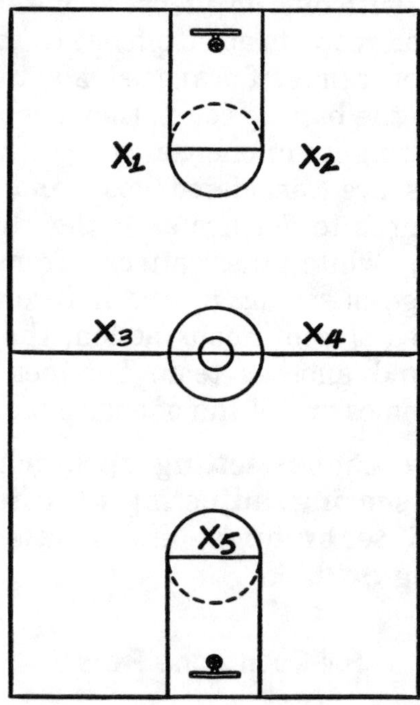

Diagram 6

Conclusion

The defenses can be changed in many ways—by verbal signals, hand signals, or by huddling on the foul line at a break in the action. Personally, I like to call defenses from the bench, so we use verbal signals. We do, however, use hand signals to vary the full pressure from weak to strong—one fist for weak and two fists for strong.

It is not necessary to change defenses every time down court in order to make them effective. In fact, it is not necessary in every game, every year, to use every defense. Certain players are more suited to certain defenses, but I firmly believe in teaching these big four to help control the game.

Of course, no total defense or defensive philosophy or strategy is any better than the sum of its individual parts. Defense must be sold to your players and it must be sold every day. As much emphasis, if not more, must be placed on defense as on offense—even though more time should be spent on offense.

Never allow a defensive mistake to go overlooked, even in an "offensive" drill. Praise the defense of your players and reward them for excellent individual and team defensive work. Make certain that your players are aware of the total defense and defensive philosophy so that they can be an integral part of your successful program.

19

The Full-Court Rotating Defense

by Bill Vining

Athletic Director
Ouachita Baptist University
Arkadelphia, Arkansas

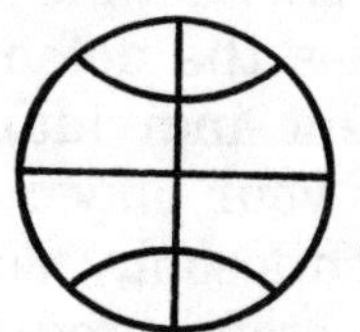

Bill Vining's coaching debut was in 1954 when he became head coach at Ouachita Baptist University (Arkadelphia, Arkansas), a position he still holds in addition to his duties as athletic director which he assumed 13 years ago. Coach Vining has compiled a 424-267 record. He has won six Arkansas Intercollegiate Conference championships, six District 17 NAIA championships, and once reached the semifinals of the national tournament. He was also named Coach-of-the-Year seven times and served on the coaching staffs of the U.S. Olympic men's basketball team trials in 1968, 1972, and 1976.

Defensive basketball seems to be the "in" thing among schools and colleges across the country. This has become necessary because of the tremendous improvement of individual offensive skills. The young players are shooting better and dribbling better—this combination makes for outstanding offensive play.

The best and only way to counter this improved individual offensive player is to develop a strong team defense. Instead of defensing one-on-one, it now takes two-on-one and three-on-one defensively to develop a sound team defense.

The Ouachita full-court rotating defense incorporates this philosophy. The theory of the defense includes pressure, stopping the dribble and covering, backcourt interception, ten-second violation, and offensive mistake. We continue this type of pressure into the front court until the ball has penetrated the 28-foot mark. The full-court rotating defense is not an easy defense to learn and it takes a great deal of team practice. In fact, it isn't even easy to explain in a way that your players can quickly comprehend and accept. Opponents sometime find it difficult to determine whether it is a zone or man-for-man full-court defense.

Throw-In

One-on-one pressure is put on offensive players who are in position for the throw-in, usually in front of the offense. The throw-in defense (option 1) is to jump and wave the hands to distract the offensive players' views. Diagram 1 illustrates this option.

Player D4 fronts his man and assists with overhead passes that may go to 02 or 03. D4 may rotate to the receiver, playing man-to-man. This necessitates a switch or rotation of the other defensive players.

D5 is the only defensive man back so he reacts conservatively. He may cover 04, requiring D2 or D3 to cover 05. However, D5 should probably play the situation as a two-on-one until D2 or D3 covers 04.

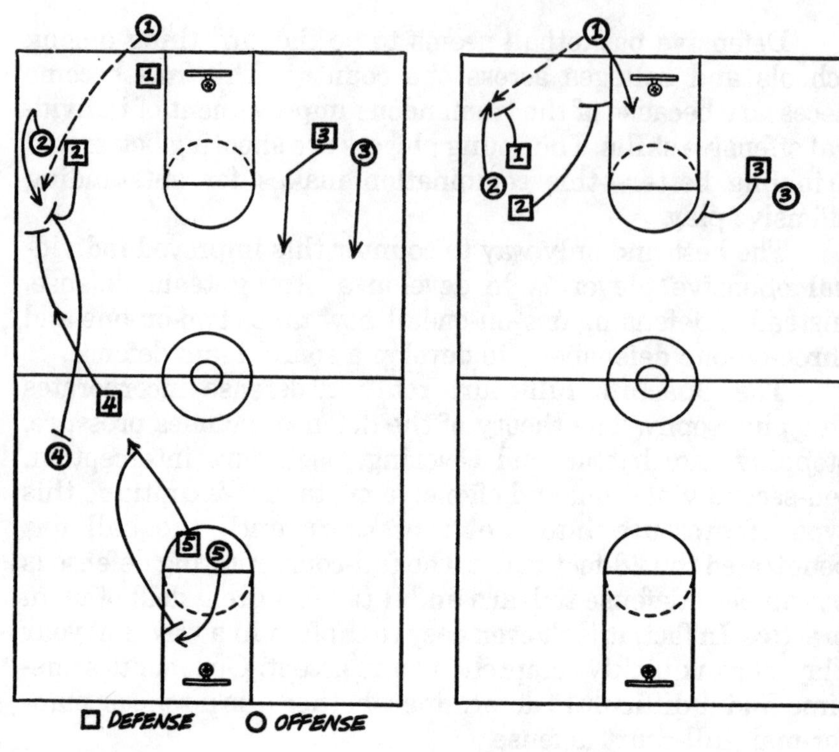

Diagram 1

Diagram 2

Added Throw-In Pressure

In this second throw-in option (Diagram 2), D1 may elect to help defend against the throw-in. If the throw-in is successful, the defensive players pick up the nearest offensive players and position themselves man-for-man. They prepare themselves for the next phase of the game.

After Successful Throw-In (or Backcourt Turnover)

If the direct throw-in has been successful and 02 begins penetration up the sideline (Diagram 3), D2 overtakes 02 and forces him to stop or reverse toward the inside. At this time, D1 is dropping back and toward the ball, anticipating 02's reverse. If 02 does reverse, D1 immediately attacks him, creating a momentary double-team. Assuming that the dribbler, 02, is stopped, D2 quickly releases and rotates to the next open man. D2 looks first to 01. If 01 is covered by D3, D2 rotates to the next man, 03. This type of switch and rotation can continue if D5 elects to switch to 03.

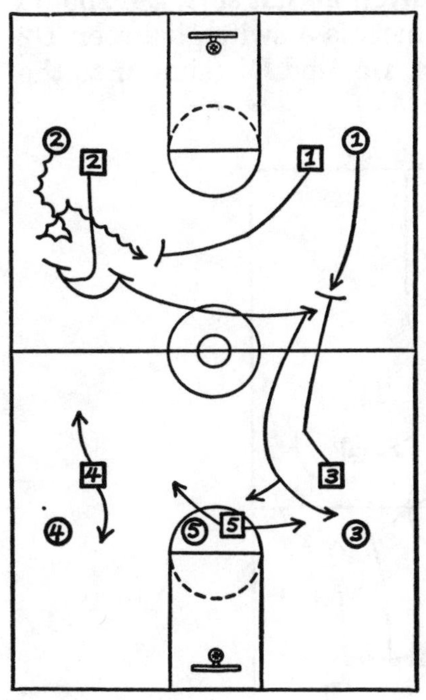

Diagram 3

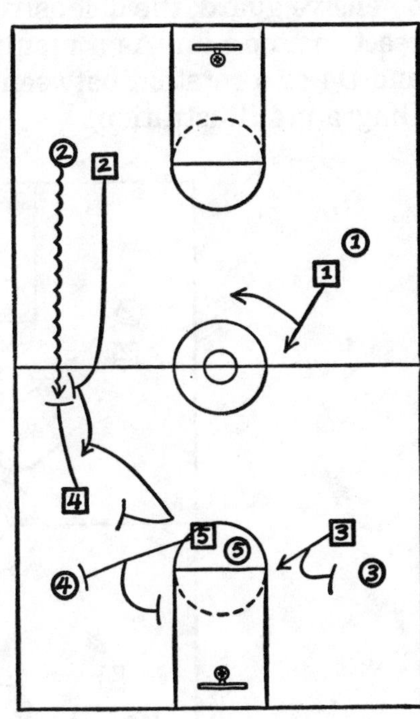

Diagram 4

If 02 penetrates the sideline and D2 is unable to overtake him, there is a second option (Diagram 4). D4 moves up to meet 02 and will if necessary, momentarily double with D2 to stop the dribbler. The rotation is set in action by D2's quick release, moving to 04. If D5 has rotated toward 04, D2 looks to the next man, 05. Again, additional switches may occur and D2 will hunt for the open man.

Many times, after a successful throw-in, one player will try to bring the ball down court by himself, waving the other offensive players down court (Diagram 5). When this occurs, the third option is initiated. Defensive guard D1 will move back only to approximately ten feet from the center line and prepare to momentarily double-team, if necessary, to stop the dribbler. The other defensive players will adjust (as in a zone) to cover the open guard, 01. If the dribbler goes away from the defensive guard, the defensive player on that side, D4, should react to stop him. As a result, there is a switch between D2 and D4 or a rotation between D4, D5, and D2 (similar to the Diagram 4 illustration).

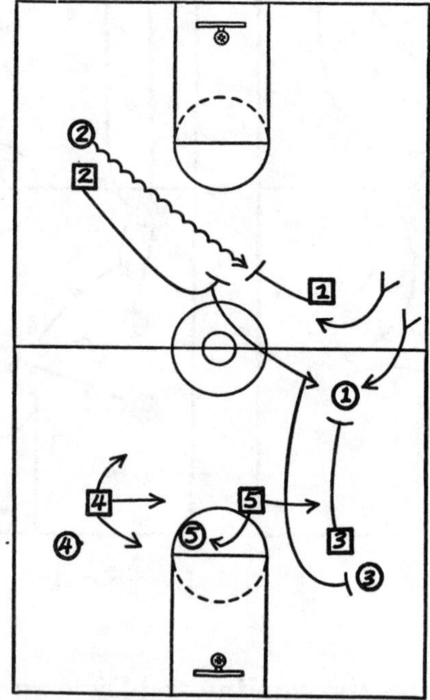

Diagram 5

This type of full-court press lends itself to the use of multiple defenses. The full-court zone or strictly man-to-man can be used to keep the offense guessing and confused. It's rather difficult for the opponents to determine whether you are in a man defense or a zone defense if you execute this properly.

This defense appears to be risky, but if you work out the proper switches and rotations it can become a real worry for your opponents. You must believe in it and your team must develop confidence in it if it is to be successful. This is true of any defense.

20

Multiple-Pressure Defenses

by Bob Kloppenburg

Head Scout and Assistant Basketball Coach
Seattle Supersonics
Seattle, Washington

After coaching 20 years of basketball and compiling a 381-162 won-lost record, Bob Kloppenburg was named head scout and assistant basketball coach of the Seattle Supersonics of the National Basketball Association.

At United States International University, we firmly believe that a team must adopt a pressure-type defense if it is to be effective defensively. Because of current jump-shooting performances, it is sheer suicide to let a team set up and take its normal shots without extreme outside pressure on the ball and passing lanes. For this reason, we teach players our multiple-pressure defenses.

NOTE: First, however, we make certain that each player is thoroughly drilled in one-on-one defensive situations from every point on the court. We feel that when our biggest and slowest men can hold their own against our fastest men from one end of the court to the other in one-on-one situations, we are ready to teach our series of pressure defenses.

We feel that each of these defenses is fundamentally sound because each gives us a one-on-one situation with little possibility of a two-on-one situation that is so common to many pressing defenses. Our purpose is not to steal the ball but to keep such intense pressure on the opposing players that they rush their game. At some point in the game, the pressure defense will begin to take its toll. This usually occurs in the second half, although it might come sooner against a weak opponent.

The coach must firmly believe in his strategy of play. He should not give up his defense whenever its effectiveness is not immediately apparent. To exert pressure properly, pressure must be applied for at least three-quarters of a game.

Court Areas

Our defenses are based on the four areas of the court shown in Diagram 1. Our number one defense covers up to the 35-foot area, which is the crucial area because it has the most high-percentage shooting spots. Our number two defense covers from 35 to 50 feet. Our number three defense covers the area from 50 to 75 feet, and our number four defense covers from 75 to 94 feet.

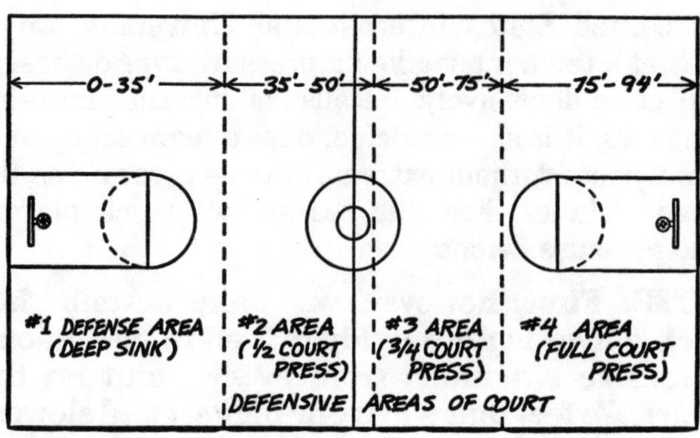

Diagram 1

We feel that the two, three, and four areas are very important to our overall defense. It is in these areas that we try to create uncommon situations for the offense. If we can force every downcourt man to dribble or move in a manner he has not practiced, we might force the offensive players into mental or physical lapses before they reach area one.

Defense Number One

Defense number one is the sinking man-to-man defense. Here are examples of how it is run.

Diagram 2

X5 pressures the ball hard. X4 sinks three to five feet inside the key circle. X3 plays the passing lane to 03. X2 plays three-quarters or fully in front of 02, blocking the passing lane. X1 sinks three feet inside of the key, facing man and ball.

Diagram 3

X4 pressures the ball hard. X1 plays the passing lane to 01. X2 plays three-quarters in front of 02, or fully in front. X3 sinks two to three feet inside the key area. X5 sinks three feet inside the key circle.

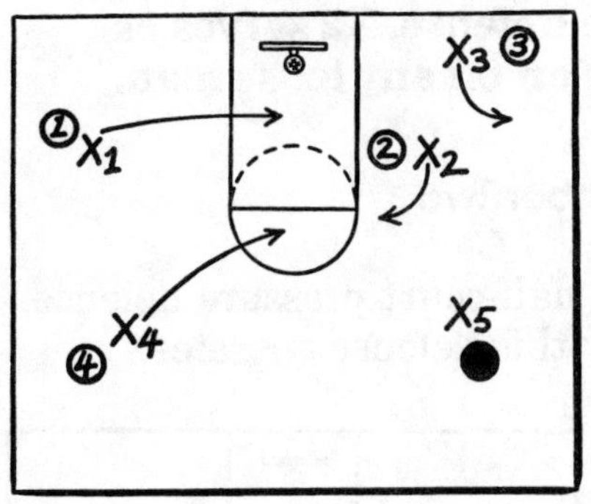

Diagram 2

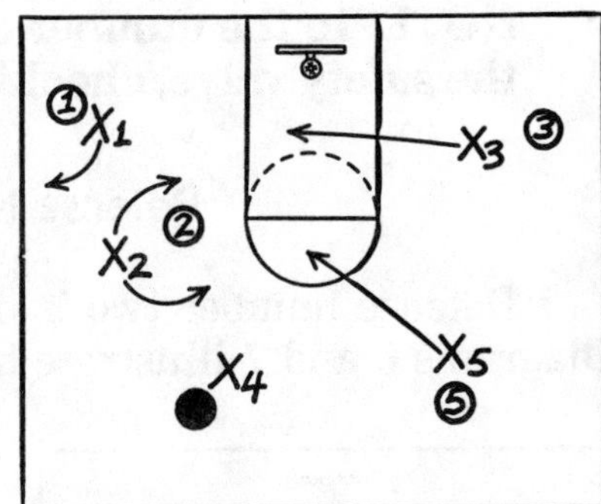

Diagram 3

Diagram 4

X3 pressures the ball hard. X5 drops off to two feet from the key. X1 sinks three to six feet inside the key area. X2 plays three-quarters or fully in front of the post man.

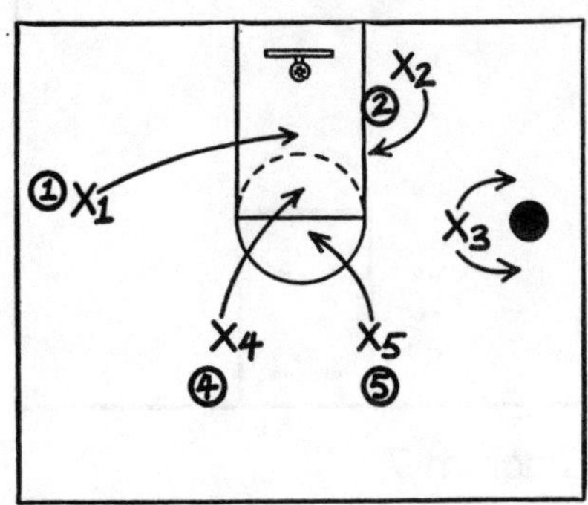

Diagram 4

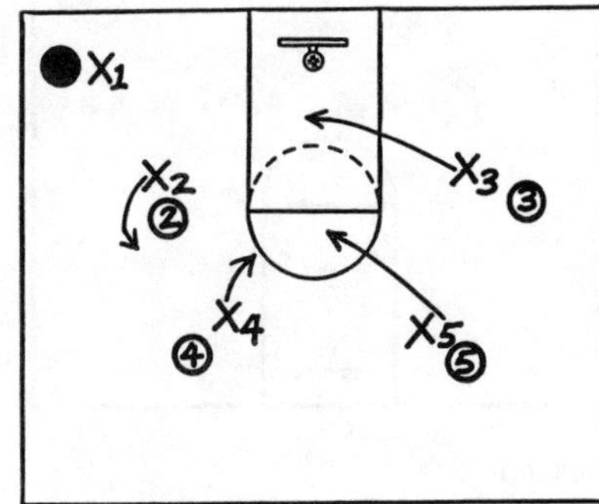

Diagram 5

Diagram 5

X1 pressures the ball hard. X2 plays three-quarters or completely in front of 02, attempting to keep the ball away from the inside area. X4 drops to a foot away from the key area. X5 sinks to a position two feet in the key. X3 sinks three to six feet inside the key directly in front of the basket.

NOTE: In the number one defense, X2 serves as the safety valve, checking off on any loose man.

Defense Number Two

Defense number two is our half-court pressure defense. Diagrams 6 and 7 illustrate how this defense operates.

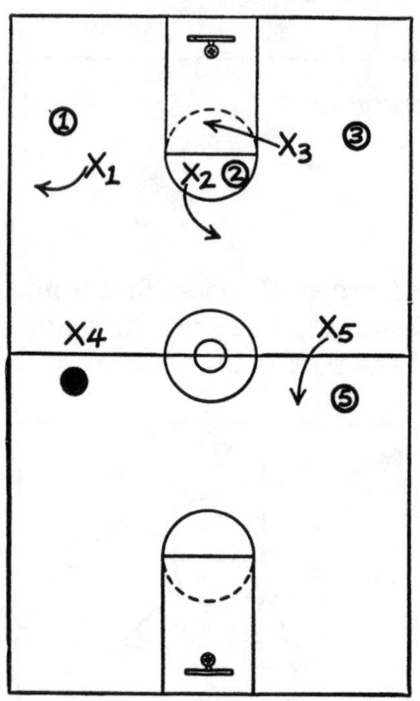

Diagram 6

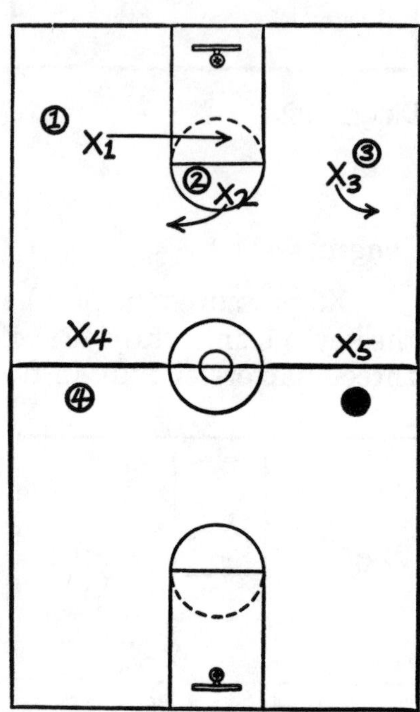

Diagram 7

Diagram 6

X4 pressures his man at the half-court line, forcing him to either sideline. X5 plays the passing lane to the right side of his man. X1 plays the passing lane to his man. X3 drops inside the key area and plays the passing lane if his man breaks to meet the ball. X2 plays three-quarters in front of his man, sometimes fully in front.

Diagram 7

X5 forces his man to either sideline and occasionally plays for a quick steal. X4 closes the passing lane to 04. X3 closes the passing lane to 03. X2 plays three-quarters around and occasionally in front of 02. X1 sinks three feet inside the key to help cover a lob pass to 02. If, however, his man breaks to meet the ball, he must close this passing lane.

> **NOTE: In this number two defense, X2 checks off on any loose man, using the arm that is closer to block the incoming pass.**

Defense Number Three

The three-quarter press is the third defense. It is shown in Diagrams 8 and 9.

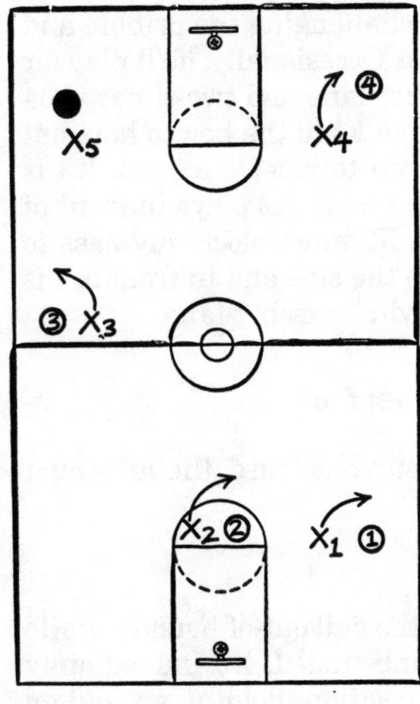

Diagram 8

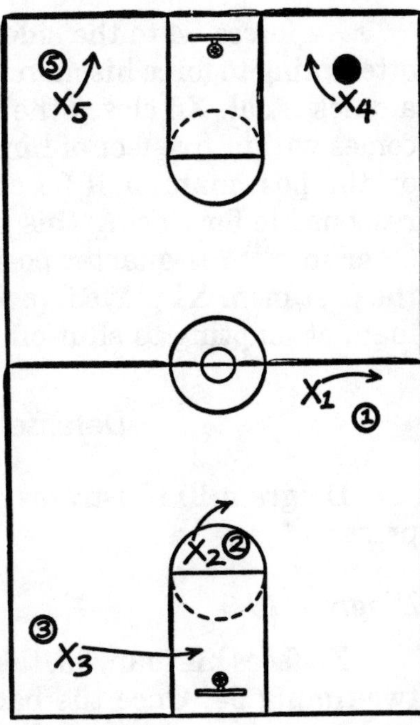

Diagram 9

Diagram 8

X5 meets his man head-on and forces him to the sideline, but he never allows his man to go down the sideline with the ball. Occasionally, X5 will play for a steal if the offensive man is slow to react. X4 plays in the passing lane of 04, two-timing the ball handler if he comes within five feet of player 04. X3 plays five feet to the side and in front of 03, closing the passing lane. X2 slides in front of 02, closing the passing lane into the post man. X1 sinks into the area near the key to help out on the post man, but if 01 breaks toward the ball, X1 must close this passing lane.

NOTE: The two front men must be quick and fast, and they must be able to react quickly when pressuring down court.

Diagram 9

X4 forces 04 to the sideline, challenging the dribble and attempting to force his man to stop. Occasionally, he'll play for a quick steal. X5 closes the passing lane and two-times if 04 comes within five feet of him. X3 sinks to the key to help out on the post man, or if 03 comes up to receive a pass, X3 is responsible for closing this passing lane. X2 plays in front of 02 or in a three-quarter position. X2 must block any pass to the post men. X1 plays five feet to the side and in front of his man, attempting to shut off this vital passing lane.

Defense Number Four

Diagram 10 illustrates our fourth defense, the full-court press.

Diagram 10

X5 faces his man, 05, taking the ball out-of-bounds, while two-timing 04. Once the ball is inbounded, X5 immediately goes into a one-on-one defensive position, holding ground on 05 all the way up the court. X4 two-times his man, facing him with his back to the ball and with his arms up. Once the ball is inbounded, he reverses quickly into a one-on-one holding-ground position all over the court.

X3 plays the passing lane, wherever his man may go on the initial pass. Once the ball is inbounded, he assumes a holding-ground position on his man all over the court. X2 plays the initial passing lane and attempts to block any pass from 05 to 02. X2 is also alert for any breakthrough, serving as a safety valve.

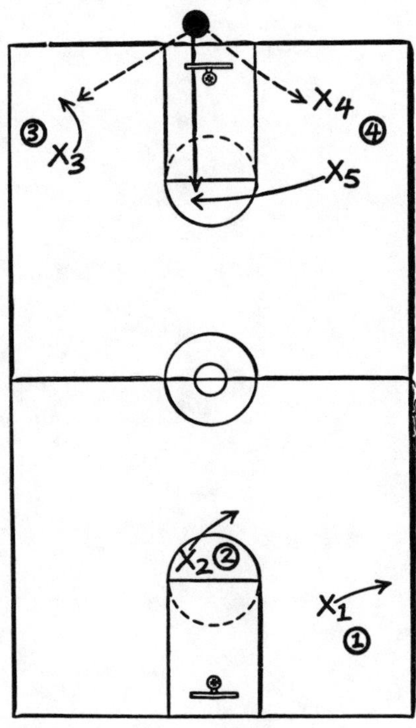

Diagram 10

X1 plays five feet to the side and in front of 01, attempting to block any pass to him.

Once the ball is inbounded, each man reverses into a one-on-one holding-ground position, keeping a distance of between five to seven feet from his man and challenging him every inch of the floor. When the ball has been successfully inbounded, the defensive men immediately take one-on-one defensive positions.

X5 releases from his two-time position on 04 and picks up his own man at the top of the key. X4 reverses and takes a head-on pressing position, holding ground on his man from one end of the court to the other. X3, X2, and X1 follow suit, occasionally attempting a quick steal.

NOTE: Once the ball is inbounded, the defense may go into the number three, two, or one defense.

21

Multiple-Pressure Defense

by Glenn Whittenberg

Head Basketball Coach
Proviso East High School
Maywood, Illinois

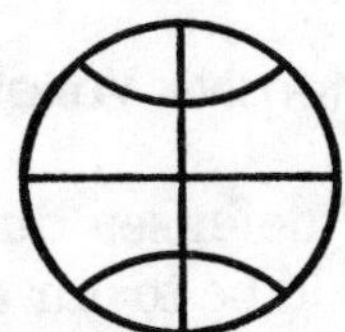

In ten years as the head coach at Proviso East High School (Maywood, Illinois), Glenn Whittenberg has won one state, three sectional, and eight regional titles. He has also won eight conference titles, four Christmas tournaments, and five Thanksgiving tournaments. Coach Whittenberg has a 241-52 career mark.

Defense wins games. So we devote most of our practice time to defense at Proviso East. With pressure defense, we try to dictate the offensive style of play. We apply constant pressure on the ball. We do not give up any part of the court without a battle.

Why pressure defense? If you asked a basketball player if he would rather bring the ball down court molested or unmolested, he would choose unmolested. Naturally, the offense would like to come down nice and easy and set up in a scoring pattern. That is why we use pressure defense, to disrupt our opponents' styles of play.

Defensive Variety

We use a variety of defenses during a game, changing whenever we think it would be to our advantage. Our greatest success has been with the man-to-man, 1-2-1-1, 2-2-1, and 1-3-1 half-court trap. Three of the many reasons for using the press are as follows:

1. To speed up the game
2. To force timeouts
3. To cause confusion among the offensive players

We also like to run, so we try to force a fast-moving, free-lance type of game from our opponents.

Selling Defense

Defense must be sold to your team and you must provide some incentive for your players to work hard enough to gain the recognition they want and need. Some players can be sold just by talking with them. Others must see some instant results. This can be accomplished by rewarding them when they do their job well.

At Proviso, we try to neutralize all of the publicity that the offensive players get from the news media and the fans by presenting awards to the defensive standouts in each game.

We also give awards for defensive excellence in practice, based on performance during certain drills.

Man-to-Man

Our man-to-man press is a face-guarding, switching press. We always press after a score when the ball must be taken out-of-bounds. We know that the offense has five seconds in which to get the ball inbounds. This gives us the valuable time we need to pick up our man and really put the pressure on him. We try to prevent the ball from getting inbounds. A typical alignment is shown in Diagram 1, with 0 representing the offense and V representing the defense.

Most coaches prefer their players to watch the belt line of the man they are guarding because that part of the body cannot fake. This is good, but I tell my players to look their men right in the eyes, because most high school players are not clever enough to use the eye fake. By watching the eyes, you may be able to learn where the ball is, because many players will be looking right at it.

In Diagram 1, V1's responsibility varies according to the game, but basically he is to worry, harass, and get in the way of the man who is standing out-of-bounds. V1 must be aggressive, quick, a good jumper, and a good anticipator. He should be able to disturb his man so much that his man will throw the ball away a few times during each game. When the ball is passed, V1 yells "Ball." This is so that defensive players who have their backs to the ball can react to the pass. After the throw-in, V1 positions his man so that this offensive man cannot get the ball back.

Another way we use V1 is to have him disregard the man out-of-bounds and concentrate his efforts on doubling with either V2 or V3. Usually, he will help defense the best ball-handling guard, forcing a weaker man to bring the ball down court.

V2 and V3 have the toughest assignments. They know that the offense is trying to get the ball to either O2 or O3. Because O2 and O3 will employ many moves to free themselves—screen, screen and roll, fake and go—V2 and V3 must be ready to talk, switch, and move to prevent the pass-in.

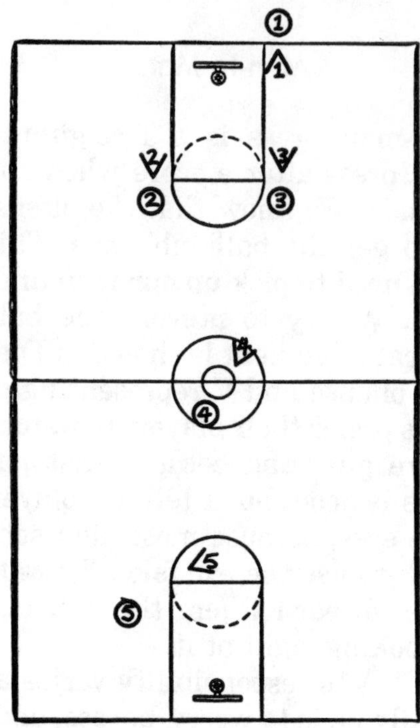

Diagram 1

NOTE: We prefer the square stance for our defensive men, as opposed to the one-foot-back method. The square stance allows easier and quicker movement in all directions than the staggered stance does.

V4 and V5 do not face their men blindly. They position themselves so that they can see their men and the ball. Their men are usually far enough away from the ball that they can use their positions without losing any advantage. Their positions should be such that they take away the largest parts of the floor from their men, making them break down the sidelines or away from the ball to get a pass. Once again, *our basic aim is to prevent any man from receiving the throw-in.*

We will switch on any man with the ball if he is coming freely down the court. He must be forced to change directions, stop the dribble, and pass. If we can make him go where he doesn't want to go, stop, change directions, pass, or go faster than he can handle the ball, then we have created an opportunity for a turnover.

When he is in an absolute face-guarding position, the defensive man has his back to the ball and must have help to know when the ball is about to come alive. In addition to V1 yelling "Ball" at the moment when the passer releases the ball, we instruct our players to time or anticipate the pass and then turn and look for the ball. We expect them to be able to count to four or five—the time allowed to get the ball in play.

NOTE: The man-to-man press is the best press in basketball because it keeps every offensive player working and doesn't allow for one or two players to stand around doing nothing as the zone presses sometimes do.

A good offensive team can adjust very easily to a stereotyped defensive team. For this reason, we employ the multiple defenses to keep the offense off-balance, allowing us the element of surprise.

Zone Defense

Our zone presses consist of the 1-2-1-1 and the 2-2-1. Both zones can be used either full-, three-quarter-, or half-court, and we try to use them at all of these positions. Our favorite zone press is the 1-2-1-1 simply because we have the greatest success with it. In the interest of simplicity, we name our alignments just the way they look in order to eliminate confusion or uncertainty among our players.

Diagram 2 shows the division of the court for full-court, three-quarter-court, and half-court zone presses. Diagrams 3-5 illustrate the alignments for the various zone presses.

With the full-court zone press we are not trying to prevent the throw-in (Diagram 3). We want to double on the ball immediately after the throw-in. We try to force the pass into one of the corners to make the double-team more effective. Many opponents, fearing the trap, will panic and turn the ball over when hit with this press.

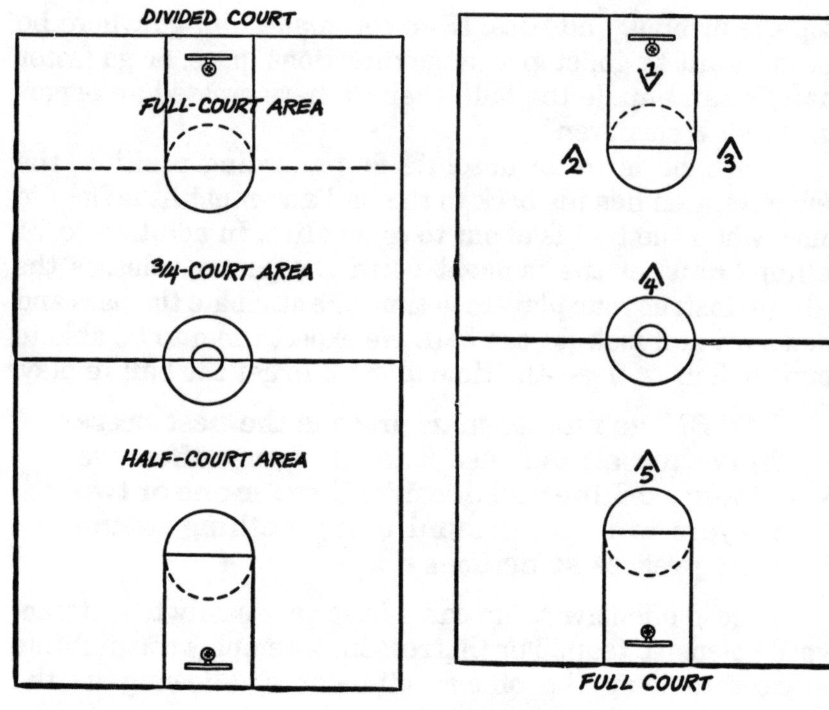

Diagram 2

Diagram 3

Our players are instructed to cover an area on the floor that depends on the location of the ball. We should keep the ball in front of the press. We do not try to take the ball away from the opposition (officiating prevents this). We do want the offense to make the mistake and "cough up" the ball without our risking a foul.

V1 should be the quickest and hardest-working guard. He is the trapper in the front line.

NOTE: V1 faces away from the ball on throw-ins to catch the movement of the offensive guards.

V2 and V3 must be quick and must play excellent position. They have outside responsibility. They must not allow the ball down the sideline. They must turn the play into V1.

The best athlete on the team should be V4. He should be agile, strong, big, and a good anticipator. V4 is the man who must intercept the passes, stop the ball when the front three men are whipped, and play great defense against the fast break to the basket.

We always seem to have one big man who is neither quick nor agile, so we try to hide him under the opponent's basket. This is V5. His responsibility is to protect the basket against any type of challenge.

If our zone press fails and we are able to stop the fast break, we always line up in a 2-1-2 or a 1-2-2 zone at the opponent's basket (Diagram 4). In Diagrams 5 and 6 the positions of all defensive men are shown in relation to the movement of the ball from one side to the other.

> **NOTE: There is an open area susceptible to the long diagonal pass. Such a pass, however, is relatively easy to recover and defense. V4 is aware of this weakness or opening and lays back, waiting to go after this pass.**

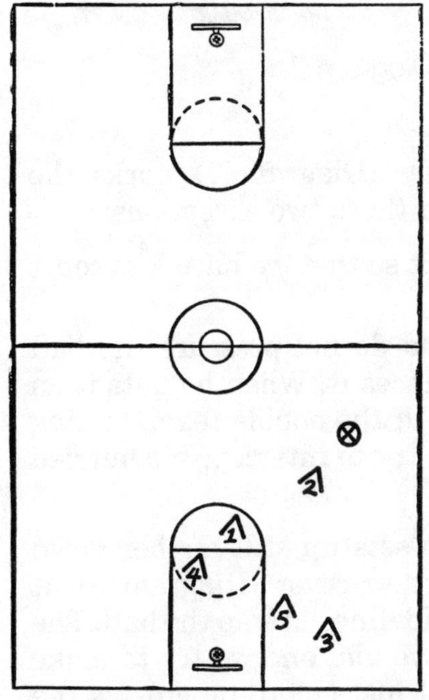

Diagram 4

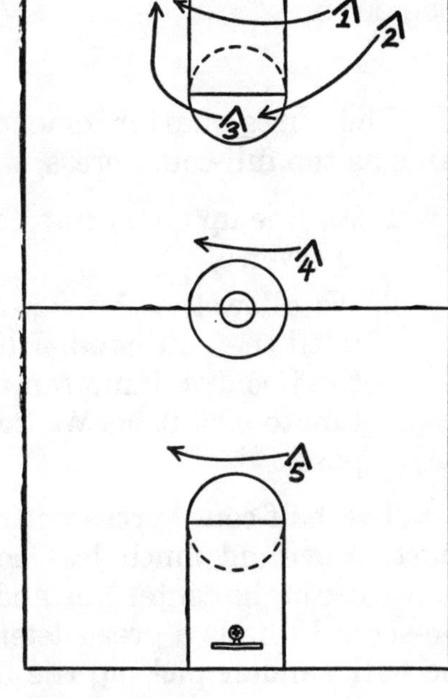

Diagram 5

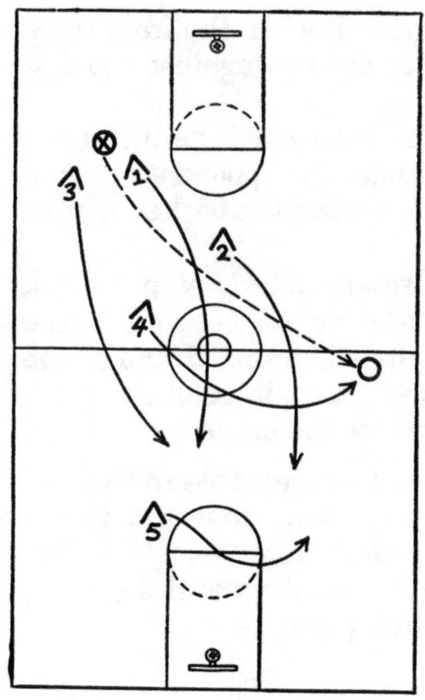

Diagram 6

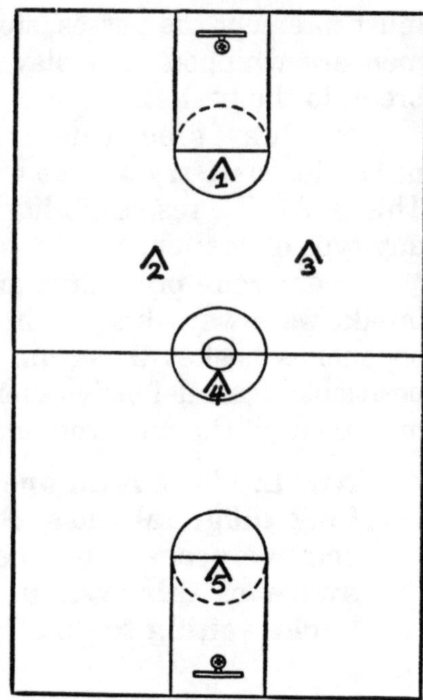

Diagram 7

The three-quarter zone press (Diagram 7) works the same as the full-court press, with these two exceptions:

1. We line up farther up court so that we have less court to cover.
2. We allow the throw-in and do not pressure the ball until the ball handler bounces it. When he puts it on the floor, we jump him with the double-team, forcing him to pick it up. We then try to intercept his hurried pass.

The half-court press or trap sets up still farther down court, providing much less court to cover (Diagram 8). It allows use of the center line and sidelines to trap the ball. The ten-second line is a great defensive aid, and we try to make the ball handler pick up the ball just before he crosses the center line. If the trap fails, we remain in the trap defense

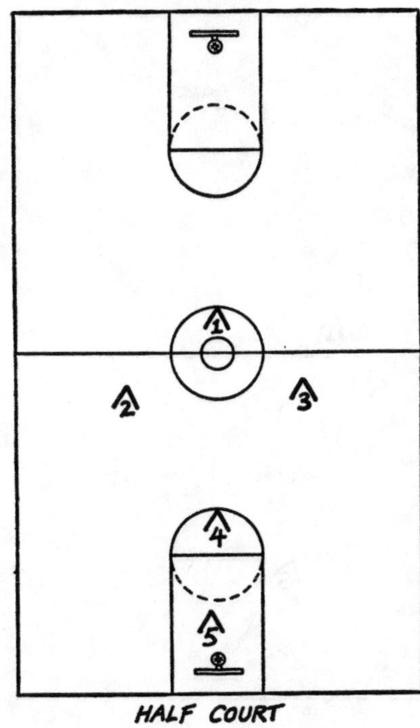

Diagram 8

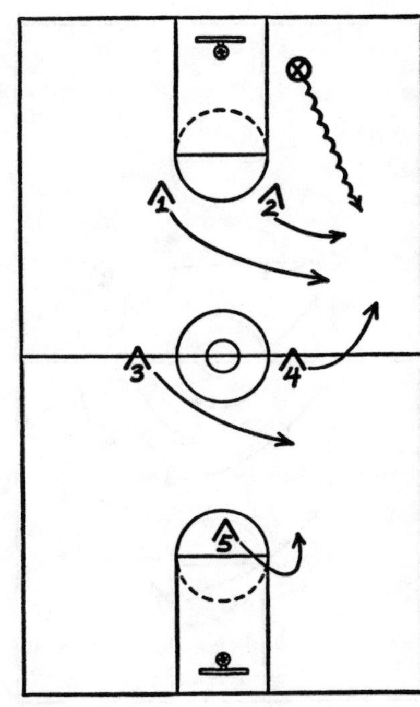

Diagram 9

until we either get the ball or the opponents score. We try to trap in all four corners of the offensive court.

2-2-1 Zone Press

The 2-2-1 zone press is used in the same areas as the 1-2-1-1, and the only difference is the alignment. The 2-2-1 is illustrated in Diagrams 9, 10, and 11.

As the diagrams illustrate, we only try to double-team the ball at the center line on either side of the court. If this fails to produce a turnover, we drop back into our 2-1-2 or 1-2-2 zone defense.

There is no big mystery about the way we change defenses during a game. The coach makes all changes. Any changes made during a game, good or bad, are made by the coach. Players should be instructed to play the game and should not have to worry about coaching.

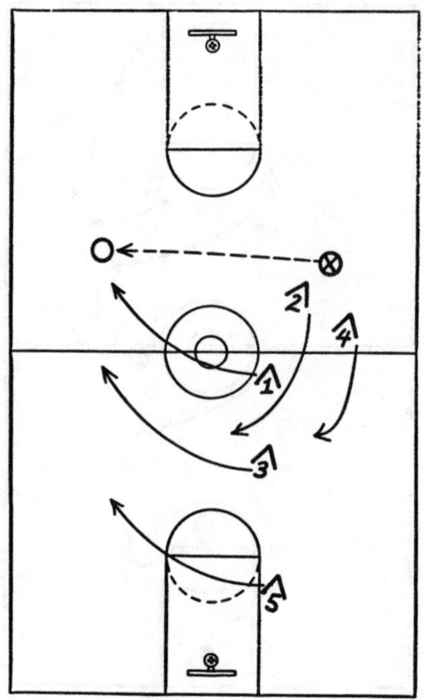

Diagram 10

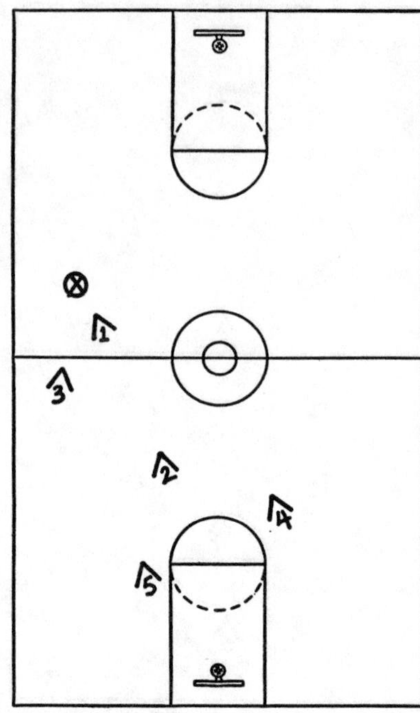

Diagram 11

Our defensive system is very simple. We want to keep it simple, believing that perfected simplicity is more successful than unconventional defenses. In conclusion, I would like to state that the basis for any successful team is conditioning, discipline, and defense—in that order.

Part Four

DEFENSIVE EXECUTION

22

Stop Percentage Shots and Penetration

by Joe Schlimgen

Former Head Basketball Coach
Emery High School
Emery, South Dakota

After coaching the varsity basketball team at Emery High School (Emery, South Dakota) to a 90-25 won-lost record, Joe Schlimgen now assists the varsity and works full-time for the football team.

Many factors contributed to our state championship in 1973, with defense probably heading the list. We used many different defensive techniques all season long, depending on our opponents and the game situation.

NOTE: We employed a full-court man-to-man press, a full-court zone press, a tight aggressive man-to-man, and some zone defense when our opponents were taking the ball out-of-bounds under their own basket.

Defense is the difference between winning and losing in high school basketball today. There are so many more great high school shooters now as compared to fifteen years ago, especially when it comes down to championship play. In fact, good defense can be the difference day in and day out.

Sagging Man-to-Man Defense

Our most effective defense was the sagging man-to-man, sometimes mistakenly described by the opponents as a match-up zone.

NOTE: My philosophy of defense is very simple: Make the opponent shoot the shot he is least likely to make, and then rebound.

There are many reasons why we used the sagging man-to-man at our school this past year. Our size was one reason; the biggest man on our squad was 6′3″ and not a regular. Actually, the team was very physical with good overall leg speed. What the boys lacked for leg speed early in the season was worked on daily for perfection before tournament time.

The second factor that influenced our defensive choice was our bench strength, especially in the early part of the season. By tournament time, we were about eight deep as far as defensive talent, but still somewhat impaired as far as offensive timing was concerned.

We could not afford the foul trouble which comes with a tight man-to-man defense. With the sagging man-to-man, we lost only three men via the foul route during our 27-game campaign to the state title. This type of defense also gave us good initial position for rebounding on the defensive boards.

NOTE: The sagging man-to-man cut down on the switching of defensive assignments that would be necessary for a tight man-to-man defense to play well against a good pick-and-roll pattern team. Switching defensive assignments when necessary is still easier with the sagging man-to-man.

Defensive Strategy

Our defensive strategy was to take away as quickly as possible the three offensive weapons which every basketball player possesses when in control of the ball (see Diagrams 1 through 5):

1. The good shot
2. The dribble
3. The pass

As far as the shot was concerned, we always worked to take away the good percentage shot. Our scouting reports would indicate favorite moves and shots of particular individuals. These shots we would also take away from them. With our height, we did not believe we could block or intimidate opponents' shots, although we did possess good timing and jumping ability. (Incidentally, we averaged six blocked shots per game.)

When the opponent (with the ball) was out beyond the 15- to 20-foot zone, we stayed back away from him a step and a half and made him prove he could shoot from that range. If he attempted a shot, we were close enough to get a hand in his face.

NOTE: If he was connecting with any consistency, we moved the defensive man up tighter to be more bothersome to his shooting. The step-and-a-half technique gave us plenty of time to react to a dribble or a penetrating pass.

When an opponent would drop a dribble, we would attack to force him to pick up his second offensive weapon. Then, depending upon whether he was within good shooting range or not, we would dictate our next defensive move. If he was within the 15-foot zone, we would stay tight and harass him, making any shot tough.

If he was outside the 20-foot mark without a dribble, we would drop off and protect against all penetrating passes. A penetrating pass to us was any pass going into the 15-foot zone. Even if a man had the ball beyond the 20-foot mark with the dribble remaining, we would drop back two or three steps to prevent the inside penetrating pass.

Nothing is more tempting to a shooter than to have an open shot from 20 to 25 feet, even though many coaches know that it's not a good shot for most high school players. I do not feel that a perimeter pass hurts a sagging man-to-man defense as it often does a zone. After a few times down the floor against the sagging man-to-man which gives up the perimeter pass, an offense tends to get lax and careless with passes. This leaves them vulnerable to interception and bad passes.

Many times our guards were instructed to meet the opposing guards a step across the center stripe and stop their dribble and penetration there. By this action we hoped to force a longer pass to the post or forwards, making interception more likely. It made their underneath men come out of good shooting range to get the ball, thus making it more difficult to start their offense.

NOTE: This also put our defense in good position to start clicking before there was a true offensive threat.

We defensed the fast break by keeping our smallest guard back; when a shot would go up, he would immediately start retreating in defense of the long pass. He was instructed not to allow an opponent behind him to receive a potential scoring pass.

Our underneath men would harass the rebounder to keep him from getting the quick release pass and retreat a step or two ahead of their men. If the quick shot release pass was accomplished, the guard who started to retreat with the shot would drop to the head of the opponents' key, again protecting against the long pass and forcing the ball to be dribbled to be advanced, allowing the rest of our defense time to retreat.

> **NOTE: When we stopped the opponent outside the 20 foot mark or out of his shooting range, we would drop back to the middle and force a neutral or digressive pass. This gains the opponent only his three offensive options again.**

Strategy Illustrated

- **Diagram 1:** Guard 1 is confronting the man with the ball to stop penetration deep in back court. Guard 2 is a step and a half inside and two steps back from his man, making a long pass dangerous.

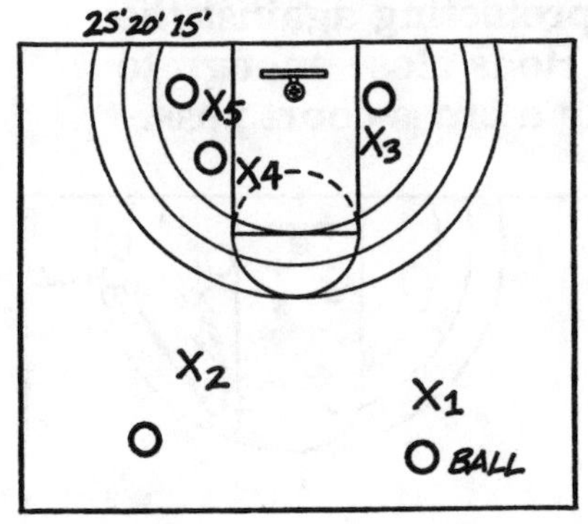

Diagram 1

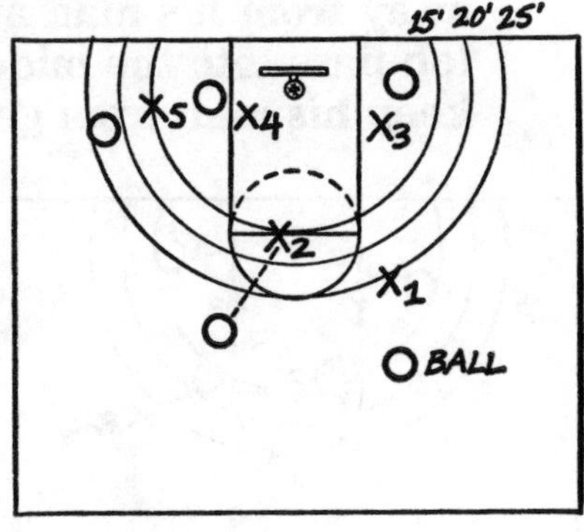

Diagram 2

> **NOTE: Three offensive men underneath are all in the 15-foot zone, so defensive men are playing tight half-man defense between their men and the ball.**

- **Diagram 2:** Guard 1 is a step and a half away from his man, who has the ball, because he is outside the good shooting percentage range. Guard 2 has dropped back to protect against passes into the 15-foot zone. Defensive man 3 is a step away and a step in front of his man, who is in the 15-foot zone.

NOTE: Same defense by man 4 while defensive man 5 is well back from his man because he is outside the 20-foot range and across court from the ball.

- **Diagram 3:** Guard 1 is confronting the ball, which has moved into percentage range, so he is up on his man. Guard 2 has the weakside guard, who is also in good shooting range, but we are protecting against penetration into the middle with weakside guard back two steps.

NOTE: Defensive men 3 and 4 are half-manning their assignments, forcing them to the outside to receive the ball. Defensive man 5 is sagging away from his man and protecting against the lob pass into the middle. He is close enough to keep his man from getting a cross-court pass.

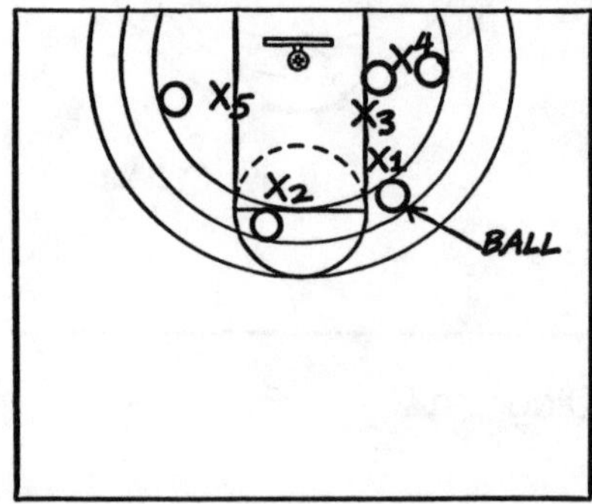

Diagram 3

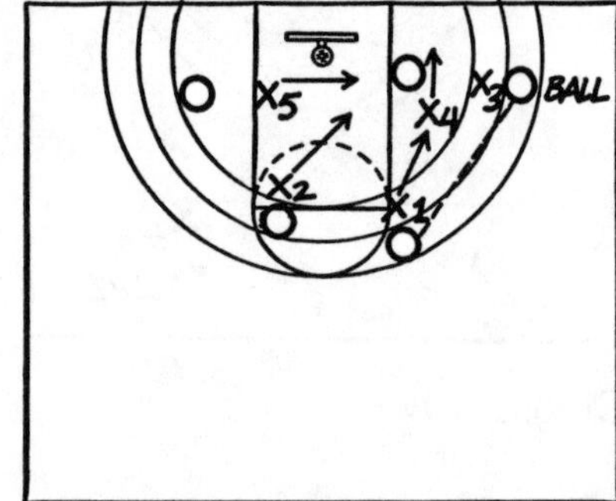

Diagram 4

- **Diagram 4:** Guard 1 is dropping away to protect against a pass into the middle. Guard 2 will be back in the middle. Defensive man 3 has forced his man outside to get the ball and is back away because of his man's range from the basket.

NOTE: Defensive man 4 is protecting against the quick pass into the pivot. Defensive man 5 is coming across to protect against the lob pass into the middle.

- **Diagram 5:** All defensive men have retreated to positions to protect against and completely cut off any pass into the 15-foot range. All defensive men are still in good position to stop their own men from getting good position for a shot.

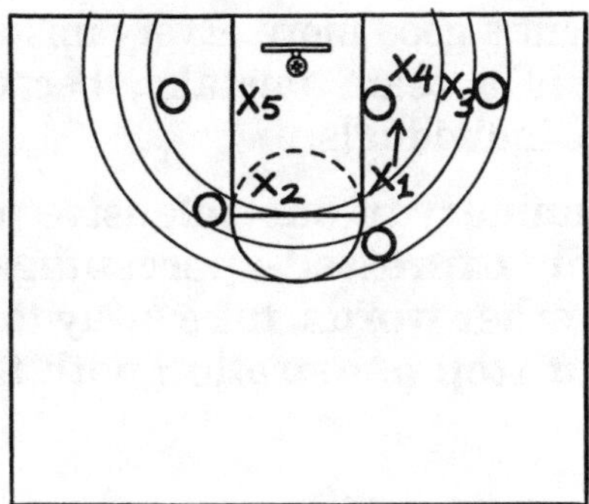

Diagram 5

Defensive Practice Sessions

Our defensive practice sessions are spent running drills, discussing information, and working on scrimmage.

- **Drills:** Our drills consist of one-on-one situations in which the defensive man has to keep his hands in the back of his shorts, various three-on-two situations, shuffle drills, shuffle and talk drills in which five men shuffle in good defensive position and direct each other to avoid collisions, and pick-and-roll drills.

- **Discussions:** Our discussions take place before, during, and after practice. It is most important to a team to discuss the "hows" and "whys" of doing things a certain way. We feel that a young man has a right to know why he is doing a drill and how it will help us to accomplish the objectives of good defense. Many times the player himself comes up with a good suggestion that might help win ball games.
- **Scrimmage:** After drills and discussions, when the scrimmage comes, the boys know what is expected of them and can always find their own mistakes and correct them. When correct procedure is used, they know they have done it right and can have that feeling of success, even if the coach should miss an error or fail to compliment a good move. Every mistake on a basketball court is a team mistake, because teams lose games—not individuals.

NOTE: A summary of our defensive philosophy can be simply expressed—percentage and penetration. In other words, take away the percentage shot and stop penetration with the dribble and pass.

23

Defense: There Are No Bad Nights

by Robert L. Hartranft

Freshman Basketball Coach
Howitt Junior High School
Farmingdale, New York

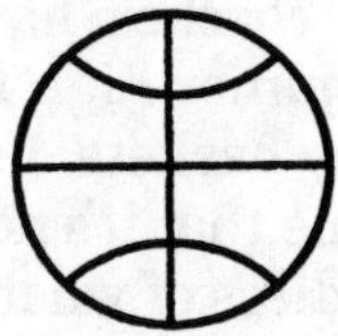

Robert L. Hartranft is the freshman basketball coach at Howitt Junior High School (Farmingdale, New York). He has compiled a 112-19 record with a current 34 consecutive game winning streak. His teams have won 71 of their last 75 games.

The title of this article is one of the maxims taught to our boys. We believe that tough man-to-man defense, taught correctly, will eliminate those bad nights. We feel that pressure defense must be painstakingly taught. Many coaches *talk* about defense and *tell* their boys to play it, but they don't *teach* them *how* to play it.

It is a difficult task to convince a boy that defense wins games. Let's face it, when players practice without a coach around, they practice shooting and dribbling—not defense. We spend 60 to 70 percent of our practice time on defense, emphasizing one basic law: *If you don't play big D, you'll sit on the little b (bench).*

Many junior high coaches have told me that playing pressure defense at the junior high level is too tough to teach and results in many easy baskets. I don't believe this and our results have convinced me that it's not true. Our defense keeps us in every game, regardless of what our offense is doing. Our boys have learned to play tough, pressure, man-to-man defense and have gone on to the junior varsity and varsity levels, improving on the same type of defense.

Teaching Defense

Here is an outline of how we teach defense to our boys.

1. Stance: Low base, feet spread approximately the width of the shoulders, weight evenly distributed (like sitting in a chair).

2. Footwork: a) Slide feet, don't cross feet.

b) Drop-step or swing-step—very important when the ball handler reverses. The defensive player must drop-step in the same direction to get an angle, coming up strong on the opponent and squaring up (recovery).

c) Recovery (as explained above).

Drill (Diagram 1)

Line up in three lines with five players in each line. The coach stands before the lines. He uses his hand to indicate the

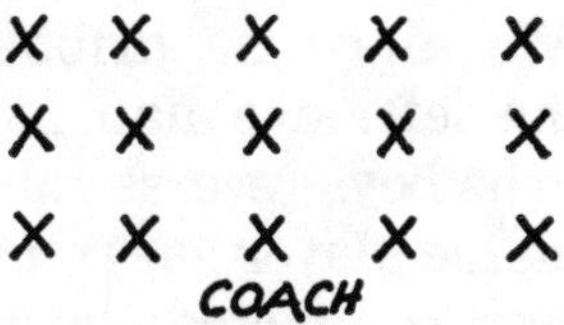

Diagram 1

direction of the slide. He indicates the drop-step and recovery by voice.

Coaching Points:

1. Check stance.
2. Player's feet should never leave the floor when sliding.
3. Blow the whistle occasionally and have players freeze. If they are leaning, they are doing something wrong. For example, feet may be too far apart, player may be picking up feet instead of sliding, player's feet may be too far forward or too far back.

This drill is a good conditioner. During a game, if a player is too high in his stance, it may indicate that he is tired, a condition that might have been prevented by this drill. When we feel that the stance and footwork drill has been mastered, we go on to our next drill.

3. One-on-one: If our opponent has not yet dribbled, we always respect his first fake, assuming he is not within shooting range, with a quick drop-step. We then recover and play him nose-to-nose. Our head is on the ball, forcing the offensive player to turn. We slide, drop-step, recover, slide, and so on. We want our opponent to make the mistake, so we put tremendous pressure on the ball.

Drill (Diagram 2)

Form two lines on one side of the basket and two lines on the other side of the basket. First, two boys on one side of the basket begin up the floor. The coach follows the boys up court, yelling at the defender: "Head on the ball," "Turn him,"

"Slide," "Recover." We allow no dribbling, with the back continually toward the defensive man. If the coach is satisfied with a boy's defense, the boys reverse roles at the other end of the court. If not, the same player goes on defense again. When these two players have completed the drill, begin the drill with two players from the other side of the basket. We use this drill every day.

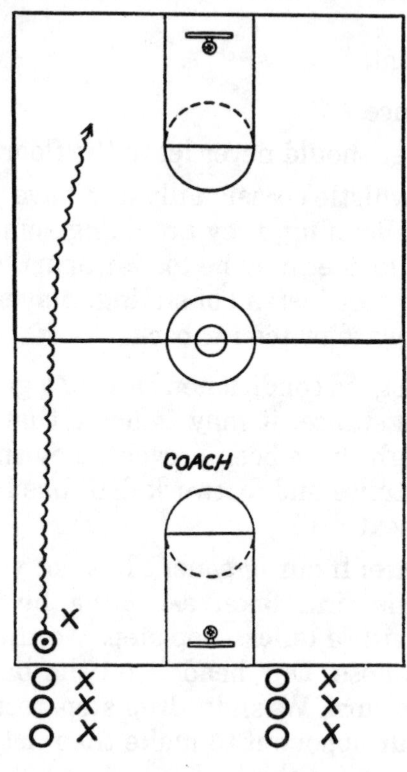

Diagram 2

Coaching Points:

1. Defensive man begins with his hands behind his back. The idea is not to steal the ball unless the dribbler puts

the ball right in front, unprotected. Let the dribbler make the mistake.

2. Head on the ball: If a man dribbles through a defensive man, it's an offensive foul. The idea is to turn the offensive man constantly.
3. Drop-step and swing-step are the most difficult. Keep working on them.
4. Encourage the defensive player: "Good job, Bill!"
5. If beaten, the defensive player runs after the dribbler, cutting him off. The defensive man doesn't slide until he has caught up with him.
6. At the end of the one-on-one, box out. The defensive player must realize that his job is not done until he has boxed his man out.

NOTE: Our defense, although much emphasis is placed on playing the man one-on-one, is still based on a five-man concept. We stress one-on-one because we want our defensive man to feel comfortable when applying tremendous pressure to the ball. When an easy basket is scored, it is usually the fault of at least three players.

4. Guard-to-guard (help and recover): We feel that our defense should always be in a help position, but players must also be ready to recover to their own man.

Drill (Diagram 3)

Begin with a demonstration, using two defensive men and two offensive men. After demonstrating, divide players into four groups of four players each. Rotate offensive and defensive players. The offensive players cannot go past the foul line extended. The defensive player who is playing the ball plays tough, pressure defense, forcing the dribbler to the middle. The other defensive man is in a help position, ready to pick up the dribbler if his teammate is beaten. The offensive man passes to the now open man. The helping defensive player must recover to his man, forcing him to the middle where he will now get help from his teammate. The defensive help player must talk to this teammate: "Help on your left," "Help on your right."

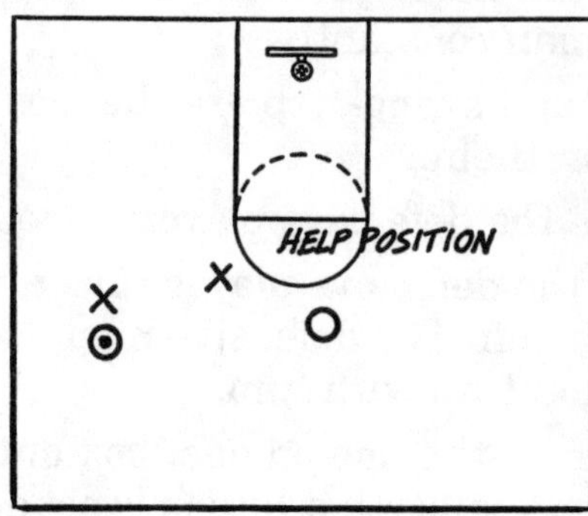

Diagram 3

Coaching Points:

1. Don't let the offense go past the foul line extended, or you will be defeating the purpose of this drill.
2. Defensive players who are on the ball must force their men to the middle.
3. The help man must be open to the ball. He must see the ball and his man. He must never lose sight of the ball or his man.
4. The help man must be one pass away from his man. This means *passing lane*.
5. When the help man recovers to his man, he should recover to the outside, forcing his man to the middle. The outside foot should be slightly back and to the outside of the other man's outside foot. This is important to teach.
6. This exercise requires real hustle.
7. At first, you can have the two offensive players in each group just pass and catch so that both defensive players learn to slide together. Timing is extremely important.

Drill (Diagram 4)

Using the same alignment as in the preceding drill, teach the players how to front a cutter. Allow the help man's opponent to cut down the middle into the three-second lane.

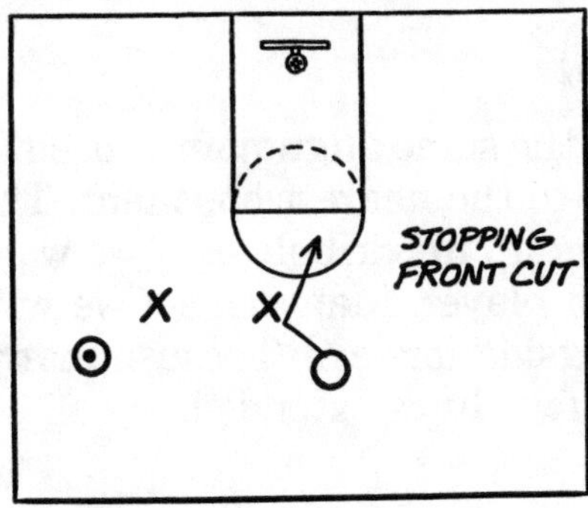

Diagram 4

Coaching Points:

1. Tell the defensive men that they are not to allow the cutter to cut in front of them. They are to step up on the cutter, forcing him to go back door.
2. If the help man is in the proper passing lane, the front cut is almost impossible.
3. When the cutter is going back door, defense opens to the ball and never turns back on the passer. Defense watches the ball as it goes to the cutter. It looks like an easy pass to make, but remember that there is a tremendous amount of pressure on the ball.

Drill

As in the two previous drills, use the same alignment. This time you'll be working on switching, hedging, and fighting over a pick.

Coaching Points:

1. We don't encourage switching at first. We prefer our boys to learn to fight over the top of the pick. We tell

the players to make themselves "thin" while going over the top.

2. The help man must alert his teammate to the pick.
3. Our help man steps back on all picks unless we are hedging or jump-switching.

Drill (Diagram 5)

Once again, the same alignment is used. We now work on denying the ball to the nearest opponent. This is used if the dribbler has given up his dribble or if we want to "shut off" a particularly good player. Many times we will also deny the ball to the strongside forward (because many offenses begin with a forward), foul lines extended.

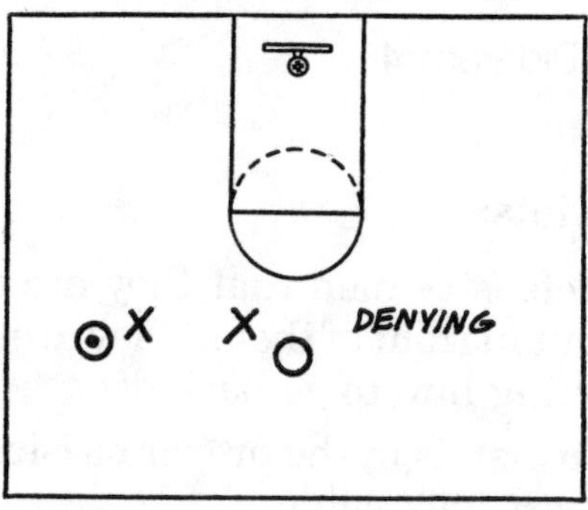

Diagram 5

Coaching Points:

1. The man on the ball calls "Deny" once the dribbler stops.
2. Player denies by getting his body slightly behind the opponent to the ball side. He uses the hand closer to the ball to discourage the pass. His inside foot should be slightly in front of the opponent to the ball side. This forces the opponent to go back door.
3. When he goes back door, the defense opens to the ball.

5. Guard-to-forward: This is similar to guard-to-guard.

Drill (Diagram 6)

When our guard is beaten, we want our strongside forward to be in a help position. This forward must stop the dribbler and still recover to his own man. This is a good conditioning drill. The idea of the drill is to let the guard penetrate so that the forward has to stop him. The guard then passes off to the offensive forward, and the help man recovers to his man. We will then let the forward drive toward the middle, and our guard must be in a help position. The forward passes off to the offensive guard, and the help must recover. Next, deny the pass to the forward. Force the forward to go back door. The forward will then open to the ball properly.

Coaching Points: See coaching points 2 through 6 for the guard-to-guard section.

6. Guard-to-guard-to-forward: Here we want to teach the concept of playing the man when he is one pass away or two passes away from the ball. Once again, the *pass away* is the *passing lane*. Stay in the passing lane to help. Try not to allow a pass through; instead, force a backdoor cut.

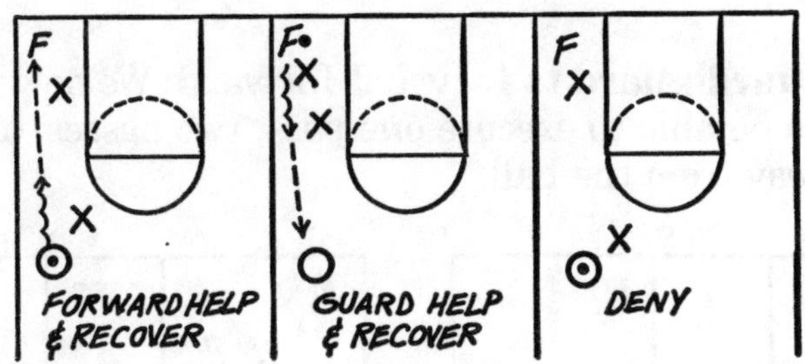

Diagram 6

Drill (Diagram 7)

Give the ball to guard 02. Make sure X1 and X3 are one pass away, in help position, and open to the ball (Diagram 7a).

Give the ball to forward 01. Make sure X2 is one pass away, in help position, and open to the ball. X3 should be two passes away, in help position, and open to the ball (Diagram 7b). (If cuts are made, defensive position dictates a backdoor cut.)

Give the ball to 03 . Make sure that X2 is one pass away, in a help position, and open to the ball. He is now the offside forward (Diagram 7c).

Coaching Points:

1. At first, let the offense pass the ball around without cutting or dribbling. The coach can now check position of body, etc.
2. The biggest problem is making sure that the man two passes away is not too low. If he is too low on his man, he will not be able to prevent a front cut. Make sure that he's in the proper position to force a backdoor cut.
3. After the position is correct, allow cutting and dribbling. Players must deny all cuts with the inside hand to the ball. This is very important because it prevents fouls.
4. Remind your players that they must always see their man and the ball. Again, we are putting tremendous pressure on the ball, no matter who has it or where it is.

7. Guard-guard to forward-forward: We now want our players to be able to execute one pass, two passes, and three passes away from the ball.

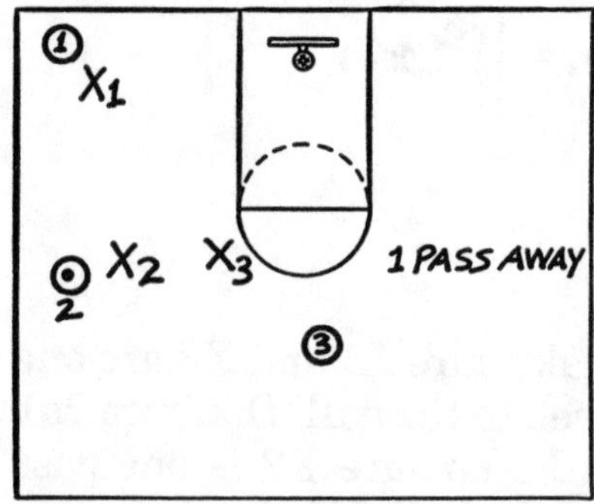

Diagram 7a

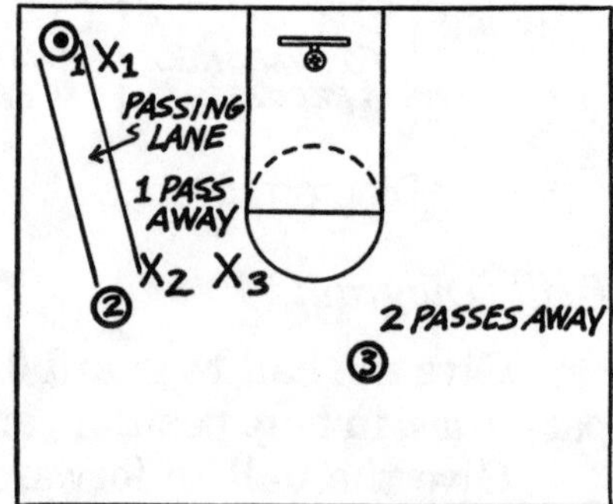

Diagram 7b

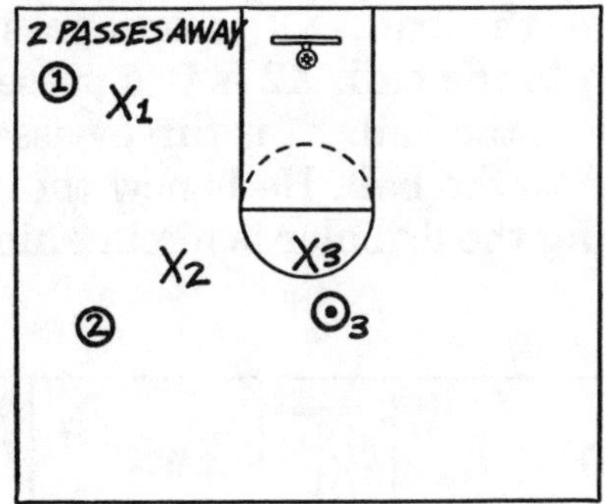

Diagram 7c

Drill (Diagram 8)

The ball is passed around slowly. Each position is noted.

02 has the ball. X1 and X3 are one pass away, in help position and open to the ball. X4 is two passes away, in help position and open to the ball. He is the offside forward (Diagram 8a).

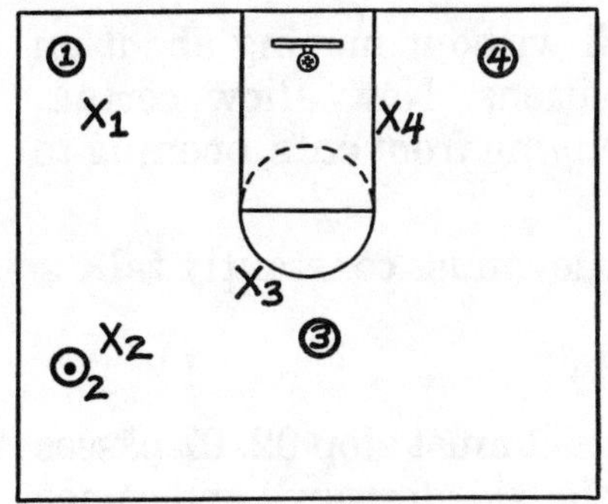

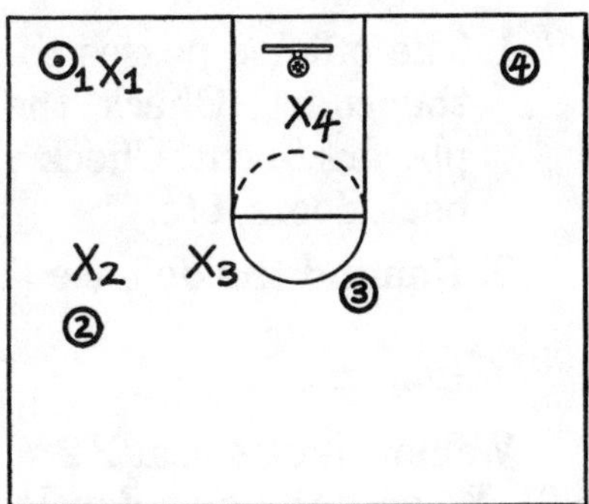

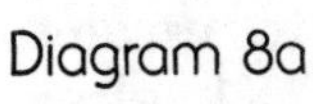
Diagram 8a

Diagram 8b

Player 01 has the ball. X2 is one pass away, in help position, and open to the ball. X3 is two passes away, in help position, and open to the ball. X4 is three passes away, in help position, and open to the ball. He is the offside forward (Diagram 8b).

Player 04 has the ball. X3 is one pass away, in help position, and open to the ball. X2 is two passes away, in help position, and open to the ball. X1 is three passes away, in help position, and open to the ball. He is now the offside forward. The man pressuring the dribbler is forcing him to the middle (Diagram 8c).

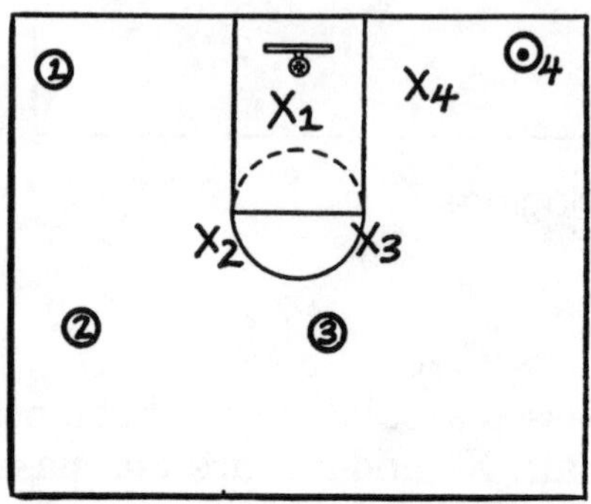

Diagram 8c

Coaching Points:

1. The offense passes the ball without moving about on the court. Check the positions. Now allow certain players to cut. Check on denying front cuts, opening to back doors, etc.
2. Remind the defense that they must constantly talk.

Drill (Diagram 9)

We now let 02 beat X2 so that X1 must stop 02. 02 passes to 01. X4 sees the play developing (offside forward) and comes over to stop 01 or take the charge. X3 drops down to prevent the pass from 01 to 04. X3 is the offside guard. X1, after stopping 02, recovers to 01 for double-team. X2 drops in to split 02 and 03.

NOTE: As soon as the ball is passed out, we pick up and pressure the ball. We get ourselves in a help position, preventing front cuts. We do not follow the cutters all the way to the corners.

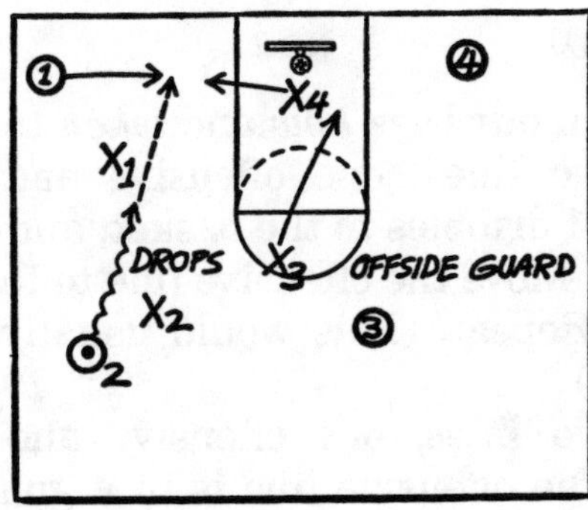

Diagram 9

Coaching Points:

1. Any baseline move by the offensive player is backed up by the offside forward. If he is in the proper help position, he should have no trouble getting there.
2. On any baseline movement, when the offside forward goes over to pick up, the offside guard must drop down into the vacated passing lane to prevent the pass or box out the offensive forward. This is critical, and it is our biggest weakness.
3. We do not want the baseline move to be used. We coach against it and turn everything back to the middle. However, you know it still does happen.
4. Every player must know whether he is an offside forward or guard. It will change quickly and he must be able to read it and adjust accordingly. The ability to read this situation takes constant practice. It is very important that all our players play out front (guard position) and on the back line (forward position). A forward never knows when he is going to be taken out front, and he may end up being in an offside guard position. He must recognize this. The same is true for our guards in reference to the backline position. This is why all of our players do these drills, whether they are forward drills, guard drills, or post drills.

Drill (Diagram 10)

We now teach our boys *how* and *when* to take a charge.

We have two lines, one offensive and one defensive (Diagram 10a). X1 dribbles to the basket, and 01 steps in and takes the charge. Move the offensive line to the baseline for a different angle. Repeat. (This would usually be our offside forward's charge.)

We have two lines, one offensive and one defensive (Diagram 10b). The offensive line is in a guard position out front. X1 drives the middle. 01 hustles over and takes the charge. (Our head-on-the-ball, nonreaching, pressure defense also draws offensive fouls.)

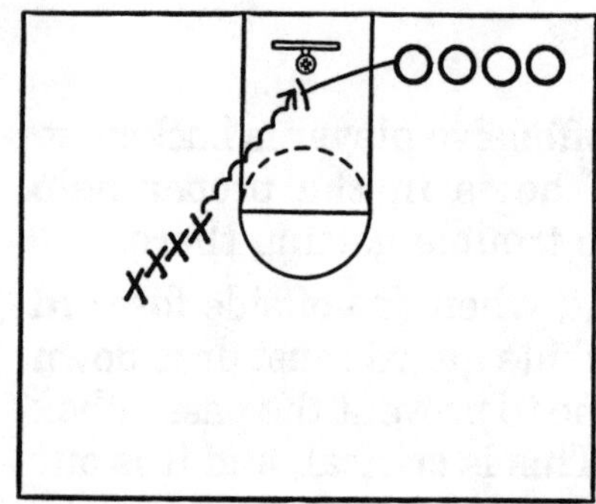

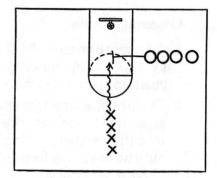

Diagram 10a

Diagram 10b

Coaching Points:

1. Hands up (not out to the sides) on all charges.
2. Fall backward; but don't overact.
3. Get the head on the ball while the opponent is dribbling. This will help prevent slight hits. We are looking for solid hits.
4. Don't try to block the shot—just get position.
5. Praise those who do well. Tell them not to chicken out.
6. Alert the officials before the game. If they don't call a foul, get on them early. Otherwise, your boys will start shying away.

NOTE: You can't take a charge if your opponent sees it coming. Surprise is the key element. Far too many times, my boys have tried to take a charge in the middle of the floor. Our opponents go right around. Last year, we took 70 charges in 14 games. In two of the 14 games, we didn't take any. Do you think the officials didn't hear about it in those two games?

Drill (Diagram 11)

Our next drill lets the offense do anything it wants—pick away, pick to, or cut through. Our defense must adjust accordingly. The coach stands out front. When a defensive mistake is made, the player is corrected, and then he runs on the sideline. Examples of possible mistakes are not opening to the ball, not fronting a cutter, not being in a help position, not taking a charge, not recognizing the duty of the offside forward or guard, and not boxing out. As soon as another defensive mistake is made, the player who was running replaces the one who made the mistake. Soon, without telling your boys, they'll say, "I know, I didn't front the cutter." It is a good conditioning drill, and it teaches the players that our defense can't allow for mental mistakes.

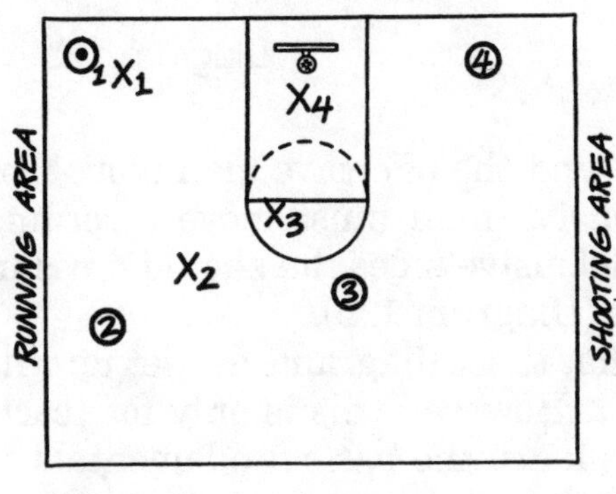

Diagram 11

NOTE: You may notice that we have been working with only four defensive players. Our fifth

man is usually the post man. All of our players must learn how to play the high- and low-post man—not just the center. We never know when our guard will be taken down low, so we must be ready for it. We want the post man to be denied the ball, whether he is high or low. Once again, we deny with the inside hand to the ball, forcing him to the middle.

Drill (Diagram 12)

The coach throws a pass to the post man. Post defense tries to prevent the pass with the inside hand to the ball (Diagram 12a).

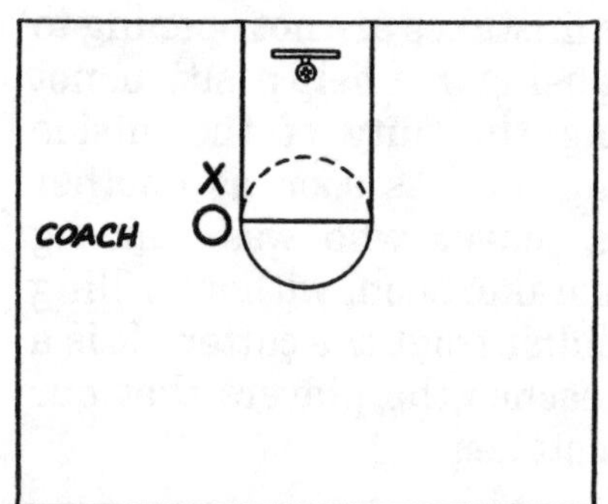

Diagram 12a

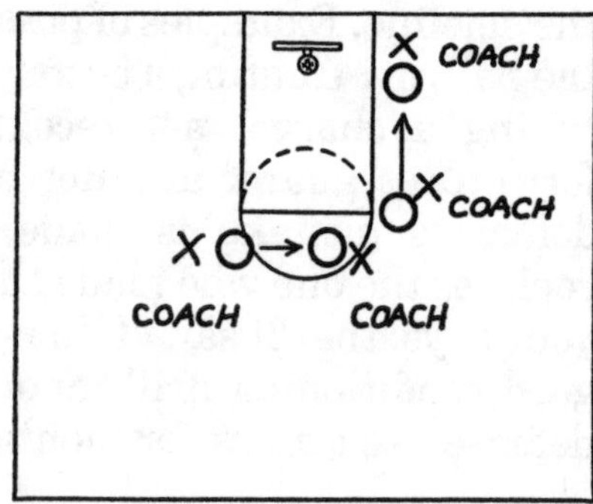

Diagram 12b

The coach and the offensive man move from high to low post. The defensive man must move accordingly, and if he must change defensive sides, he should cross in front with a step-over move (Diagram 12b).

I realize that these diagrams are set up with a particular offense in mind. However, this is only for teaching purposes. Once your boys learn the basic fundamentals of this defense, they will apply them to any offense you come up against.

As you can see, this defense, if played correctly, requires great teamwork and intelligent movement. It must be broken down and taught step by step. Remember, be patient. Don't move on to the next drills until the ones you are working on are done correctly. Keep going back to these drills for reinforcement.

You must always pressure the ball. We pick up at the mid-court line and pressure it wherever it goes. You will have to hound your players constantly to keep pressure on the ball. They are afraid that they are going to get beaten. Stress that they will be getting help. I almost never yell at the man who was beaten unless he was beaten baseline. It is usually the help man or the offside forward who is criticized and corrected.

Al LoBalbo, former coach at Fairleigh Dickinson University (Rutherford, New Jersey), once said, "Don't expect your boys to do something in a game that you didn't teach them in practice." This is something that I heartily believe in.

24

Pressure Defense Fundamentals

by Richard J. Zaranek

Head Basketball Coach
St. Clare of Montefalco School
Grosse Pointe Park, Michigan

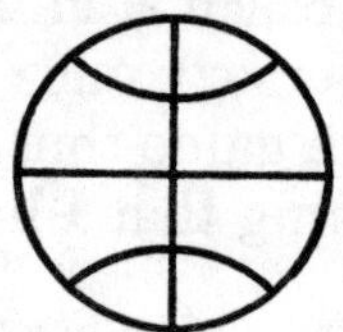

Presently the head basketball coach at St. Clare of Montefalco School (Grosse Pointe Park, Michigan), Richard J. Zaranek has been coaching for 12 years. In that time he has won seven league, two regional, and three district titles. Coach Zaranek has a 159-49 won-lost record.

When I began coaching basketball at the grade-school level several years ago, there was no question in my mind about the defensive philosophy I wished to impart to my team. It was my belief that the best defensive results could be obtained by employing a man-to-man defense with strict adherence to assigned tasks and by discouraging switching unless absolutely necessary.

I believed that a dedicated, aggressive coverage compensated for the weaknesses of this defense, such as the fact that little or no help is afforded the defensive man who is assigned to the man with the ball, and also the weakness of this defense in the convergence aspects. For the next three years I continued my "You cover your man, I'll cover mine" defensive philosophy, and with this formula we experienced one third-place finish and three championship seasons. So, one may ask, why change?

For the most part, the big men were becoming increasingly more difficult to defend against because they were developing more agility and quickness. We needed to formulate a defense that would stop the big man from scoring. This led me to go to what we call pressure defense, a decision I have never regretted.

This system of pressure defense was introduced to me by Ray Ritter while I was working as one of his assistant coaches at Grosse Pointe North High School. Coach Ritter developed this pressure defense system at Grosse Pointe North and has enjoyed much success with it.

Characteristics of Pressure Defense

Pressure defense requires a less stringent individual approach but embodies greater team responsibility. Switches are more frequent, the help side or weak side converges in the basket area, and help is afforded the man playing the ball whenever possible. This defense incorporates the switching defense and many zone principles into its assigned man-to-man responsibilities.

Advantages of Pressure Defense

Pressure defense has several advantages. By applying constant pressure on our opponent at all times and in all areas of the floor, we force him into errors. It also helps us to establish the tempo of the game. We are able to play "our" game.

Along these same lines, pressure defense takes the opponent out of his normal pattern of play. Offensive patterns that have been worked upon so much the previous week are now forced into change, and this causes confusion for the opponent. This defense also helps to minimize differences in size. Good opportunities to start a fast break are created, and most of all, from a motivational standpoint, we find that pressure defense is fun to play.

Ten Fundamentals

We have compiled a list of ten fundamental areas that must be mastered by each of our players in order to realize success with our pressure defense.

Terms

First, it is essential to understand the terminology of our three basic concepts: middle third, line-of-ball, and the perimeter rule. Middle third (Diagram 1) is simply defined as the area in the middle one-third of the floor. Line-of-ball (Diagram 2) is the imaginary line extended from the position of the ball parallel to the baseline. Finally, our perimeter rule (Diagram 3) encompasses the area within a 17-foot radius from the basket.

Stance

Our second essential fundamental is the stance. We work very hard on perfecting our defensive stances, making sure that:

a) The player is square to his opponent and balanced.

b) The player is close enough to his opponent to touch him with his hands.

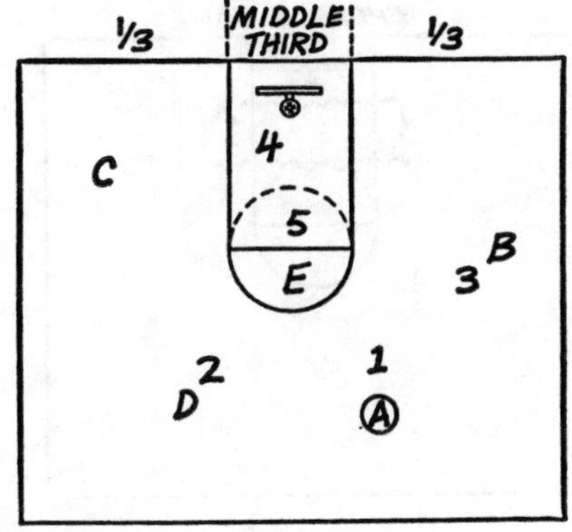

Diagram 1

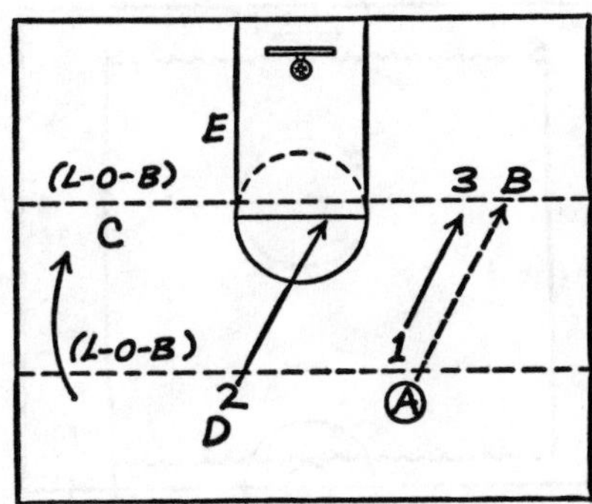

Diagram 2

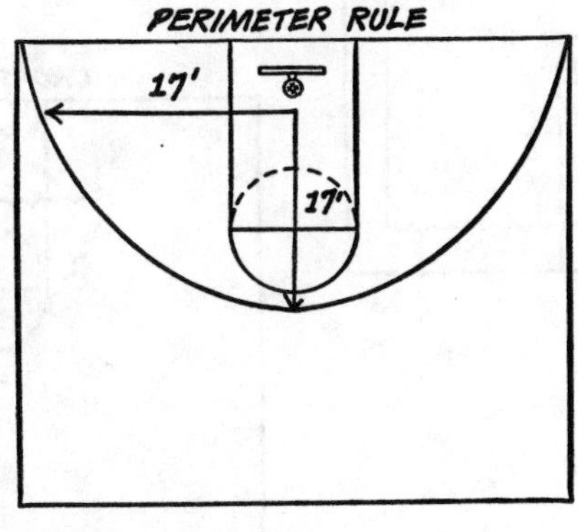

Diagram 3

c) The player's head is always in the middle of his body, his back is straight, and his tail is down.

Next we work on the shuffle, where we stress keeping the feet apart, the hands inside, and the palms up while using the drills shown in Diagrams 4, 5, and 6.

Pressure Series #2

The next six essential fundamentals for our pressure defense are what we call our Pressure Series #2. Here we learn to defend against the dribbler, screener, shooter, cutter, wing, and post.

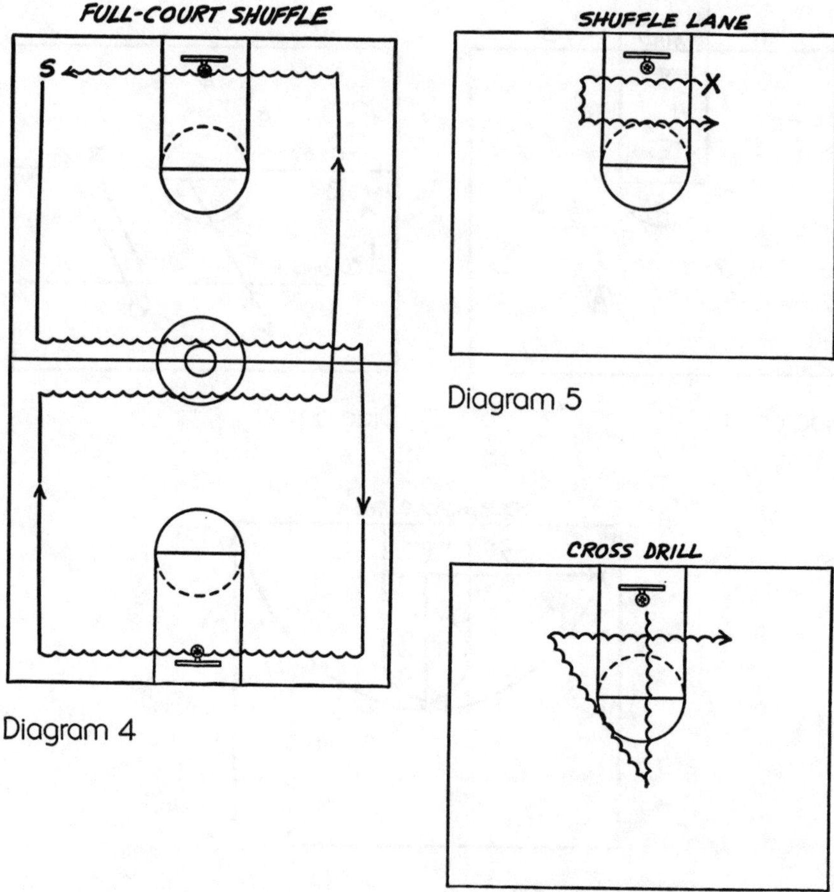

Diagram 4

Diagram 5

Diagram 6

Vs. Dribbler

For defending against the dribbler, we use the diagonal dribbler drill (Diagram 7), keeping four things in mind:

1. Keep the ball between the legs.
2. Stay square to the baseline in back court. Stay square to the basket in front court.
3. Try to draw charge.
4. When the dribbler picks up the ball, yell "Lane" and go belly to belly.

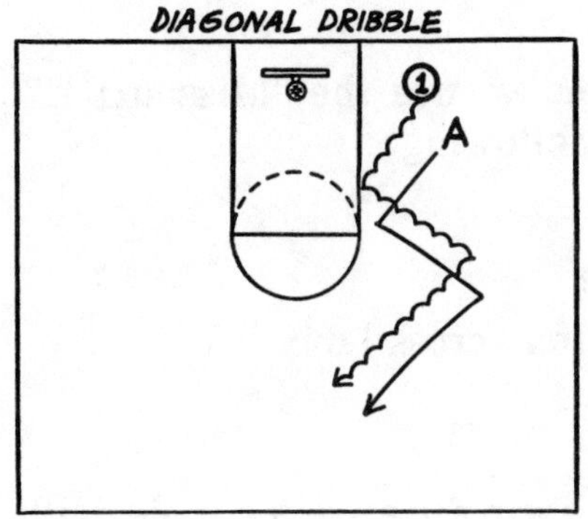

Diagram 7

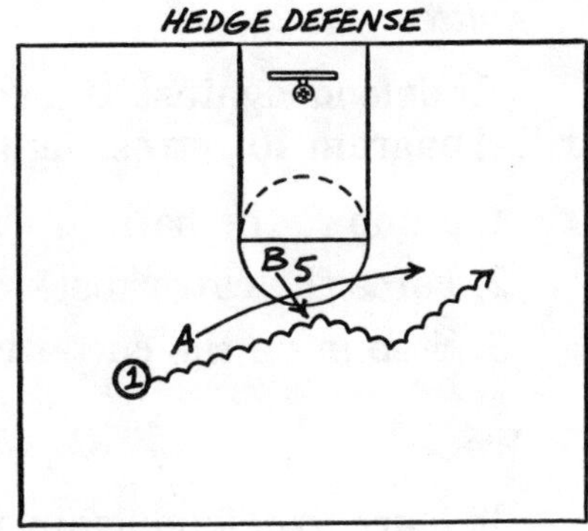

Diagram 8

Vs. Screener

The drill we use to defend against the screener is called the hedge defense. Here we always hedge to the ball (never away from it), step into the dribbler's path, and then retreat to our own player (Diagram 8).

Vs. Shooter

To learn how to defend against the shooter, we use a drill called the lane defense (Diagram 9). We restrict the offensive man to the lane. The defensive man should stay square and take away the rocker step, keeping a hand in the shooter's face and then blocking out.

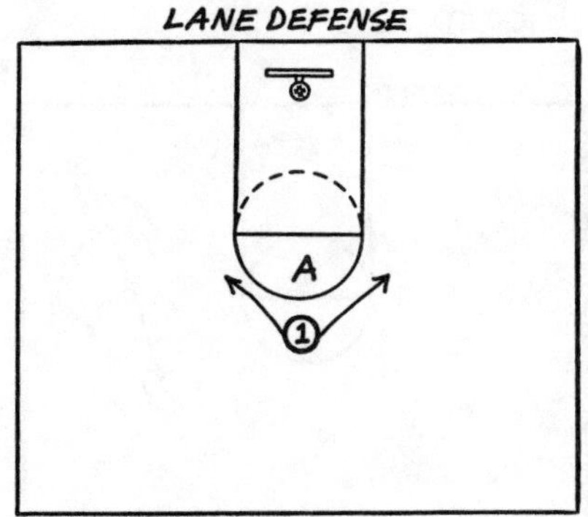

Diagram 9

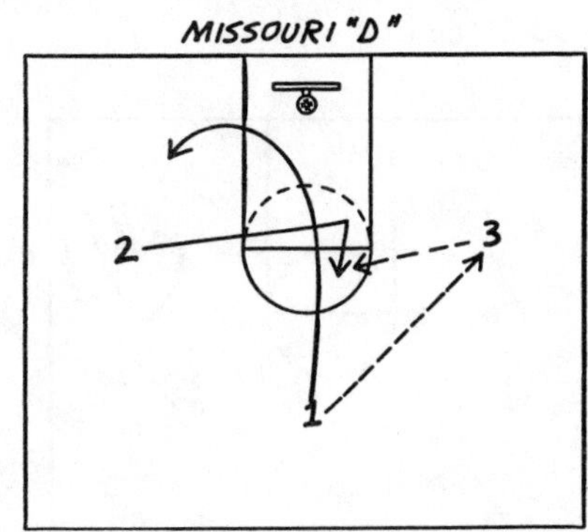

Diagram 10

Vs. Cutter

To defend against the cutter, we use the "Missouri D" drill (Diagram 10), stressing the following:

1. Jump to the ball.
2. Force the cutter back door.
3. Step in on the cutter coming across lane.

Vs. Wing

To learn to defend against the wing, we use a simple drill called "Get It" (Diagrams 11-14), stressing the following:

1. Hand in the passing lane.
2. Hand behind the wing.
3. Force back door.
4. Open to the ball on baseline cuts.

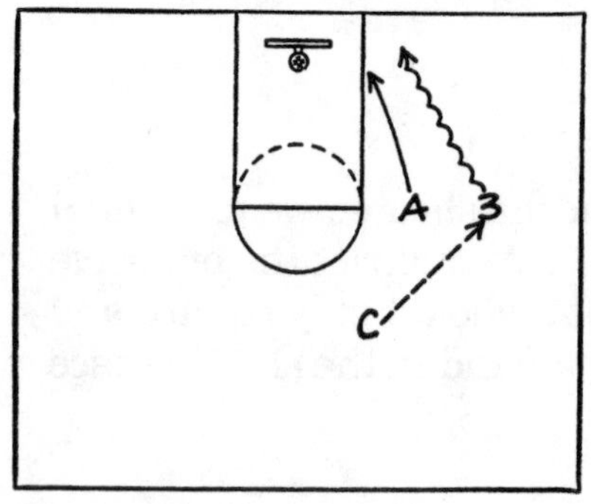

Diagram 11

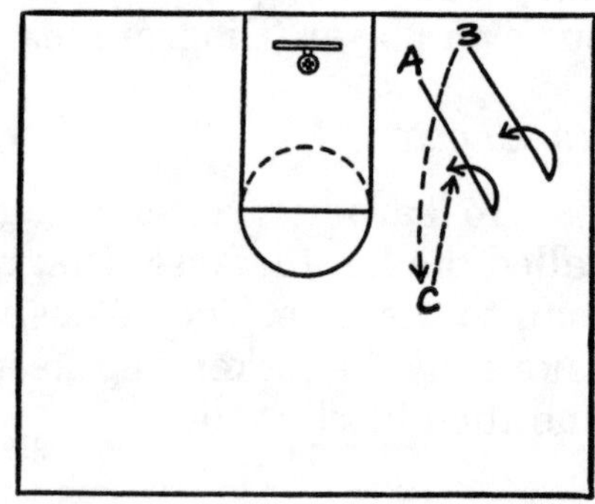

Diagram 12

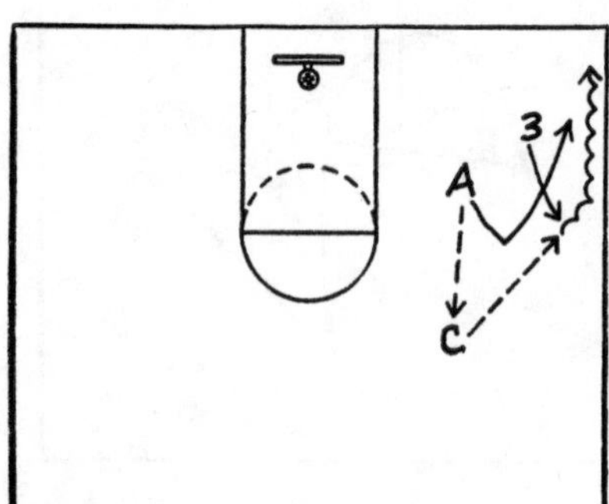

Diagram 13

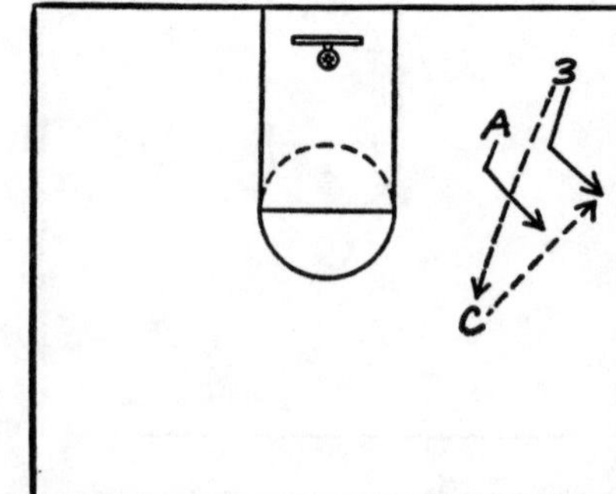

Diagram 14

Vs. Post

To defend against the post, we want our post man to front everything inside 15 feet, and when the ball is passed from point to wing, the defender is to go over the top side of the post (Diagram 15).

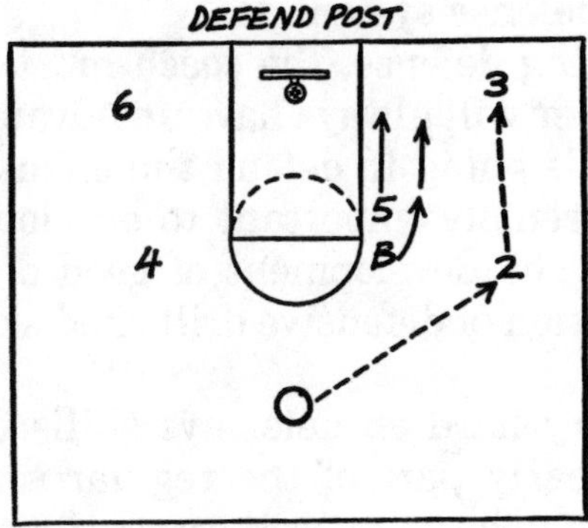

Diagram 15

Four-Corner "D"

Our last fundamental defensive drill is one that encompasses several of our defensive skills. We call this our multiple "D" drill, or four-corner "D" (Diagram 16). Here we are working on middle third and line-of-ball concepts, helping and recovering, jumping to the ball, defending the double-deep post, the double clear, and dropping for backside support.

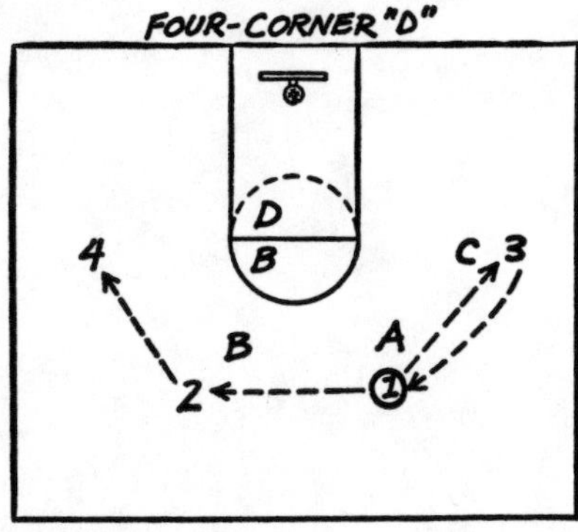

Diagram 16

It is our feeling that these ten areas must be mastered by *every* player on the squad. We feel that mastery of these fundamentals will help our team in every phase of the defensive game. Of course, there are many other drills that we use to cover the other facets of defense; however, these ten drills are the basis on which we build all other defensive drills in our pressure defense system.

When teaching defense, the coach must remember that the offensive player will always have an advantage, and if the defensive player is going to defend the offensive player adequately, it is extremely important to develop the necessary defensive skills. The development of good defense can only come from repetition of defensive drills and skills throughout the entire year.

We work very hard on defensive skills during the preseason and the early part of the regular season, and even when things seem to be going well we continue to work on our defensive skills until the end of the season. We feel that a letdown in defensive work in the latter half of the season will cause a deterioration of defensive play at a very crucial time when league championships are being decided and when state tournaments are beginning.

25

Your Defense Should Fit Your Personnel

by Bill Peters

Former Head Basketball Coach
Fairview High School
Sherwood, Ohio

Bill Peters coached basketball at Fairview High School (Sherwood, Ohio) for 11 years. He had a 97-80 record with one district, two sectional, and two conference championships. Bill resigned after the 1977-1978 season to devote full time to the teaching of high school mathematics.

During the past six years, Fairview High School basketball teams have compiled an overall record of 86-34. Defense has contributed heavily to this record. The overall defensive average for the six-year span has been 60.3 points per game. The defensive averages have ranged from a low of 55.4 to a high of 63.4 during this period.

Make Your Defense Flexible

I think that the main reason for our defense's consistent success year-in and year-out is that we have been flexible enough to adjust our style of defense to the personnel that was on hand. Too many coaches want to use the same defense every year, regardless of the type of players they have. This might be fine for college coaches who can recruit a particular type of player, but high school coaches must work with the talent that is at hand. High school coaches must be willing to adjust their defense to fit the personnel that they have available.

My first year as a varsity coach was during the 1969-1970 season. We had only one returning letterman, a 6′3″ junior center. We had two senior guards, a junior guard-forward, a junior guard, and two sophomore forwards in addition to the letterman, who were good enough to make contributions as varsity players. Both seniors and the junior guard were 5′9″, the junior guard-forward was 6′2″, and the two sophomores were 6′2″ and 6′1″.

I had previously been a junior high coach and a high school assistant coach. I had had success in using a 1-2-2 defense and a 1-2-1-1 full-court press. Going into my first year as a varsity coach, I felt that I could be a success at any level with the combination of those two defenses. At mid-season of that year, we had a 5-3 record. I was satisfied with our record, but not with our defensive play. I realized that we must change our style of defense in order for us to improve over the last half of the season.

I decided to change to a 2-3 defense with a 2-2-1 full-court press. We were immediately an improved team. We had a 7-4 record for the remainder of the year, beating some of the best teams in the area along the way. Even though our won-lost record after changing defenses was only a little better, we were definitely a much better team.

Why I Chose the 2-3 Defense

There were several reasons why I decided upon the 2-3 defense. One was to improve our defensive rebounding. A 2-3 defense puts three men in good rebounding position, whereas a 1-2-2 defense has only two. Another reason was to give us better coverage on the corner shots. In the 2-3 defense, the back men do not have to move as quickly to cover the corner shooters as they do in the 1-2-2. Yet another reason was to allow the players to help each other out better. We were an inexperienced team and made many mistakes. The 2-3 defense allowed the side men in the back to cover up for mistakes by the guards, and it allowed the center to help everyone out. The center had to be strong on defense because just about the only way to cover up for him was by fouling.

In the first part of the season, we had used the 1-2-1-1 full-court press as a weapon. Because of our inexperience and lack of speed, it was sometimes a disaster. In the last part of the season, we used the more conservative 2-2-1 full-court press only when we were in trouble. It helped us at times but was not exactly a major reason for our successful defense.

An Experienced Team

For the following year we had an experienced team. We used the 2-3 defense in every game except one. The one exception was a game in which we lost two starters to injuries in the first half. We then switched to a man-to-man defense and made up a large deficit. Unfortunately, we lost the game by one point. The 2-3 defense was a huge success throughout the year. We lost only three other games, two of them in overtime. We finished the season with a 17-4 record and won the first sectional championship in the school's history.

Our defensive average for the year was 59.5 points per game. Our reasons for using the 2-3 defense were the same as they were the previous year. The fact that we had a year of experience at playing it made it much more successful. Again, we resorted to the 2-2-1 full-court press only when we were in trouble.

When practice opened for the 1971-1972 season, we had four key players returning from the successful team of the previous year. They were a 6′3″ senior center, a 6′2″ senior forward, a 5′11″ senior guard, and a 5′11″ junior guard-forward. It seemed as if we would be hard to beat once again. It also appeared as if we should use the same defensive strategy. Unfortunately, we had two problems. The senior center and the junior guard-forward had sustained injuries in other sports between basketball seasons.

I used the two injured players as much as possible, but at mid-season we had a 3-5 record. Not only were we being beaten, but we were being beaten badly. We had used several defenses during this time, but none was successful.

Drastic Changes

I decided to make some drastic changes after the eighth game. By this time, it was evident that the injured center was not going to be able to help us. Therefore, I replaced him with a 6′5″ inexperienced junior. I relegated the injured junior to a role of sixth man and replaced him in the starting lineup with a 5′9″ junior. The 5′9″ replacement is probably the quickest boy I have ever coached. The 6′2″ senior and the 5′11″ senior were two of the other starters. The fifth starter was a 5′11″ senior forward who had been one of the few pleasant surprises of the season up to that time.

I also decided to change our defense to what I call a "2-3 match-up zone" defense. We had four quick players to go along with a relatively slow 6′5″ center. Only one of the other four starters was over 5′11″. The center was quick enough, aided by his size, to do a respectable job in the middle. The other four starters were quick enough and aggressive enough to be able to match up with men coming into their area. I would say that good speed and a lack of overall height were the main reasons why I chose this particular defense. I might mention that I would never have chosen this defense had I not had the 6′5″ center. I do not feel that we could have gotten away with this defense without a big man in the middle.

Instant Success

The changes that I made were an instant success. We won ten straight games before losing a heartbreaking two-pointer in the sectional tournament. We finished with a 13-6 record and a defensive average of 61.6 points per game. The defensive average was astonishing considering that we gave up almost 70 points per game for the first eight games. I have never seen a team go from so bad to so good almost overnight. I received more satisfaction from coaching that team than ever before. I also think that I turned in my best coaching performance during that season.

Five senior lettermen returned for the 1972-1973 season. These included a 6′6″ center, a 5′11″ guard, two 5′10″ guards, and a 5′9″ forward. Along with these lettermen, we had a 5′8″ senior guard and a 6′6″ sophomore center. Again, big things were expected of us.

We started the season with the 2-3 match-up zone defense. This time it was not successful. After nine games, our record was a disappointing 3-6. Most of the games were close for the first three quarters, but the fourth quarter would be a disaster. Our main problems were lack of hustle on defense and poor defensive rebounding.

For the tenth game, we played a relatively weak team. We beat them by about 20 points. The boys were happy; I wasn't. We were still making the same mistakes. I knew that there were few teams on the remainder of the schedule that we could beat if we didn't improve.

Again, I decided to revamp our starting lineup and change our defense. The five players I decided to start were the 6′6″ sophomore center, the 5′11″ guard, one of the 5′10″ guards, the 5′9″ forward, and a 6′1″ sophomore forward who had been moved up from the reserve team.

New 1-3-1 Defense

Our new defense was to be a 1-3-1 half-court press. We would also play a 1-3-1 defense if the opposition beat the half-court press. Again, size and speed played major roles in my decision. Both guards and the 5′9″ forward were very quick. I also knew that I could get them to hustle and to be aggressive. I played the 5′9″ forward and the 5′10″ guard on the side positions of the 1-3-1. They both were very strong boys for their size and could drop down to rebound on the weak side. The 6′6″ center was ideal for the baseline position. He was tall but, more important, he was very quick. The 6′1″ sophomore was slow, but was aggressive enough to do an acceptable job in the middle position.

Just as in the previous season, our fortunes immediately took a 180-degree turn. We won eight straight games before losing in the sectional tournament. Along the way, we captured the first outright conference championship in the school's history. Our final overall record was 12-7, and our defensive average for the year was 61.3 points per game. This was an amazing figure considering that we gave up about 70 points per game for the first ten games of the season.

Reviewing the Situation

Looking back on the last nine games of that season, I can see some mistakes that I made. In the first six games in that stretch, we played outstanding ball while beating some very good teams. In the next two games, we played weak teams. We defeated them but we did not play well. Both teams beat our half-court press and also picked up too many offensive rebounds. A lack of hustle and a lack of aggressiveness on our part were the main reasons. I should have made some changes, but I didn't. Superstition on my part probably kept me from taking action. We had won eight straight games using this defense, and I hated to change. The time of the season (we were entering tourney play) also was a factor. Trying something new during the first game of the tourney didn't seem to be the right thing to do. We played the 1-3-1 half-court press defense in the tourney game, and we were beaten badly. Our defensive play was very poor.

If I had it to do over, I probably would do the same thing. I look upon tourney play as an opportunity for a team to exhibit the things that they have mastered during the regular season. The 1-3-1 half-court press was the only thing that that team had mastered to any degree. The boys had confidence in it. If I had changed, I am sure that they would have lost confidence in my coaching ability. I don't think they would have put their hearts into anything new. To sum it all up, at the time of the season when our troubles fell upon us, it was a hopeless case! I don't think we could have played well with or without a change.

Inconsistency

The 1973-1974 basketball season at Fairview can be summed up in one word—inconsistency! We defeated some very good teams and lost to some very poor teams. Our final record was again 12-7. We lost two overtime games and also a two-pointer on a shot in the closing seconds. So we quite easily could have finished with a good 15-4 record instead of a fair 12-7 mark.

Our defensive average for the year was 61.8 points per game. We used the 2-3 match-up zone defense for most of the season. It, too, was inconsistent. We did not have one player who individually was a good defensive player. Inexperience played a big part, as four underclassmen started for a good portion of the season.

Following the 1973-1974 season, I evaluated our team carefully. In particular, I evaluated our defense. We had been using some form of zone defense for all of my five years as a varsity coach. Our junior high, freshman, and reserve teams had also been using zone defenses most of the time. Perhaps we had forgotten how to play defense, man-for-man.

I greeted four lettermen when practice opened for the 1974-1975 season. I thought all four had the potential to be very good ballplayers. They were a 6′8″ senior forward, a 6′3″ senior center-forward, a 6′0″ senior guard-forward, and a 5′9″ junior guard. Three other players were good enough to play varsity ball. They included a 5′9″ senior guard, a 6′0″ junior center forward, and a 5′10″ junior guard.

We started the season by introducing what I call a "denial man-to-man, full-court press." The 6′8″ boy guarded the opposing player, who took the ball out-of-bounds. The other four players picked out a man and played in front of him, trying to deny him the ball. If the opposition beat the press, the boys played man-to-man on the opponent they had been guarding on the full-court press. If the opposition beat the press consistently, we removed the press and played a straight man-to-man defense on preassigned opponents.

Object of the Full-Court Press

The object of the full-court press was twofold. One objective was to get the opposition to make numerous ball-handling errors and to disrupt their set offense in general. The other objective was to get our team to move, both on offense and on defense. The previous year we had been guilty of standing around too much on both ends of the floor. I have always believed that the actions of a team on defense set the pattern for their actions on offense. In other words, "If you move on defense, you will move on offense."

The press was not much of a success for the first objective. It probably cost us more baskets than we scored as a result of it. Most of the time we had to remove it early in the game.

The press was a success for the second objective. We moved on both ends of the court and were very aggressive both ways. We began all but four games by using the denial press. There were only three games all year in which we stood around, and all three were games which we did not begin with the denial press. Once we started with this particular press, our movement continued throughout the game, regardless of whether we removed the press or not.

We won our first six games of the year and then lost our next two. The losses were by two points and one point, respectively. We used the denial press and the man-to-man defense in all eight games. We used it effectively, but we were not improving. Too many teams were scoring too many points against us. We were not a high-scoring team; therefore, we could not afford to give up too many points.

Team Evaluation

I began to evaluate my team to decide on a new defense. We had only two boys with any significant height. Therefore, there was no object in putting any other players along the baseline. I decided to use a 1-2-2 defense. Along with this, we used a 1-2-2 three-quarter-court press and a 1-2-2 half-court press. We always started out with our denial press and man-to-man defense. We would then change to our 1-2-2 defenses. The three-quarter-court press caused the opposition to turn the ball over quite frequently. It also kept the opposition from setting up their offense on numerous occasions. The 1-2-2 defense also allowed us to dominate the defensive boards and to execute a number of successful fast breaks.

We won our first 14 games after switching defensive tactics. Our winning streak was stopped by a two-point loss in the regional tournament. We had captured conference, sectional, and district championships along the way. It was the first district championship in the history of our school. Our final record was 20-3. Our defensive average was 55.4 points per game, which was a new school record.

I have presented a summary of each team I have coached. I did this for several reasons. First, I wanted to show that we have not been a team of "giants." We have always had fair size, but never anything out of the ordinary. Second, we have not always had good teams right from the start of the season. Third, we haven't been successful on defense every year. The 1973-1974 team never played consistently well on defense for any length of time. Fourth, it gives the readers an opportunity to compare their teams with the teams I have had.

Conclusion

In conclusion, I would like to offer the following suggestions:

1. Constantly evaluate your defense throughout the season. Consider the quality of the teams you have played and the quality of the teams you are going to play in future games. If you feel that the defense you have been using is good enough to defeat the rest of the teams on your schedule, then stick with it. If you don't feel that way, you had better change. Remember that games in the future are more important than games in

the past. A team that never improves can never be a great team.

2. In evaluating your team, the two most important components to consider are the overall size and the overall quickness of the team. If you have two big men, a 1-2-2 might be best. You might try a 2-3 defense if you have three big men. If you have one or two big men and three quick players to go with them, a 1-3-1 might work. A man-to-man may work for any team with good speed, regardless of size.
3. Always try to get your best defensive rebounders in good rebounding position. For instance, never put your best rebounder out front on a 2-3 defense.
4. Evaluate your team after the completion of each season. Consider what type of ballplayers you will have for the next season. Develop a good idea of what type of defense might be successful. (It took me five years to learn that I should do this.)
5. Don't start to think that there is only *one* type of defense that will work for you. Be willing to change. Many coaches have had success with more than one kind of defense, and so can you.
6. No defense will work if you do not have players who are willing to hustle and be aggressive. A player with limited ability might become a good defensive player by hustling and by being aggressive, but a player with outstanding ability will *never* become a good defensive player if he is not willing to hustle and be aggressive.
7. The last thought I would like to leave with you is this: There is no magic formula for coaching. What works for one coach might not work for another, and what works for one coach one year might not work for that same coach the following year. A coach has to do what he thinks is going to make his team the best at the end of the season. If one thing doesn't work, then try something else. Never give up on yourself or your players, and never let the players give up on you or themselves!

26

Floor-Position Defense

by Richard Jarrett

Head Basketball Coach
Metairie Park Country Day School
Metairie, Louisiana

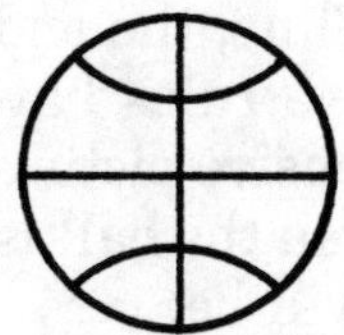

Richard Jarrett has built a 197-75 record as the head coach at Metairie Park Country Day School (Metairie, Louisiana). Coach Jarrett has been at Metairie for ten years.

If you are a believer in helping-team defense and have trouble getting your players to understand when to execute weakside or ballside responsibilities, take a look at *floor-position defense.* This gives the defensive player a better picture of his floor position and responsibilities in relation to his offensive man and the ball. If the three simple floor-position rules are followed, your defensive players (away from the ball) will have the angle on the ball. This makes floor positioning much easier for your players to understand.

I divide the court into three areas: harassment, contesting, and overplay. Each area has its own simple rule and, if the rules are followed, the defensive man will always have help either from the sideline, the endline, or his teammates.

These three defensive rules have enabled my teams to understand the total defensive picture. Using these rules, my players know to which area the ball is guided, and what their respective assignments will be.

HARASSMENT AREA RULE: Guide the ball to the sideline.

The harassment area is located from the baseline to the back court to a point in the mid-court area. In this area, the defense guides the ball to the sideline. The defense is then free to run and jump, double-team, or use any other defensive maneuvers according to the game strategy. The defense must keep the ball from coming down the center of the court. Depending upon the tempo I choose for a game, or the team we are playing, we may vary the place where we pick up offensive men. The main point to stress is to guide the ball to the sideline (Diagram 1).

CONTESTING AREA RULE: Force the ball to the sideline and stop the dribble.

The contesting area rule is similar to the harassment area rule, except that the defense must *force* the ball to the sideline. When the rule is in effect, it makes playing the helping-team defense 100 percent easier, since the defense knows where the ball will be on the floor.

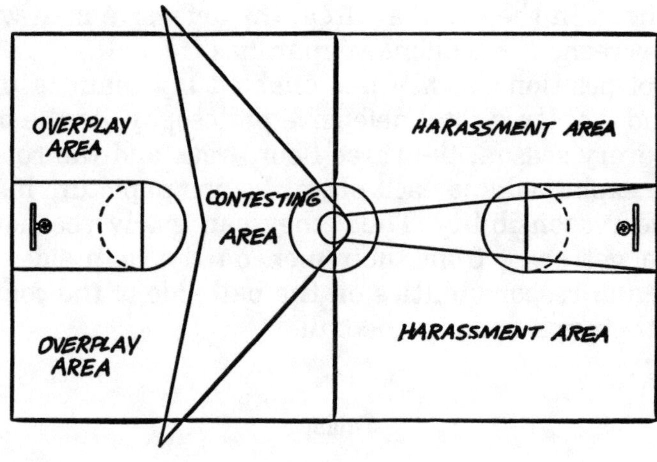

Diagram 1

OVERPLAY RULE: Overplay all passing lanes and force the ball into the middle, either by pass or by dribble.

The contesting area is located just above the half line and about two or three feet above the top of the key. In this area, the defense is playing tight pressure and will *force* the ball to the sideline to try to stop the dribble. The defense will key on a reverse dribble and try for a steal or a double-team.

If the dribble is stopped near the sideline, the ballside and help-side defense is easy to initiate. This is due to the ball position in relation to the court position of the offense. The help-side defense can pick up a good angle on the ball and their offensive men, and also be in a good position to help the ballside defenders cut off the passing lanes. Also, if there's a backdoor play, there's help from a help-side man.

The overplay area is located between the top of the key and the baseline. Pressure defense will be applied *constantly* in this area, on and off the ball. Defensive men overplay the passing lane on the ball side of the court and force a backdoor situation. If the offensive man has the ball in this area, *never give up the baseline*. Force the ball into the lane area to receive help. In the overplay area, the defensive man will go over all screens if his offensive man has the ball.

Floor-position defense has enabled my team to understand and develop a total defensive philosophy. At the beginning of every season, the three floor areas and the rules for each are explained and each player begins to picture his own defensive responsibility. Thus, they can easily see how far they can get away from their men on the help side, their position and responsibilities on the ball side of the court, as well as their positions on the ball.

Drills

With floor-position defense as a solid background, I then break down into individual defensive drills. I use one or more of the following three drills, two to four days a week, 15 minutes a day. At the start of the season, I may stay with a drill up to 30 minutes to keep weak players in the drill for a longer period of time.

Full-Court Run-and-Jump Drill

This drill is used to teach the harassment area rule in addition to player movement on the run-and-jump (Diagram 2).

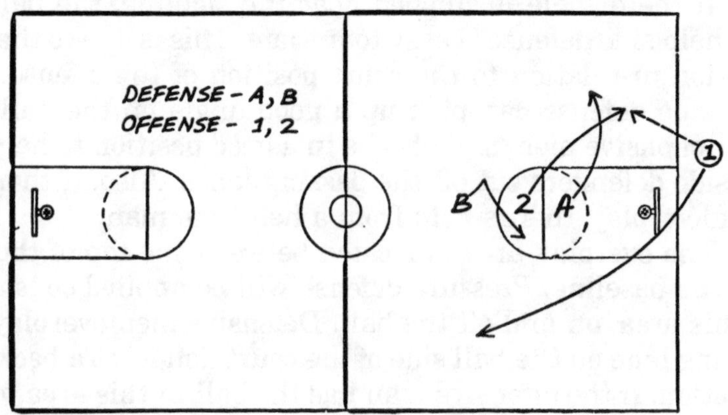

Diagram 2

The defense puts front and back pressure on player 2 and will only let him receive the ball at the baseline corner position. After the inbounds pass, 1 will go to the 28-foot line (Diagram 3).

Defensive man A guides player 2 to the sideline. Defensive man B will double-team at the sideline and player 2 will pass to 1. Then 2 goes to the half line. A must try to beat the ball to 1 at the 28-foot line and must keep him from dribbling into the middle of the court (Diagram 4).

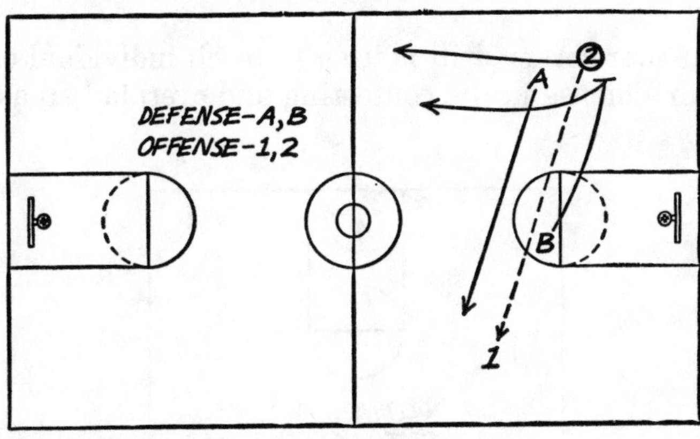

Diagram 3

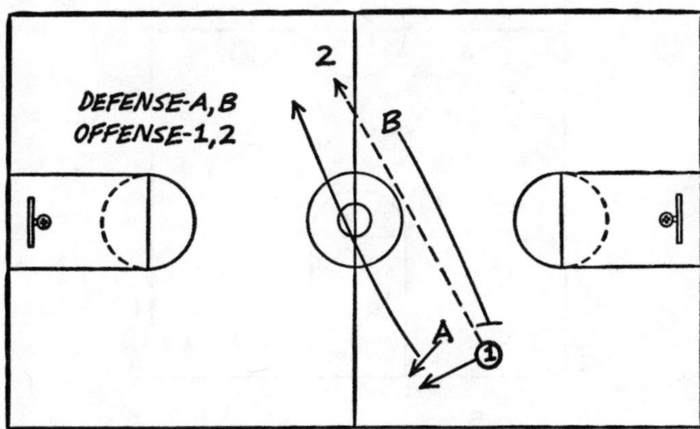

Diagram 4

B again tries to double-team. A must beat the ball passed to 2. After the pass, 1 goes to the 28-foot line. The players continue to zig-zag down court and another group starts after the first group crosses the half line.

At the beginning of the season, the defensive men cannot touch the ball but can only play body position defense. The offensive man who receives the pass cannot take off until he is guarded. This restriction is lifted after the defense gets its best timing on the run-and-jump.

Four-Corner Drill

The four-corner drill is used to teach individual on-the-ball team defense in the contesting and overplay areas (Diagram 5).

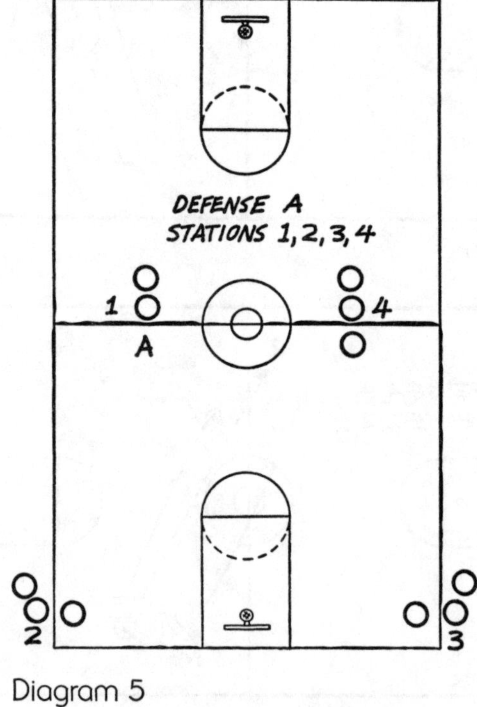

Diagram 5

The defensive player starts at station 1. He must force the offensive man to the sideline, stop him, and then turn him in to the middle. The offensive man must drive and try for a lay-up or a ten-foot or closer jump shot. The defensive man must stay with him and play body position (no steals), block out the shot, and recover the ball.

The defensive man then moves to station 2. He must not give up the baseline and must force the man into the middle, staying to block him out and recover the ball. The defensive man then rotates to stations 3 and 4 where he must play defensive strategy as in stations 1 and 2.

During this drill, I'm not overly concerned about whether the shot will be made, but most good one-on-one players will score. I am mostly concerned with body position and defensive rules in the drill.

In positions 1 and 4, the player must take his man to the sideline, turn him, and then play him close, blocking out the shot. In positions 2 and 3, the defensive man must not give up the baseline, but must force his man into the middle and then block out. If they do these things, they are playing team defensive rules!

Three-Man Team Defensive Drill

This drill involves three defensive players at three different positions. Each one plays helping-team defense on the ball side and the help side. I have the players go through each position on defense four times and then rotate to another station. All ballside and help-side rules must be followed closely in this fast-moving game situation drill (Diagram 6).

I start this drill by holding the ball myself. My offensive men must be ready to move when I look at them.

At station 1, A must force the offensive man into a backdoor situation by overplaying the passing lane and then trying to defend against it. He has help from B and C. After four turns, A rotates to station 2.

I do not even have to throw the ball—I just make sure that the defensive movements are carried out properly. If a pass is made, a game situation is started and play continues until a basket is made or the defense recovers the ball. The defensive help must recover to their men after play is stopped. I then look to station 2 or 3 for an offensive play.

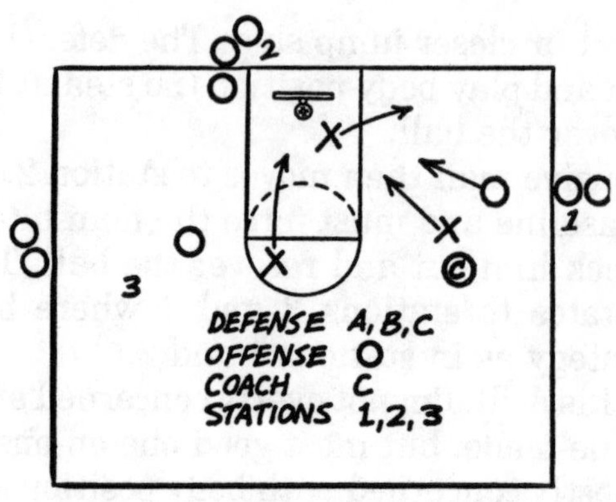

Diagram 6

Station 2's defensive man must not let the offensive player flash post and receive the ball. Again, I do not have to throw the ball—I just have to make sure that the defensive movements are carried out properly. If the ball goes to the center, the defense collapses around the ball.

Station 3's defensive man must prevent his offensive player from moving directly to the ball—and still be able to stop a backdoor play. Again, I don't throw the ball—I just watch those defensive movements!

From here, I continue to rotate around the stations. After each player has had four turns at one station, he moves to the next one. I use this drill two or three times per week—and always the day before a game.

27

Staying Aggressive in a Defensive Transition

by Ernest Zafonte

Head Basketball Coach
Dover Plains High School
Dover Plains, New York

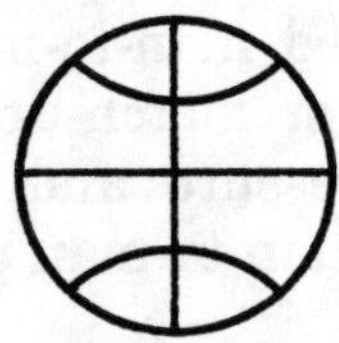

After six years as the junior varsity coach at Dover High School (Dover Plains, New York), Ernest Zafonte was moved up to the varsity program in 1978. His record for his first two years as varsity coach is 28-8, with one league championship and two trips to post-season play.

For a press to be really effective, strong team pressure must be applied and momentum must grow. The transition from the press to a preassigned defense can be a major stumbling block in meeting these objectives. Little can hurt a team's momentum more than an easy basket scored in the confusion of this transition. Many coaches have confessed that they are hesitant to press because "we don't get back well."

For the past few seasons, pressure defenses have been a major part of our game. We have been noted for our aggressive man-to-man defense and zone presses.

It is my feeling that on the high school level the players should be instructed in how to play sound, smart man-to-man. Once they have mastered man-to-man principles, they can learn any type of zone or match-up easily. The concepts of strongside (ballside) pressure and weakside help are the backbone of aggressive man-to-man play and paramount in a successful zone press.

Formation

Zone pressing and falling back man-to-man kept us aggressive but left us susceptible to mismatches, unguarded men, and poor defensive team positioning. Falling back into a standard zone (2-1-2, 3-2, and so on) tended to disrupt our press defense (hence our whole defensive pace) by having a player or players pass up the second or third trapping opportunity for the safety of a zone position.

We have reduced transitional mistakes by adopting the floor positioning and slides of the 1-3-1 half-court press while falling back on defense. We like to press out of a 2-2-1 formation, with our front line a stride in from the foul line (Diagram 1).

The inbounds pass is allowed but is always directed toward the outside. We concentrate on keeping the ball away from the middle while forcing our opponents up the sidelines. It is on the sideline that we look for our double-team opportunities. Diagrams 2 and 3 show the trapping assignments as the ball moves up court.

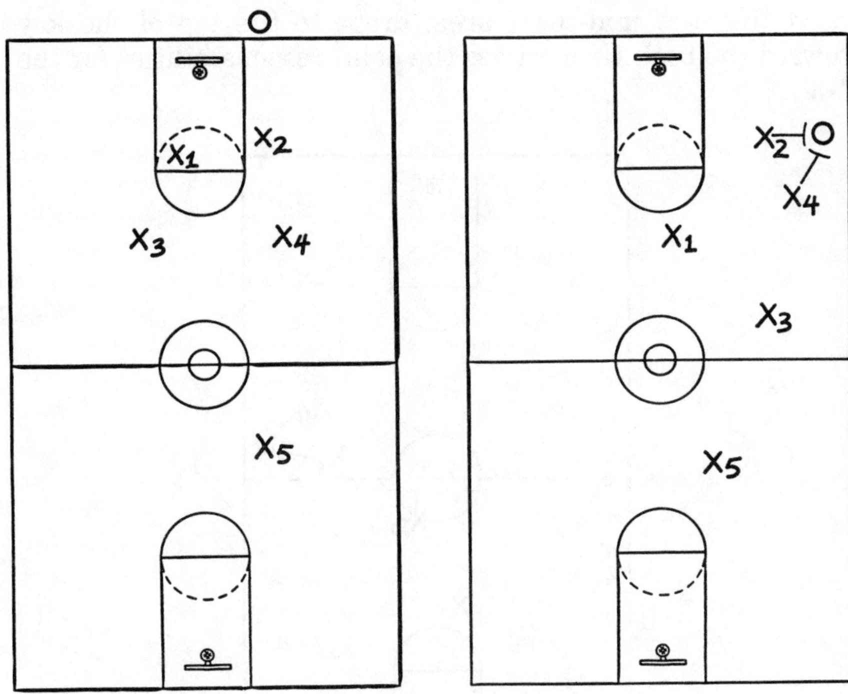

Diagram 1

Diagram 2

After the ball has passed the mid-court trapping area (Diagram 3), we will be thinking more along the lines of 1-3-1 half-court trapping principles. We use the 1-3-1 slides as they would apply to positioning after the ball has advanced past mid-court to a wing position.

Adaptation of 2-2-1 to 1-3-1

Player 1 is our quickest player. At the transitional stage from the 2-2-1 into our half-court pressure, he will be in the area at the top of the key.

After the ball has left the mid-court traps, 1 will slide parallel to the foul line (ball side). His responsibility off the 1-3-1 movement is the baseline. Our 2 man, who had been patrolling the mid-court area, drops to the top of the key toward the ball. He assumes the point responsibilities for the 1-3-1.

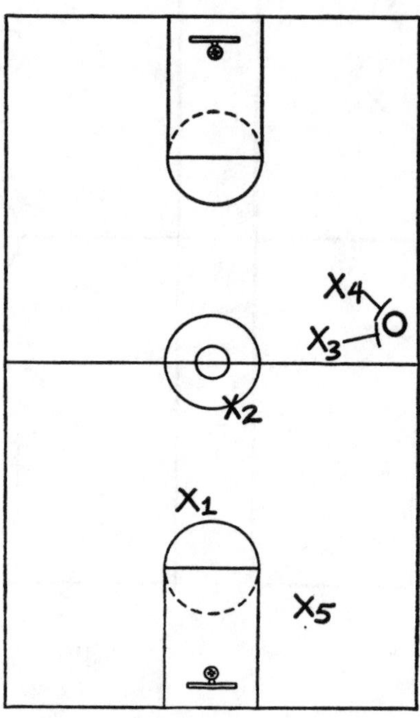

Diagram 3

Our 3 man, who had the sideline trap in Diagram 3, flows to the wing area off the foul line extended. It is his job to provide pressure toward the sidelines. The 2 man is looking to double-team if the occasion arises. The 4 man, when entering from court, assumes the off-wing slides of a 1-3-1 zone. (If the last trap was on the other side of the court, 3 and 4 exchange roles.) The 5 man is up on the foul line fronting all post men. Diagram 4 shows the eventual alignment.

If the ball (now in 3's wing area) is brought out in an attempt to set up, 2 attacks aggressively and tries to trap with his wing. We perform the standard half-court slides from this ball position.

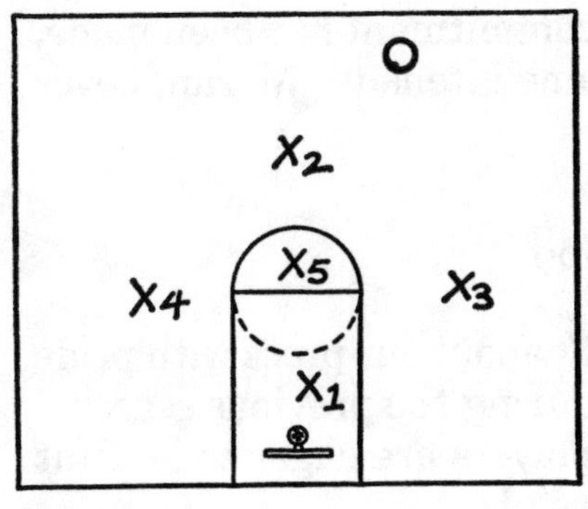

Diagram 4

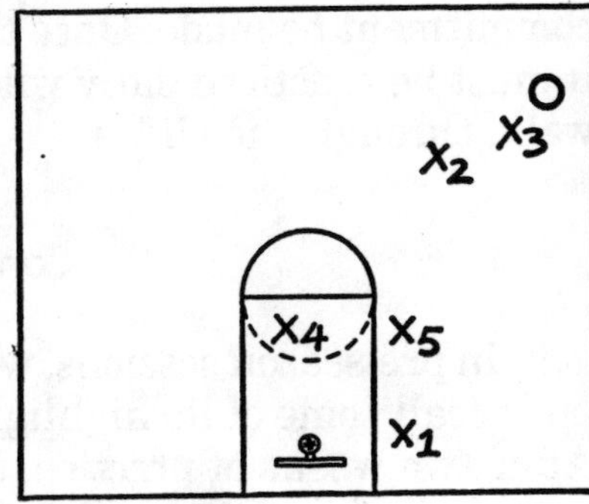

Diagram 5

Fall-Back Procedure

Most times the play is not set up after it crosses mid-court because most teams try to go on the offensive. Knowing where to go and being aggressive pays off here. Player 3 is playing his man aggressively to the outside (Diagram 5). Players 2, 5, and 1 have lined up in the post area, leaving the corner as the next obvious pass. Player 1 jumps out, 5 slides down, and 3 is given the option to double-team, if the occasion arises (Diagram 6), or play the passing lane.

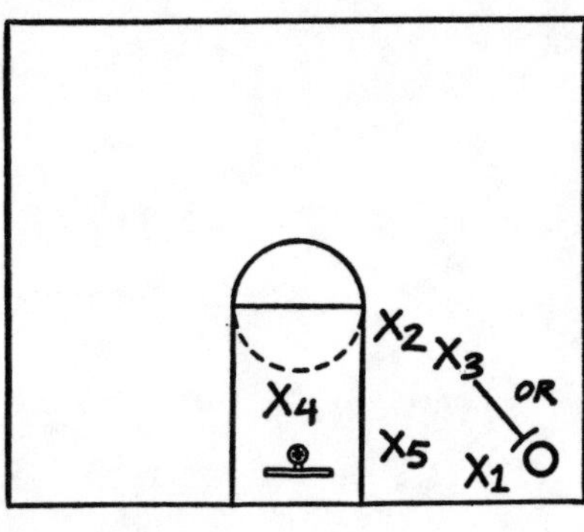

Diagram 6

Before attempting to install this press fall-back procedure or any pressure tactic, it is important that a team commitment be made. Once this commitment has been made, it must be practiced daily with game intensity. We run, never walk, through the slides.

Conclusion

In pre-season sessions, we talk about our press with pride and recall some of its highlights during the previous seasons. After two weeks of practice, the players are eager to learn it and prove that they can be successful.

It is not until we have mastered our full-court movement that we introduce our 1-3-1 fall-back. The 1-3-1 gives players bolstered confidence and aggressiveness in their press.

When introducing the 1-3-1, we teach it as a half-court press. This procedure allows the players to see the slides and movements of their teammates. Seeing it from the standard 1-3-1 formation allows them to see whom they help and who helps them. This pays off when they come back on the run, confident that they have help.

Using this fall-back procedure, we have cut down considerably on our transitional mistakes and have kept up our pressure and momentum.

28

Using a Code for Pressure Defense

by Holt Browning

Head Basketball Coach
Trenton High School
Trenton, Florida

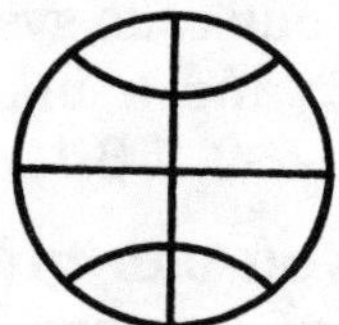

Holt Browning has been the head basketball coach at Trenton High School (Trenton, Florida) for the past ten years, and he has compiled a 137-69 won-lost record. In 1979, he won county, district, and regional honors. During these ten years, 15 of Holt's athletes have signed basketball scholarships.

In this sophisticated day and time, when players and coaches are getting smarter, you have to use more than one defense and press to counteract your opponent. A press seems to do many things to the opposing team; namely, it hinders their offense from setting up as they normally do, it disrupts their game plan (especially if they are a patterned team), it demoralizes them, and it gives the defense some easy lay-ups.

Adopting a Code System

Since we have several presses and defenses, we number each one so that we can call out numbers instead of the defense itself. We call this our code system. We use three full-court presses: 1-2-2, 2-1-2, and a man-to-man. We also fall back into three defenses: 1-2-2, 1-3-1, and a man-to-man.

NOTE: Of course, you can give any press any number. Our system is very simple, and the players pick it up rapidly.

The first number is the press you are using and the second number is the defense into which you are falling back. So, if we called out a "twenty-three," we would be in a 2-1-2 full-court press and fall back into a man-to-man.

REMEMBER: The code must be memorized in order for it to be effective.

DEFENSIVE CODE SYSTEM

Press	Fall Back
11 = 1-2-2	1-2-2
12 = 1-2-2	1-3-1
13 = 1-2-2	man-to-man
21 = 2-1-2	1-2-2
22 = 2-1-2	1-3-1
23 = 2-1-2	man-to-man
31 = man	1-2-2
32 = man	1-3-1
33 = man	man

The offense seems to be off-balance, never knowing what's coming next.

NOTE: We also have a half-court press, which we have given the number four.

Here are some important points to emphasize about the code system:

1. Call out the defense when you're on offense so that you don't waste that split-second.
2. Never give up on the press. Be positive, and sell the press to your players.
3. Find the opponent's weakness; it's there.
4. Be in top condition.
5. Occasionally, press after a missed basket.
6. Work on the press for at least 30 minutes per day.

The 2-1-2 Full-Court Press

One of our most successful presses has been the 2-1-2 full-court press. Diagram 1 shows the basic setup. Players X1 and X2 will usually deny the ball being thrown in by fronting their men.

Sometimes we let the ball be thrown in, but our rule here is to force the ball to the side. Player X3 is our trap man. He will trap on both sides. If the ball gets in, X1 will force the ball down the side (Diagram 2). When this happens, X3 has the job of stopping the ball. We tell X3 to meet the dribbler. After he picks him up, we are in position (Diagram 3). Player X2 will move back and get between the ball and the nearest man to the ball, around the half-court line. Player X2's responsibility is to pick off the cross-court pass. Player X4 will play between the ball and the nearest man to the ball, on the trap side. Player X5's main job is to prevent the lay-up and slow the ball down until help arrives. He is also in position to pick off the long lob. If the ball goes to the other side, it's just the opposite.

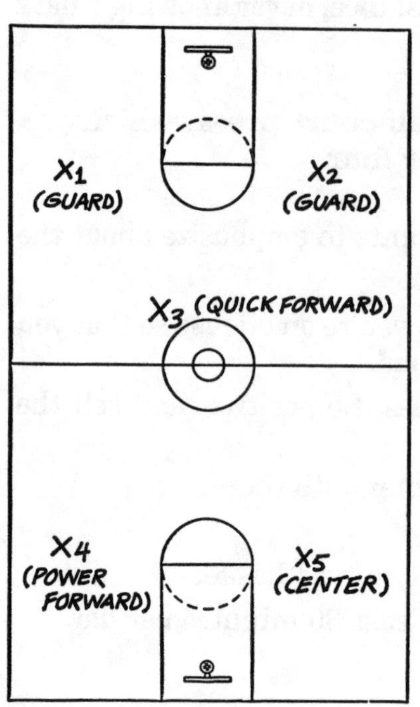

Diagram 1

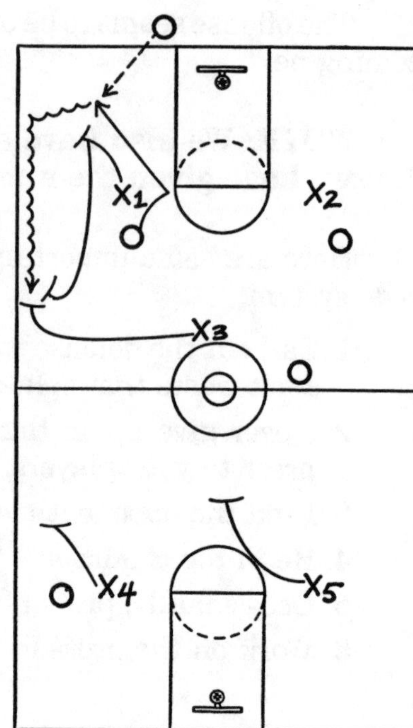

Diagram 2

NOTE: We stress in our players' minds that we are not actually trying to steal the ball, but are trying to force the other team into committing turnovers. These turnovers include the bad pass, five second violation, double-dribble, traveling, and ten-second violation.

Let's face it. Winning basketball games, like winning in any sport, boils down to three things: personnel, scheduling, and coaching. Once in a while, the coaching aspect will be more important than the scheduling. It is up to the coach to have his team physically ready to play the game. To some extent, he can mentally prepare them, but that depends on the coach's experience and his nature.

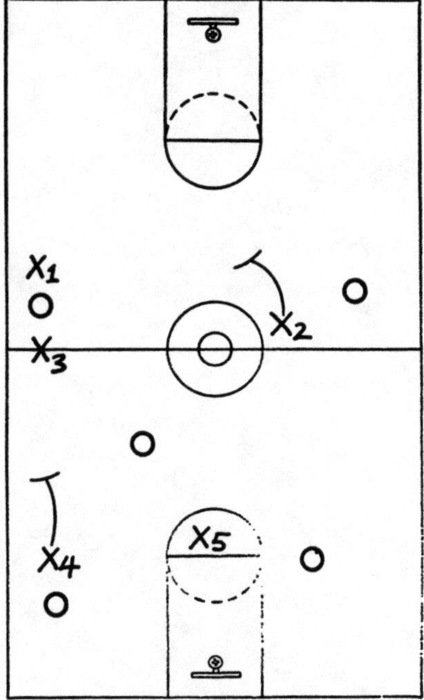

Diagram 3

Part Five

DEFENSIVE DRILLS

29

The Daily Dozen (Parts 1 and 2)

by Jim Gudger

Head Basketball Coach
East Texas State University
Commerce, Texas

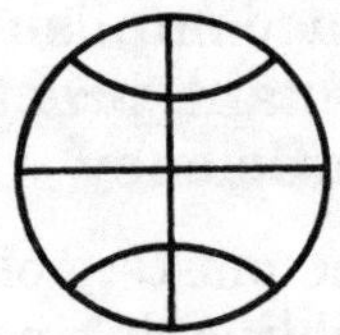

Jim Gudger is one of the most knowledgeable coaches around today. Currently the head coach at East Texas State University (Commerce, Texas), Coach Gudger has won over 500 games on the college level and another 58 on the international level. He has traveled abroad extensively, coaching U.S. teams in international competition, coaching foreign teams, lecturing, and leading clinics. In addition, he supervised the first two Olympic Development Camps, coached the 1971 Pan American team and, coached the victorious NAIA teams in the 1967 Pan American and 1968 Olympic trials. He has written a book for Parker Publishing Company, entitled *Modern Basketball*.

Part 1

On many occasions when I am speaking or conducting clinics, I make this statement: "Do not overlook the little things." Mastery of the little things is paramount in making daily progress in basketball or, for that matter, any sport.

The little things are the basics, the fundamentals, the foundations of the game. To improve a skill or skills, we must first master the fundamental concept of that particular skill. Secondly, we must apply those fundamentals through constant repetition and practice.

NOTE: Knowledge of fundamentals will provide a player with the confidence, poise and relaxation necessary to accomplish the task at hand. Repetition or constant practice will insure a higher degree of efficiency.

It is only through the mastery of the "little things," such as passing, jumping, dribbling, faking, footwork, agility, body balance, and shooting, that we can have a good basketball team. As coaches, we are not honest with our players and ourselves if we fail to remind our players constantly of daily attention to fundamentals.

The Setup

An important part of our daily practice session is a series of drills which we call our "Daily Dozen."

Our first idea was to make this series the very first thing our players did when they came onto the floor. It was usually unsupervised because some players reach the floor before others. Even though much emphasis was placed on the importance of this series, we soon found that only a few players were getting the full benefit of these drills for various reasons.

We have now changed our thinking and administer the series under a coach's supervision. We divide our squad equally on six baskets and assign two specific drills to each basket. Team members move to the next station upon completion of the drills at the preceding station. We continue this progression until all players have completed all six stations.

In order to prevent our drill session from dragging, we attempt to challenge a young man to improve daily on a series of skills that are basic to the game and that will eventually endow him with the poise, confidence, and desire necessary for top-flight performance.

Recordkeeping

At times, we keep accurate charts at each station and rate our players daily or weekly on their efficiency of performance and improvement.

Place your first rating on the locker room bulletin board and watch for changes in performance at the next rating period. You will notice individuals working on their own time in weak areas in an effort to move up the chart and replace someone else.

> **NOTE: We feel that a daily application of these drills will definitely improve a player's touch, quickness, ball handling, jumping, agility, body balance, hand and eye coordination, and faking. The intangibles involved are discipline, motivation, and challenge.**

A Valuable Learning Experience

Teaching and improving skills in basketball closely follow the lines of the association concept of learning:

1. The experience must be presented so that a vivid memory of the facts and details remains.
2. Frequency of application or repetition insures steady progress.
3. The duration of the learning process has a definite bearing on retention factors.
4. Current, fresh application better prepares an individual for sharp, effective performance.

This is how the "Daily Dozen" series works. The first six drills are described in the following paragraphs.

Rim Touches

This is an excellent jumping and coordination drill for all players, regardless of their size (Diagram 1). It serves as a good warm-up drill. But its greatest value lies in the fact that daily we test and challenge our jumping muscles and progress to the most difficult aspect of the jump in the last phase of the drill.

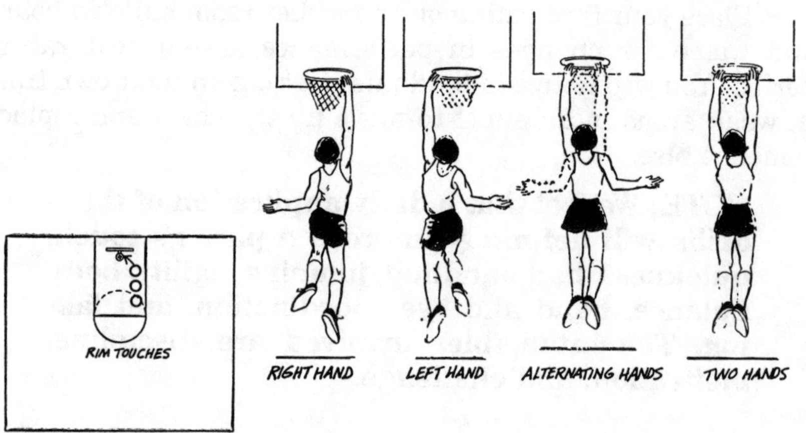

Diagram 1

1. The player faces the basket and jumps to touch the rim five times with his right hand. He may jump from a position in which his feet are stationary, or he may take one step and jump.
2. The player jumps to touch the rim five times with his left hand, using the same technique as in step 1.
3. The player jumps five times and alternates hands. He starts with either hand and uses the same techniques

described in steps 1 and 2. If he starts with his right hand, the drill will be right-left-right-left-right.

4. The player jumps five times with two hands. This is the most difficult because it follows 15 previous jumps. The important point here is that the upward thrust must come off two feet. The upward thrust in most instances in the first three jumps will be off two feet; however, we *insist* on this for the two-hand jump.

If a player is too small to touch the rim or if his jumping ability is inadequate, we ask him to pick a spot on the backboard, use this as his target, and strive to get higher on each successive effort.

I prefer to have two players work on this drill at one time. When player 1 completes five jumps with the right hand, player 2 steps in and performs the same stage of the drill. When he finishes, player 1 steps back in for five jumps with his left hand. This continues until all four steps have been completed by both men.

All 20 jumps may be performed by one individual in succession after the proper techniques have been mastered. This drill is a good challenge if properly supervised.

Tapping Drill

This drill helps to improve touch, rhythm, agility, and coordination (Diagram 2).

1. The player faces the backboard about two steps in front of the board. He tosses the ball onto the board and taps it against the board ten times at maximum height. He should try to use good rhythm and touch and strive to complete this stage of the drill without a break in the motion.
2. Same as step 1 but with the left hand.
3. Same as steps 1 and 2 but with alternating hands.
4. Same as steps 1, 2, and 3 but with both hands.

The important effects here are rhythm, timing, and

touch. A small player may also use the board, but his touch and timing must be excellent because the distance between the ball and his hand is greater than that of the tall player or super jumper.

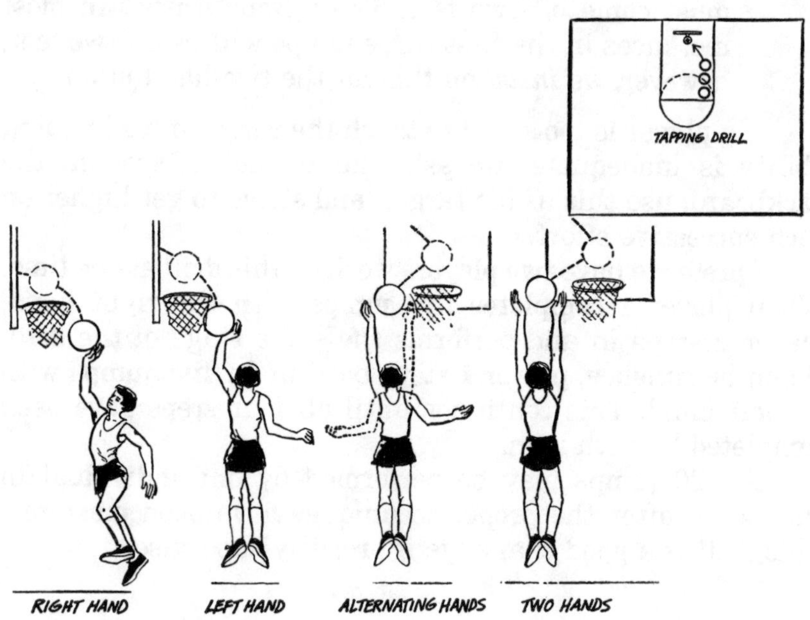

Diagram 2

Again, I prefer two players to alternate, ten taps each. When an individual becomes exceptionally accomplished with this technique, we ask him to do the 40 taps in succession—right hand, left hand, alternating hands, and two hands without a break.

Hook Shot Drill

The player should take a position with his back to the basket (Diagram 3). He should be one step in front of the rim, holding the ball waist high with two hands.

He will then take a short step to the right on his left foot and shoot a short hook shot, using the backboard. He must maintain his balance, catch the ball as it comes through the net (the ball should never touch the floor) and, with two short rhythm steps, roll in and shoot a short hook shot with the opposite hand.

Diagram 3

He continues this action until he makes 20 baskets. Misses are not counted.

This is an excellent drill for improving agility, rhythm, timing, touch, and concentration. It is a great help in improving the steps and rhythm of the weaker hand.

Again, the ball should never touch the floor.

Flip-Flop Drill

This drill is executed best with three players: one ball handler, one obstacle, and one shooter (Diagram 4).

1. The ball handler stands one step in front of the basket (facing the basket) with the ball in two hands.
2. The obstacle is one step behind the ball handler and facing the basket.
3. The shooter is one step behind the obstacle and facing the basket.

Diagram 4

4. On a signal, the ball handler flips or hangs the ball about shoulder height at a 45-degree angle to the determined side. The shooter moves forward, takes the flip, and shoots a lay-up. He immediately comes under control, quickly turns, and cuts behind the obstacle to the opposite side for a lay-up with his opposite hand in a half-circle pattern. This action continues until the shooter has made ten baskets. Misses do not count.
5. The ball handler should never wait for the shooter. Immediately upon catching the ball as it comes through the net, he should flip it as described to the opposite side. It is the shooter's challenge to be there. It is important that a lay-up and not a jump-shot technique be used.
6. When the first shooter finishes, he becomes the obstacle, the obstacle becomes the ball handler, and the ball handler becomes the shooter.

The results should be improved quickness, agility, touch, footwork, and concentration.

Saddle Drill

The player stands with his heels on the foul line and his back to the basket, with the ball held waist high in both hands (Diagram 5).

Diagram 5

1. Choosing the right side for his first move, he should execute a slight head-and-ball fake to his right. At the same time, he should execute a deep drop-step with his left foot, quickly turn to the left foot, and drive hard directly to the basket for a right-hand lay-up.

2. Same action to the opposite side.

The player should complete ten of these moves to each side. On each move, he should strive to make that move quicker than the one before. Improvement in quickness, quick drives, and faking should be noticeable.

Two-Ball Dribble

The player stands at one end line with a basketball in each hand (Diagram 6). Choosing his own pace, the player begins to dribble the two basketballs alternately toward the other end line.

Diagram 6

Progress will be slow at first, and the player will be prone to dribble the balls simultaneously. As the alternating technique is improved, speed should also improve.

The desired effect is accomplished when the player is able to sprint-dribble to the opposite end line, make the turn, and sprint-dribble back to the starting point without losing a ball or breaking the dribble.

This drill is very effective for improving hand-eye coordination, reflex action, agility, and ball control.

Part 2

If a player is adequately schooled in the "little things" and has the necessary desire and physical stamina to play, he should be an asset to any team.

All coaches do not have the same resources for attracting prospective players. High school coaches do not even have the opportunity to recruit. However, regardless of our situation along the line, we can all take positive steps to prepare and improve the players we do have available.

Wiggle-Waggle Drill

The player stands at one end line with the basketball.

1. Choosing his own pace, he drops his hips and takes a long step forward on his left foot. With the ball now in his right hand, he passes the ball under his left leg from the inside into his left hand (Diagram 7).

Diagram 7

2. Now his right leg has come forward. With his left hand, he passes the ball from the inside, under his right leg, into his right hand.
3. The player continues this process at his own pace until he reaches the level where he can move swiftly from end line to end line, turn, and return to the starting point without an error.

The technique is to keep the hips down and the body low, step long, and place the ball with the hands. Players should not attempt to lift their legs to step over the ball.

VARIATION: This drill may also be performed by placing the ball under the legs from the outside. It is a slight change and a bit more difficult.

Repetition of this drill improves coordination, agility, body balance, and ball handling.

Pickup Drill

This drill must have at least three people involved. It is more satisfactorily performed with four.

1. Place a ball on each wide lane divider. Place a helper behind each ball and under the basket (Diagram 8).
2. The player takes a position in the middle of the lane between the two balls.
3. On a signal, or whenever he is ready, the player steps toward the ball with his right leg. The left leg is extended on the line between the ball and the basket.
4. From this position, the player reaches down and picks up the ball with both hands. He does this without moving his left foot and without turning his body. He drives the ball toward the basket, using the power move technique.

The player repeats these moves, alternating sides, until he has made 20 baskets.

NOTE: It is important that the participant not open his body to the basket. Instead, he should

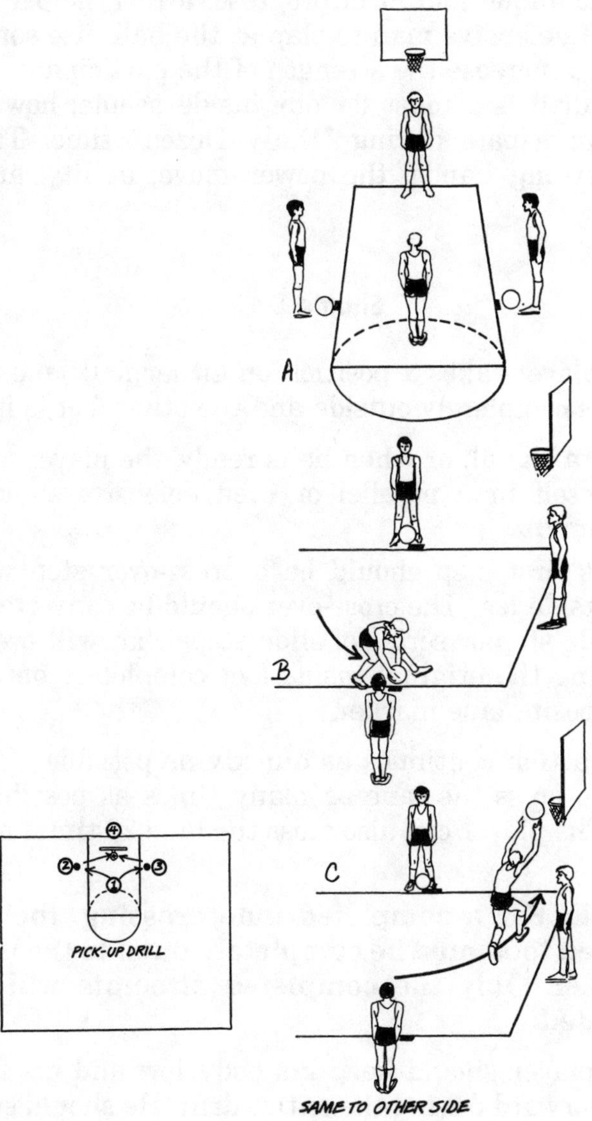

Diagram 8

practice the technique of protecting the ball with his body, with his back to the court and a firm grip on the ball.

As technique and form progress, a fifth helper may be added as a defensive man to slap at the ball, use some body contact and increase the strength of the participant.

This drill is a must for our inside people; however, all players participate during "Daily Dozen" time. The drill develops strong hands, the power move, agility, and body balance.

Shuttle Drill

The player takes a position on either foul lane marker. One foot is completely outside and the other foot is inside.

1. On a signal, or when he is ready, the player positions himself in a parallel or even defensive stance (Diagram 9).
2. His first step should be a cross-over step with the outside leg. The cross-over should be converted into a slide step or series of slide steps that will eventually bring the original inside foot completely outside the opposite lane marker.

This action continues as quickly as possible. The challenge is to cross the lane as many times as possible in 30 seconds. The player can also cross the lane 20 times and time the effort.

NOTE: For a completed lane crossing, the extended foot must be completely outside the lane marker. Only the completed attempts will be counted.

The player should keep his body low and his face and shoulder forward during the entire drill. He should strive for speed and agility.

Drives

Place a chair or other obstacle on each side of the court at a 45-degree angle to the basket and approximately 20 feet

Diagram 9

away. Line up as many players as necessary behind one of the chairs.

1. Using various stages of the rocker step, the first player will drive to the basket in quick, explosive starts for a driving lay-up. All of his efforts should be programmed for technique and the attempt to make each drive quicker and faster than the one before (Diagram 10).
2. After the player completes the drive, he moves to the opposite side and prepares to make his next drive.

Ten drives are expected from each side. Chairs may be moved and starting points adjusted.

The player should always keep speed, quickness, footwork, and ball control in mind and should strive to make each drive quicker than the one before.

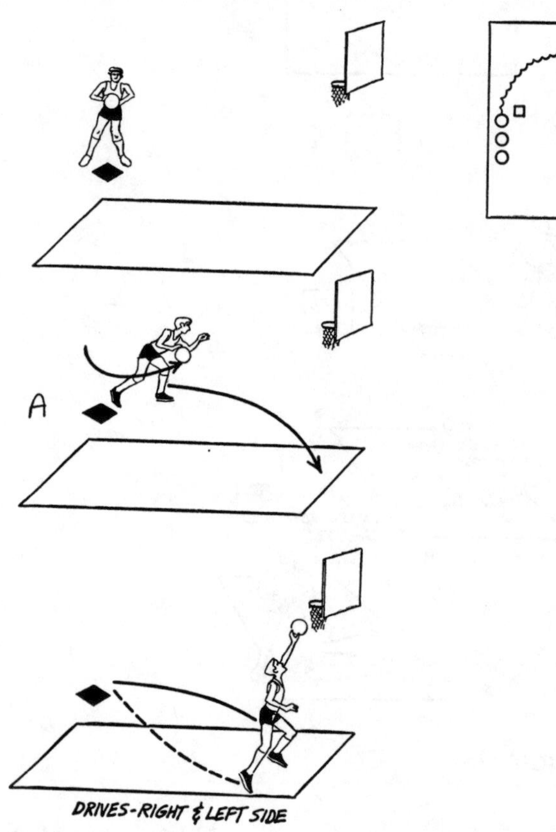

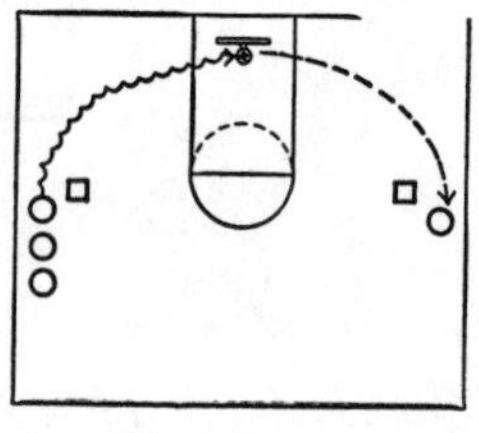

Diagram 10

Quickie Touch Drills

Our eleventh drill is actually a series of quickie drills which we think produce an improvement in touch and ball handling (Diagram 11).

1. Stand erect, feet together, and merely feel the ball by wrapping it around the body, right hand to left hand. Start at waist level and go as high and as low on the body as possible. These continuous wraps in a circular

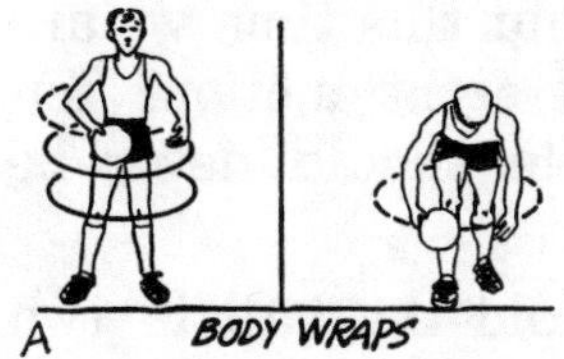

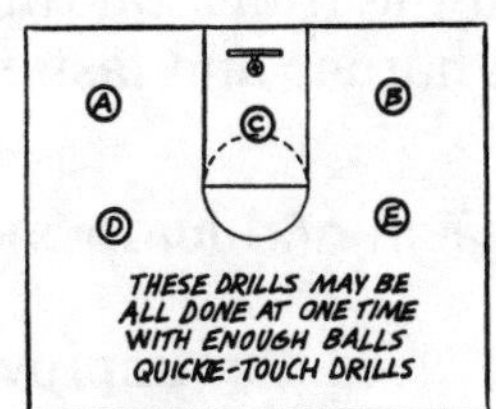

A
B
C
D
E
THESE DRILLS MAY BE
ALL DONE AT ONE TIME
WITH ENOUGH BALLS
QUICKE-TOUCH DRILLS

Diagram 11

motion around the body should be performed ten times as fast as possible.

2. Stand erect with feet spread and the ball held in two hands in front of the body. To begin the drill, drop hips and place the ball between legs from the inside into the opposite hand. Continue in a figure-eight motion for at least ten complete figures.
3. Same as step 2, but each time the ball goes between the legs it should go with a short bounce from one hand to the other. Ten complete figure-eights with two bounces to each figure.

4. Same position in steps 2 and 3, but this time we are dribbling the ball in the figure-eight motion. Ten complete figures and the dribble should never be broken.
5. Stand erect with feet spread. Hold the ball in two hands in front of the body. Bounce the ball with two hands between the legs and catch it with two hands behind the back. After catching the ball behind the back, bring it to the front. Do this ten times. Work to bounce the ball harder and faster.

Short Turn-and-Jump Shots

We find this drill good for improving the short high-percentage finesse shots close to the basket. These important shots may not present themselves too often, but a team must be successful when the opportunity does arise. This drill gives us daily contact with such shots (Diagram 12).

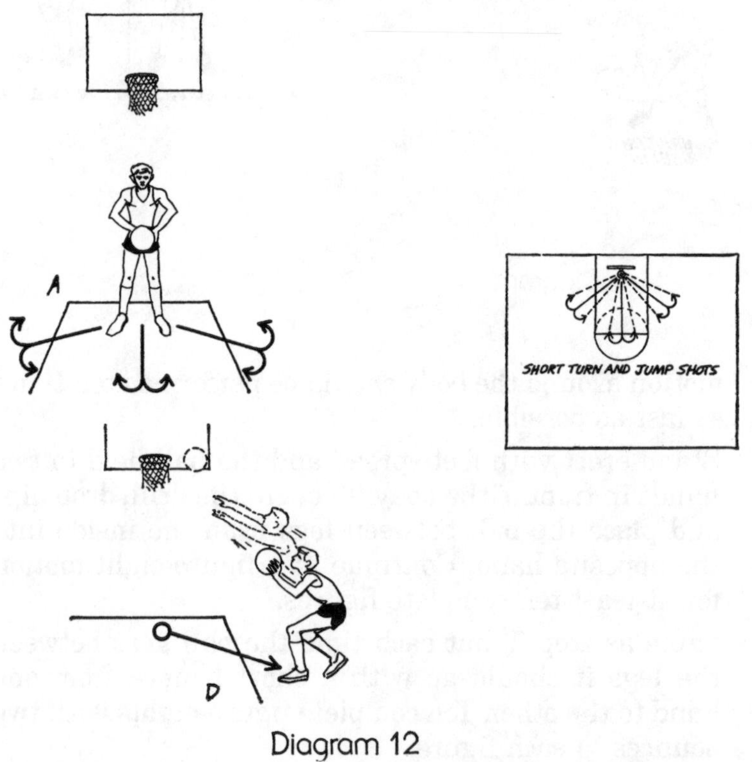

Diagram 12

1. The player should stand directly under the basket with ball in hand.
2. He takes one dribble away from the basket to the left at a 45-degree angle, jumps using all of the techniques of the jump shot, and banks the ball off the board into the basket. He repeats this until he has made ten baskets.
3. The player dribbles straight forward and lifts the ball over the rim. Finesse is important.
4. The player dribbles to the right at a 45-degree angle and uses the backboard.

The player must make ten successful baskets from each of the three positions. The goal of the drill is good shooting form, good shot technique, quickness, and elevation of the shot.

Conclusion

A working squad normally has between 10 and 15 players. With this group divided among six baskets, using the station method, the "Daily Dozen" can be completed easily in 20 minutes. I think most coaches will agree that this is 20 minutes well spent.

I have not emphasized the value of the "Daily Dozen" as warm-up drills or as conditioners. But check your players after a few days of the drills. I think you will be pleased.

30

Four Basic Drills for Improving Individual Defensive Skills

by Bill Leatherman

Assistant Basketball Coach
James Madison University
Harrisonburg, Virginia

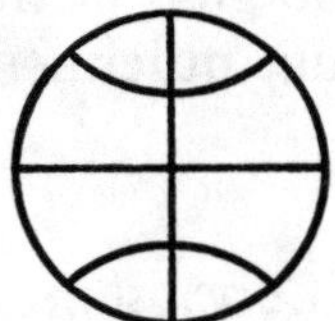

After 13 years as a high school coach, Bill Leatherman joined the staff of James Madison University (Harrisonburg, Virginia) as an assistant basketball coach. On the high school level, Bill compiled a 161-116 won-lost record.

A prerequisite for winning "team" man-to-man defensive play is for the squad, as individuals, to master defense. We constantly talk about and build our team defensive philosophy, such as ballside play, weakside play, sagging, help and recovery, but any way we look at it, outstanding individual work within the unit is the key to our defense.

I feel that a team using any variation of a man-to-man or zone defense can benefit from several drills which we use daily during the season. The amount of time spent on these drills varies from day to day depending on how well our players master the skills.

Approximately 70 percent of our practice each day is allotted to defensive work. There are many defensive drills that we can use to correct various weaknesses our staff detects, but there are four basic defensive drills that seem to reach most individual problems. We use two of the four basic drills each day.

Simple Defensive Strategy

Our defensive style is not complicated, but there are certain rules we must master:

1. The *charge drill* teaches absolute protection of the baseline and the art of drawing the offensive foul, as well as the correct way to turn each play to the inside.
2. We never allow a cutter to cross the lane toward the ball unless we have fronted him. We use the *talkside drill* to teach this technique.
3. The *trio drill* is used primarily by our guards to teach fighting over the top of the screen, sliding through, and proper execution of the jump switch.
4. The *towel drill* is used to create mental defensive toughness and proper defensive play through positioning of the body. This is a favorite drill of our good defensive players—and they really can gain the respect of their teammates by demonstrating their skills. The best part of the *towel drill* is that it can be done by

any player regardless of his ability—if he learns that "guts and pride" are the primary ingredients in becoming a defensive standout.

Our players really enjoy these drills. Since they are all competitive drills, they are fun and challenging. I hope you will find them helpful when working with your squads. I know they'll improve your defensive game!

Charge Drill

A chair is placed about two or three feet outside the free-throw lane and about six feet in from the baseline. The offensive player (0) begins about three steps in front of the defensive player (X). Player X passes to 0 and the ball is returned for a second pass. Player 0 will receive the second pass just prior to making his cut around the chair (Diagram 1). He is instructed to drive hard to the basket for the lay-up at all costs. Player X, after making the final pass, must hustle to the baseline with good defensive positioning. We encourage contact, but X is required to use the proper defensive position. Player X should not make the initial contact, but should "take" the contact from 0.

Two balls should be used to keep the drill moving, and the players rotate lines. This drill encourages defensive toughness.

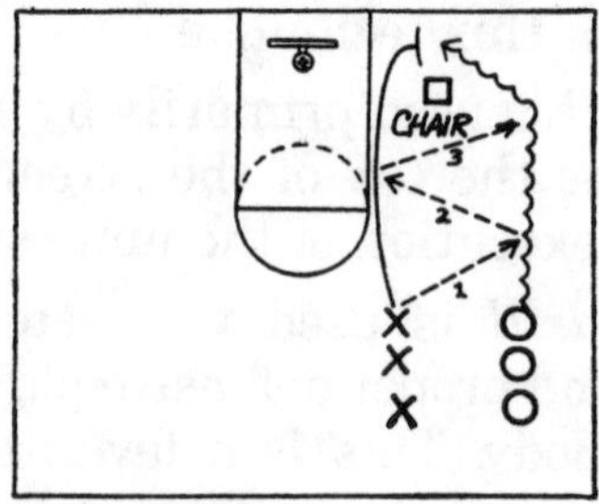

Diagram 1

Talkside Drill

Players 01, 02, and 03 are in a triangle around the top of the circle facing the basket. Player 02 has a basketball locked between his knees. Player 01 (who has another ball) passes off the dribble to 02, who passes immediately to 03. Player 01 cuts across the lane to receive a pass from 03 (Diagram 2).

Player X1, the defender, must maintain a good defensive position on 01, by denying him the passing lane from 03. This phase of denying the passing lane enables us to condition ourselves to front all people inside the lane.

NOTE: In our team defensive scheme, if everyone fronts properly, we will always have a player behind any man in the lane, provided we have driven the ball to the side.

Player X1 is actually defending against two basketballs. This is designed to improve defensive quickness and inside recovery. Player 01 may make a quick return cut to receive a pass from Player 02, who uses the ball between his knees.

When X2 (under the basket) sees 01 cut back and 02 remove the ball from between his legs, he shouts "back" to X1. Player X1 must listen for this signal from X2. At the same time, he must maintain the proper defensive position on 01. In addition to serving as a defensive and a passing drill, the talkside drill also encourages our players to talk while working on defense.

Trio Drill

The trio drill is appropriately named because our defensive players must use three different maneuvers to stop their men. The defense is always instructed to be close enough to touch their men (Diagram 3).

The offensive players, 01 and 02, are using the screen-and-roll effect. The defensive players, X1 and X2, must try to fight over the top of the screen and slide through with the help of their teammates. Or, if the front defensive man (in this case, X1) appears to be beaten, X2 (the back man) will initiate the jump switch. Player X2 will shout "Switch."

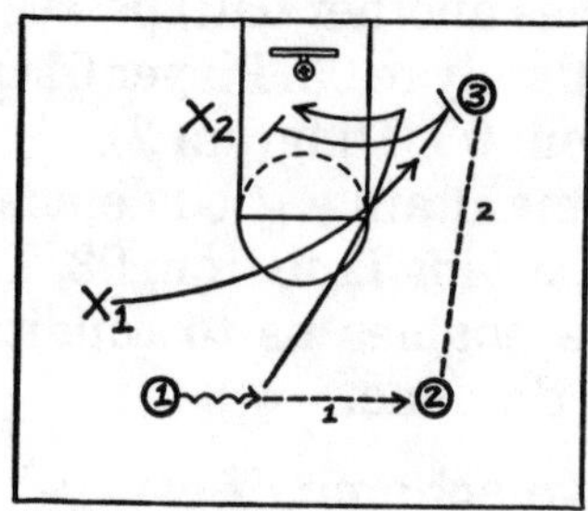

Diagram 2

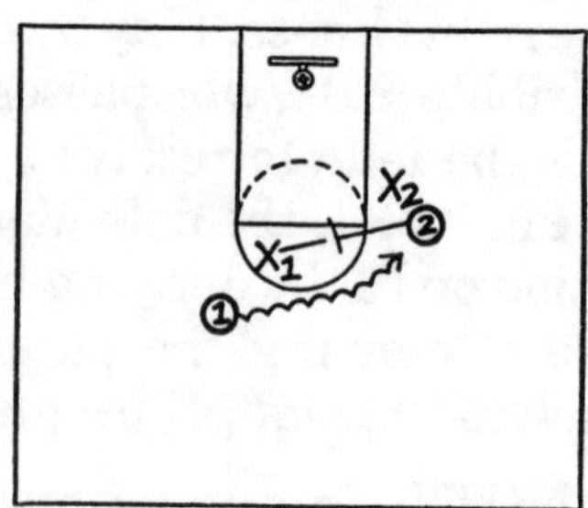

Diagram 3

> **NOTE: Emphasize to your players that X1 cannot call the switch. Players X1 and X2 must be working together and only the back man can call for a switch. The switch is used only as a last resort.**

Obviously, X1 will get more defensive work, so we rotate the four players into this position. This drill will help guards learn to stay a half-step ahead of their offensive men. You can use this drill as a two-on-two series for intersquad competition.

Towel Drill

This is one of our more difficult drills for conditioning of the legs while at the same time teaching positioning of the body while on defense. We use the entire court and have most of the squad active simultaneously (Diagram 4).

Player X assumes the defensive stance facing the offensive man who has a ball. Player X has a towel rolled up and placed around his neck. He grasps both ends of the towel and pulls himself "down" into the stance. His elbows are extended out to serve as antennas and for body balance.

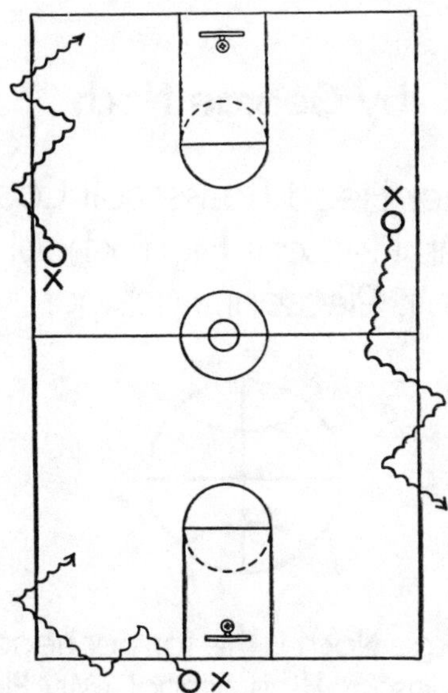

Diagram 4

Player 0 will dribble around the outside of the court in a zig-zag pattern going from side to side. He is instructed to stay within three feet of the line, while X, the defender, is instructed to keep his body in front of 0 at all times.

If X loses his balance, he must hustle back and assume his position guarding 0. Player 0 will make a real effort to get around X. If X should lose his balance, 0 will not wait for him.

Any player can perform this drill, regardless of ability. It can help many players to gain confidence in their defensive skills. We have several combinations of players working at the same time and rotate the offensive and defensive positions.

31

Defensive Drills for a Feeder System

by George Noch

Former Head Basketball Coach
Mt. Pleasant High School
Mt. Pleasant, Michigan

George Noch is the former head coach at Mt. Pleasant High School (Mt. Pleasant, Michigan). When he resigned, he was the "winningest" coach in the school's history, with over 200 wins. His teams won one regional, four district, and five conference titles.

Here are drills for teaching good man-to-man defense. Each drill teaches and progressively develops your players' skills. Other drills may be used by the coach, but these drills are recommended as the foundation.

In addition to the techniques, each coach should be aware of the terminology used in these drills. This is important because it allows coaches at all levels to use the same terms to describe the same actions. This makes for consistency from year to year, which benefits both players and coaches.

The most important thing to remember is that the techniques of defense should be stressed at all times—not just when the players are practicing them. These techniques should become part of the players' skills and part of the team's play.

1. Toss It Out and Play Directional Defense (Diagram 1)

Objective: To teach each player to use the proper footwork when approaching a ball handler. The second phase is to teach a player to direct the offensive player's moves.

Technique: One foot should be closer to the player being guarded than the other foot, the knees should be bent, the arms should be in palms-up position.

Procedure:

1. Players X1, X2, X3 are under the basket on defense. Players 01, 02, 03 are within shooting range on offense.
2. Player X1 has the ball and gives it to 01. Player X1 must get to 01 to prevent the quick shot and any subsequent offensive move. Make sure that the defense approaches using the one-foot-forward shuffle.
3. Players X1 and 01 play until 01 scores or X1 gets the ball. Each player then goes to the line opposite from where he

started (i.e., offensive man goes to the end of the defensive line, and vice-versa).

4. After the correct footwork is drilled, the coach should have the defensive man dictate the direction of the offensive man. This is called "directional defense." The defensive man should:
   a. Make the offensive player go left.
   b. Make the offensive player go right.
   c. Make the offensive player go to his weak hand.
   d. Make the offensive player shoot outside.

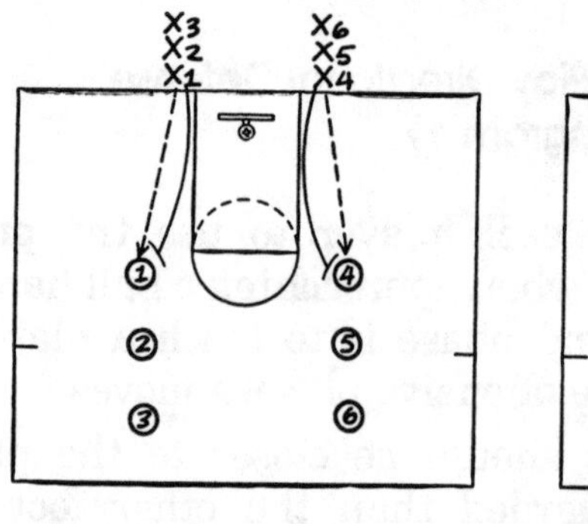

Diagram 1

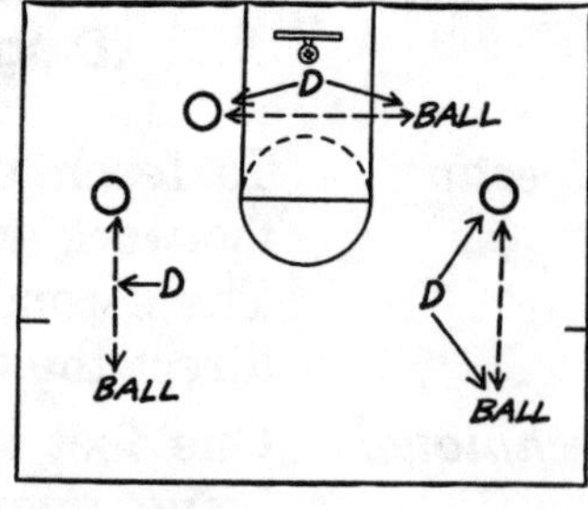

Diagram 2

2. Triangle of Defense (Diagram 2)

Diagram 2 illustrates the fundamental formation that the defensive man wants to be in, in regard to his man and the ball, after each position change his man makes. Several rules can help a player achieve his goal:

1. A player should always be *one step* off the base of the triangle or one step off the passing lane.
2. The formation should be *ball-me-man*. In other words, never let the man get between you and the ball.

3. Open up to the ball. You should be able to see the ball and the man you are guarding.
4. The farther your man is from the ball, the farther you may be away from him. However, always maintain your position one step off the base of the triangle.

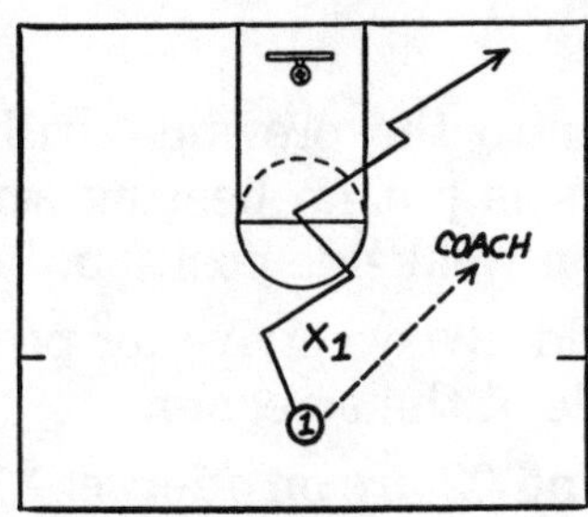

Diagram 3

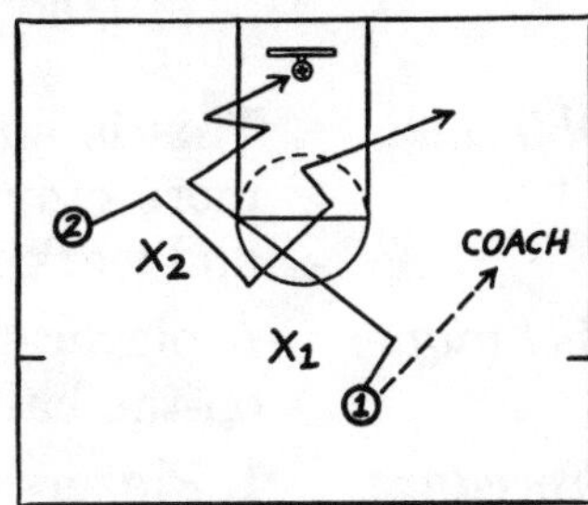

Diagram 4

3. One-on-One with the Coach (Diagram 3)

Objective: To teach each player the correct defensive position in an everchanging situation.

Technique: The coach should not throw the ball to the offensive player the first time he gets open. It is better to give both the offensive and defensive men time to work before going in to the one-on-one play with the ball.

Procedure:
1. Player 01 has the ball and tosses it to the coach. Player X1 is guarding 01.
2. Player 01 makes any cut he wants in any direction he wants. Player X1 must maintain proper position and prevent the pass.
3. On the pass from the coach to 01, 01 and X1 play until 01 scores or X1 gets the ball.

4. A player goes from offense to defense and then to the end of the line. The starting position for the offensive player may be changed to suit the coach.

4. Two-on-Two with the Coach (Diagram 4)

Objective: This is similar to the previous drill, but more emphasis is put on beating screens and working on weakside position.

Technique: A player should always strive for position on the ball side of the screener.

Procedure:

1. Players 01 and 02 are on offense: X1 and X2 are on defense. Player X2 must not let 01 pass the ball to 02.
2. After 01 passes to the coach, 01 and 02 may make any cut to get open. The coach passes the ball to the open man, but only after several cuts have been made.
3. It is very important that a defensive player does not follow his man's fakes away from the ball. Switching should not be allowed at first, but should be taught as progress is made.

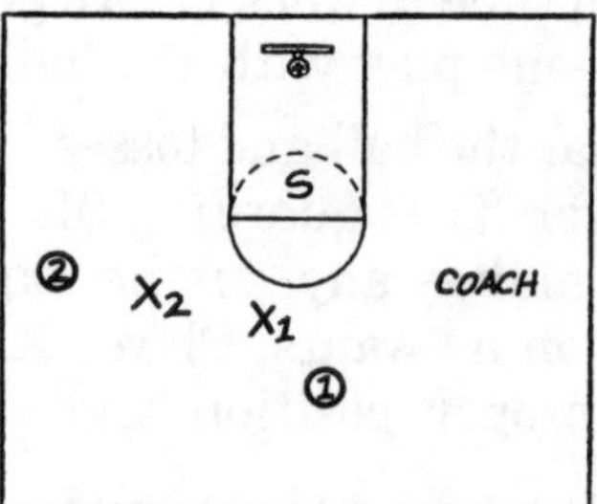

Diagram 5

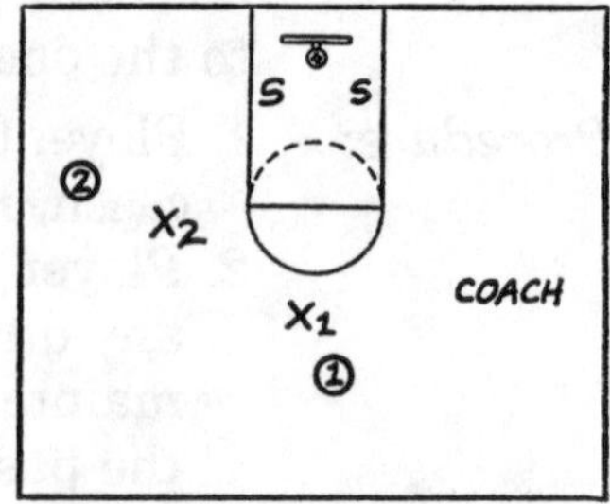

Diagram 6

4. Additional screeners may be placed as shown in Diagrams 5 through 7. Managers usually make good screeners.

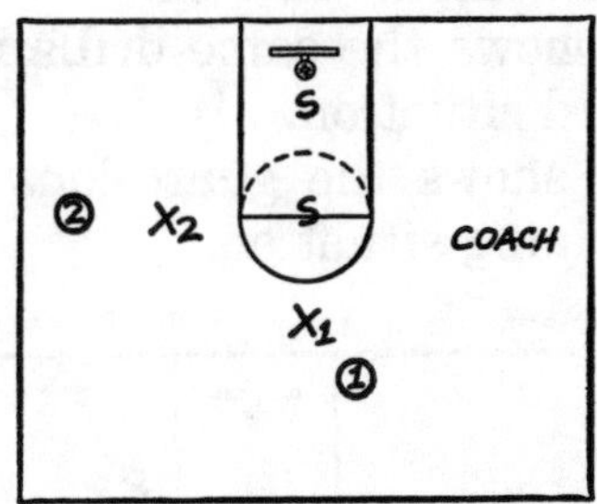

Diagram 7

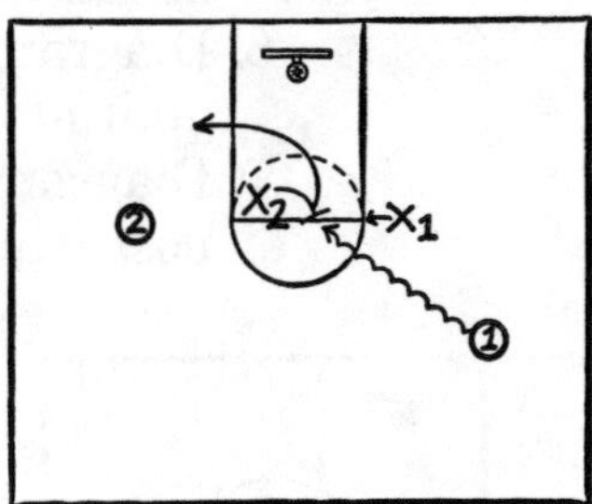

Diagram 8

5. Helping Drill (Diagram 8)

Objective: To teach each player to assist a teammate on defense and still be responsible for his own man.

Technique: Make sure that the helping player uses a shuffle step and maintains good body position. Reaching with a hand is not good enough.

Procedure:

1. Player X1 must make 01 drive to the middle.
2. Player 02 must be in shooting range, and in the beginning he must remain stationary.
3. As 01 drives, X2 must shuffle to stop his drive. When 01 passes to 02, X2 must return and prevent the shot by 02.

4. This drill then becomes a two-on-two drill, until the offense scores or the defense gets the ball.
5. Initially, 02 is allowed to drive to the basket. Later, 02 should be allowed to backdoor X2 without the ball.
6. Diagram 9 shows the same drills in a guard-forward situation.
7. Diagram 10 shows the guard-forward-post man-helping situation.

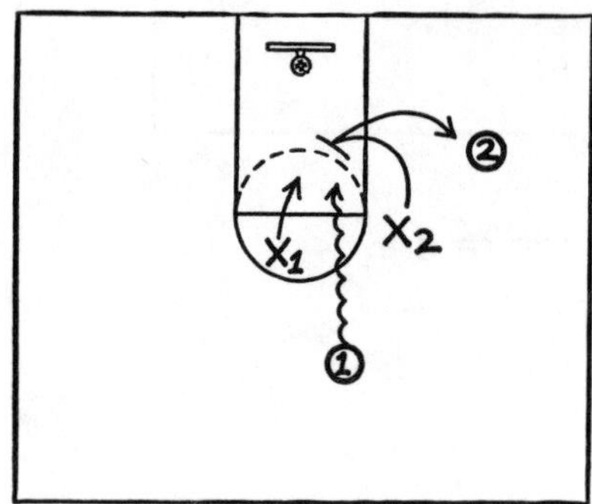

Diagram 9

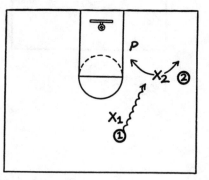

Diagram 10

6. Cut the Lead—Fronting (Diagram 11)

Objective: To reinforce the triangle of defense. To learn to prevent a pass. To learn to cover the backdoor cut.

Technique: The defensive player must overplay on the ball side at least half a step. He must learn to shuffle without unnecessary head movement to see the ball. He must open to the ball or close to the man when the backdoor cut is made.

Procedure: 1. Two groups go at the same time, but the offensive player must work to get open somewhere in the area of the free-throw line extended and the free-throw lane line.

2. The coach has the ball and should not pass too soon. Make both the offense and the defense work on technique.
3. On the pass, it is two-on-two completion. It will help if either defensive man yells "Ball," when he sees the pass made.
4. Make sure that the defensive man away from the pass releases and uses proper triangle defense techniques.
5. You can add one or even two screeners in the key.
6. Players go from offense to defense and also change sides on the floor.

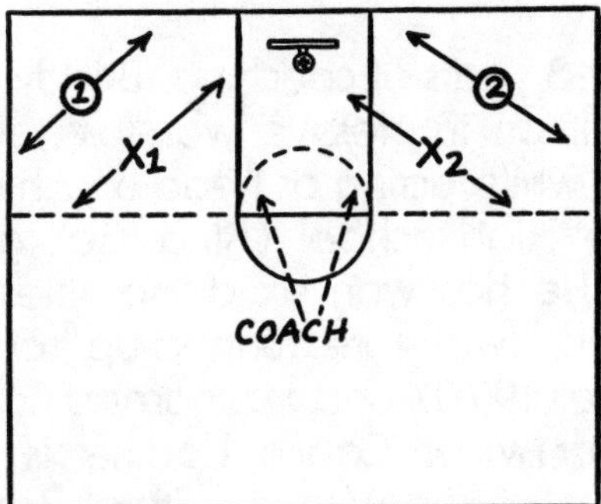

Diagram 11

There are other drills that are very suitable for working on defense. Constant work in the one-on-one, two-on-two, and three-on-three situations, both half-court and full-court, is very good. The key to success, however, is having the proper techniques taught early, reinforcing them at all levels, and never allowing them to be done incorrectly. Defense can be the foundation of a team's success.

32

Drills to Improve Defensive Aggressiveness

by Buddy Updike

Head Basketball Coach
King George High School
King George, Virginia

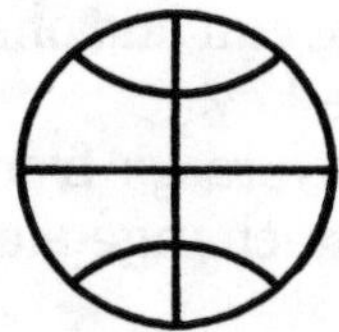

In 13 years of coaching, Buddy Updike has built an impressive won-lost record of 219-83 while acting as head coach at King George High School (King George, Virginia). He has won six district titles, three regionals, two state runners-up, and one state title (1970), and was named Coach-of-the-Year twice. Coach Updike is also a member of the Virginia State Basketball Coaches Committee.

With the approach of every basketball season, I start reviewing my defensive philosophy and begin to search for new drills to improve our defensive aggressiveness.

Aggressiveness on defense is essential to our basketball success. Our teams are never large, and since we play teams with much taller personnel, we feel that we must go after people full-court rather than play a sagging type of man-to-man defense.

I have picked the seven drills that we use primarily to encourage aggressive defensive play. I believe that these drills will help any coach to develop aggressive players.

One-on-One Full-Court Drill

After dividing the squad into two groups, the coach gives each squad member a number and places them across the end line. The coach stands at center court with a ball and calls two numbers. The two players charge out to half-court, diving for the ball. The player who gets the ball becomes offense and the other is defense.

They play full-court one-on-one to a score of five. Both players may fast break, but both are required to press full-court constantly. This drill is also a great conditioner (Diagram 1).

Circle Drill

Six players are put into a circle around the foul line. The coach stands outside the circle and throws or bounces a ball into the circle. All six players must retrieve the ball (Diagram 2).

After a player has three retrieves, he steps out of the circle. The rest continue until the last two players compete. The last man runs two "suicides" while the rest of the squad cheers him.

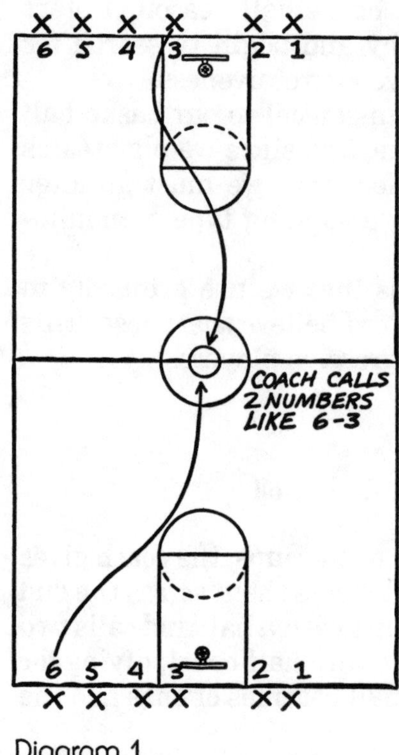

Diagram 1

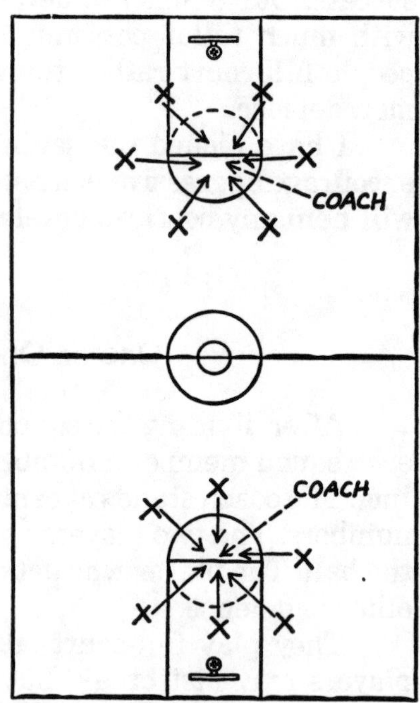

Diagram 2

Draw-the-Charge Drill

This drill encourages our players to keep good defensive position on the end lines and sidelines until charged by an opponent. The entire team of 12 players line up, one behind the other, on the end line. (Diagram 3).

The coach passes to the second man in line. The front man assumes a defensive stance about three feet from the ball handler. The ball handler fakes and drives the sideline hand. The defensive man must cut off the sideline and take the charge. He does this for each man until he draws six charges correctly as judged by the coach. If he does not draw the charge correctly, he stays on defense until he does.

We then put another man on defense. We teach our players to take the charge, hit the floor, slide back, and groan.

Two-on-Two Full-Court Drill

This drill is used to teach our defensive guards to attack one-on-one, then jump into the double-team and recover to help. The whole team plays this, big men as well as guards (Diagram 4).

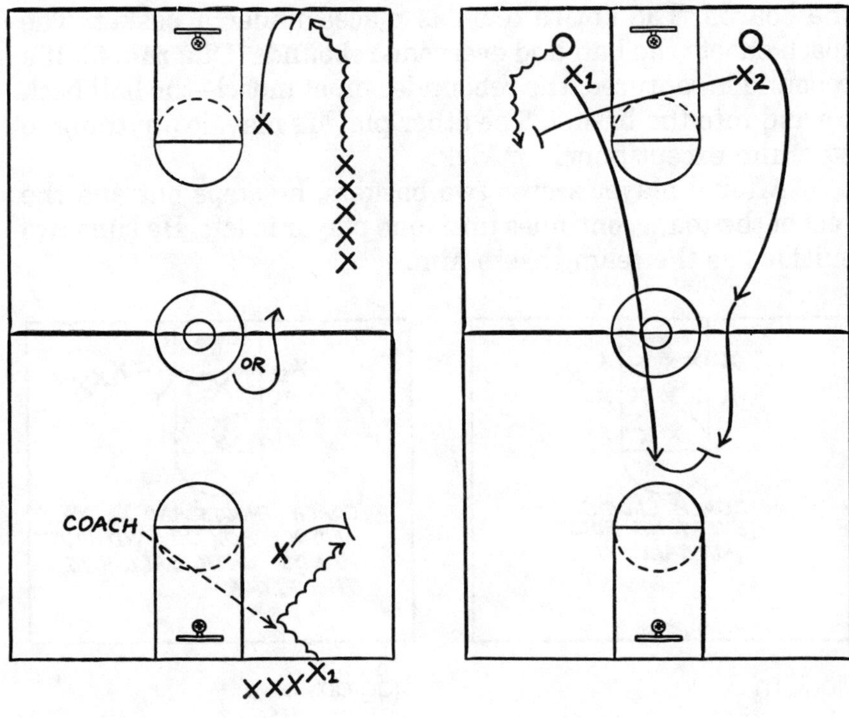

Diagram 3 Diagram 4

The assistant coach gives the ball to the offense. The two offensive players try to bring the ball up any way they can—

by screening, crossing, cleaning out, and so on. The defensive men try to stop the ball handler one-on-one and then cover other men to prevent a pass to him, or they may run and jump the ball handler.

As soon as the trap is sprung, we release the original defender. He protects the basket as best he can to cut off the other offensive player. This drill encourages teamwork and teaches our defenders the proper time to trap.

Muscle Rebounding Drill

This drill is used to accustom our players to contact on the boards. The entire team is placed under a basket. The coach shoots the ball and everyone rebounds (Diagram 5). If a rebound is captured, the rebounder must muscle the ball back up and into the basket. The other players may do anything to stop him except punch or kick.

After a player scores two baskets, he steps out and the rest of the team continues until one player is left. He runs two suicides as the team cheers him.

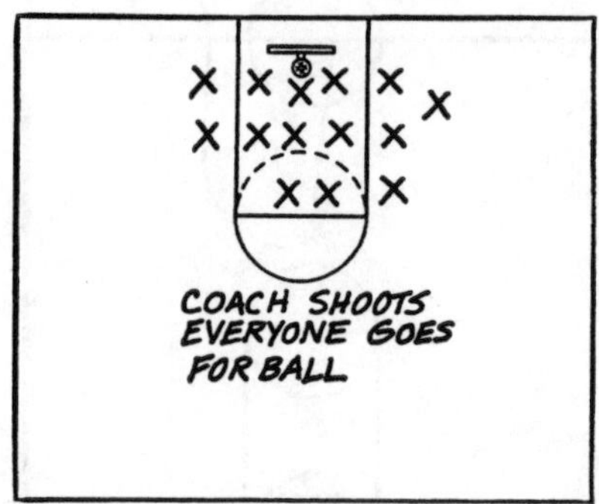

Diagram 5

Diagram 6

Box-Out Drill

Three lines are placed under the basket. The first men in line step out and assume a defensive stance (Diagram 6). The coach shoots the ball. The three defensive men pivot and box out until the ball bounces on the floor. They then go to the end of the line and three more take their places.

Five-on-Five Box-Out Drill

The first team plays defense on the second team while the coach shoots the ball. The second team crashes the board, trying to get an offensive rebound or to keep the ball alive. If they get an offensive rebound, they put it back up and score a point. If the defense boxes out and gets the fast break outlet pass out safely, they score a point.

We play to five points or seven points and then switch the offense to defense. Suicides are run by the loser after every five or seven points.

Conclusion

We use these drills daily during the season after we have taught the proper fundamentals. These drills will make any team more aggressive. We feel that this is the key to our success.

33

Defensive Drills Build the Skills That Help Win Games

by Frank Holz

Basketball Coach
Urbandale Junior High School
Urbandale, Iowa

Frank Holz is the basketball coach at Urbandale Junior High School (Urbandale, Iowa). He has a career won-lost record of 107-32.

Although offense is labeled the more glamorous aspect of the game of basketball, defense is really the backbone of success. Good defense must be taught and stressed as an important aspect to beginning as well as advanced players. Players must understand the principles of defense and be able to execute basic defensive moves.

Man-to-man defense is the origin of all defense. Zones may be employed occasionally for specific purposes, but on the floor it breaks down to an individual confrontation of offense and defense.

Mental and Physical Conditioning Are Important

Before defense is properly played, it must be broken down, explained, understood by the players, practiced, and executed. Conditioning is thus an important factor in playing good defense. A player must be in excellent physical condition if he expects to play sound defense. In addition to physical conditioning, he must work on mental alertness, reaction, and quickness. A good defensive player must be able to adapt to a changing situation and recognize the offensive possibilities.

Basic body position is the first step in playing defense. A player must practice positioning daily. Our players position themselves with feet slightly wider than shoulder width. The knees should be bent sharply, similar to a number 7. The back should be straight with the head erect to view as much as possible.

A choice of two hand positions may be used. One has a hand up near the ears and a second position is with the hands at the sides of the knees.

The first position is used when the defensive player is guarding an offensive man who has used his dribble and must pass or shoot. We also use this in a recover move when guarding a driver. This shows that the player is getting body position and not reaching on defense. The second position is used when guarding a dribbler who is moving outside. It allows the defender to dig for the ball and maintain body balance.

The first position is often responsible for forcing the offensive player to throw a lob or poorly controlled pass. When the other players learn to play the passing lanes on a dribble-used situation, the defense can come up with several steals during a game. This position also puts the defensive man in good position to make the offensive player shoot over him. His hands are already up to distract the shooter.

Footwork Is Important

Footwork is very important in defense. A good defensive player will not allow his feet to come too close together. By keeping his feet apart, the player allows himself a broader base to work from, which will give him quicker and better body control.

The shuffle step is the basic foot movement. Players may prefer a staggered stance, toe to heel, especially if they play defense on the side of the court. If a player is playing on the side, such as a forward, the foot kept back should be closer to the baseline. This will make recovery toward the baseline much easier. If a player is beaten on the drive, he should at least force his man to the middle of the floor where he can get help from a teammate.

The shuffle step must be practiced in different directions. An approach-retreat and a side shuffle are both required. This step is then combined with a quarter- and half-turn pivot so that the player is able to change direction quickly. All of the movements and changes in direction are practiced with at least three hard shuffle steps. We feel that the first three steps will determine whether the defensive man has recovered or forced the offensive man to stop or change direction.

Up until this point, my focus has been primarily on individual defense from the guard or forward position. We have also assumed that we are defending the player on offense who has the ball. Now we would like to briefly discuss defensive position and play in guarding a player who does not have the ball.

Guarding a Player Without the Ball

The defensive player must know his own abilities in terms of speed and reaction. His speed, along with the abilities of the offensive player, will determine how far away from his man he can play. This in turn will determine how much he can play helping defense.

The defensive player must be concerned with two things. First, he must position himself some distance away from his man, but remain close enough so that he can adjust or recover should the offensive player move or get the ball. Second, he must try to position himself where he can help a teammate.

General Rules of Team Defensive Play

The general rules we have used to develop team defensive play are as follows:

1. If the player guarded is one pass away from the ball, then the defensive man plays a step toward the ball and a step off the imaginary line between the ball and the player guarded.
2. If the player is two passes away, the defender plays two steps toward the ball and one off the line.
3. Whenever the ball is on the side, the guard (two passes from the ball) sags into the lane area.
4. The forward on the opposite side of the ball must also help defend the post area.
5. In all cases, the defensive player must position himself to see both the player he is guarding and the ball.
6. Whenever the player with the ball has used his dribble, the other defending players move into a position to overplay the passing lanes to the players they are guarding.

Defending the Post Area

The post area is played differently. If the opposing post player is the main scoring threat, we will try to keep the ball from him. We front the post man with our post and get help from either the guard or the forward cross-court away from the ball. Diagrams 1, 2 and 3 show fronting the post and where we get defensive help.

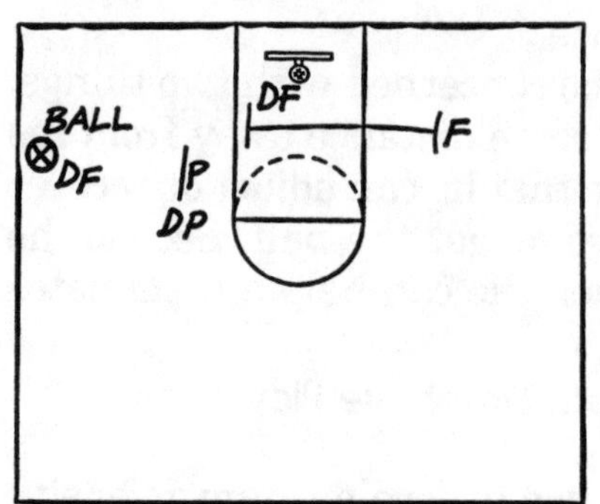

Diagram 1

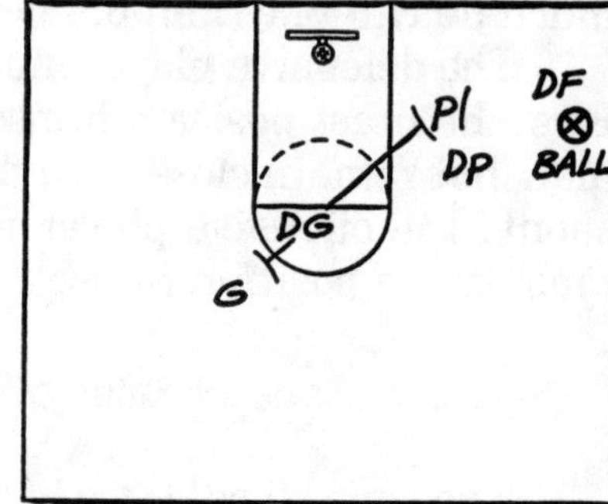

Diagram 2

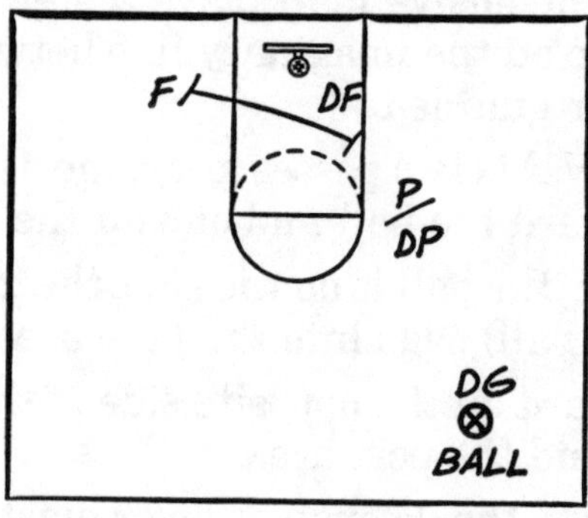

Diagram 3

We will not front the post if the post man goes out above the free-throw line after the ball.

Help on defense will always come from the side of the floor away from the ball. Therefore, if a cross-court pass is made, our players will be quick enough to react or recover and defend the player receiving the ball.

All five players on the floor must continually adjust to the men they are guarding as well as to the location of the ball. The coach must explain and convince his players that each one has a defensive responsibility and that if one of the players momentarily loses track of where he is supposed to be, an easy basket could result.

Mistakes will be made and some easy baskets given up. If the players are willing to work hard, they can usually cause many turnovers and get many steals by playing our type of helping defense.

Developing Defensive Skills

Our first drill for developing defensive skills is the body positioning drill. Proper footwork and body position are stressed. The players line up in rows of three or four.

As the players get into their defensive positions, you should check to see if their positions are correct. Bent knees, straight back, head erect, feet shoulder width, and hands up should all be stressed. On your command, the players "foot fire" in place and on their toes. When you give a hand signal, the players should execute a quarter-turn from their foot fire and return to their foot fire.

You must make certain that the players do not hop or spend too much time floating in the air. Their feet must remain close to the ground so that they can move quickly. Three or four 15-second spurts for the drill daily will help establish good body position and reaction.

Add Shuffle Steps

The next step in this sequence is to add the shuffle steps. The objective here is to develop the player so that he can change direction by reacting to the offense and shuffle over to cut off a driving movement.

The players foot fire in defensive position. On command, they execute a quarter-turn, three shuffle steps (in the direction in which you point), and three shuffle steps back to their original positions. You may want your players to practice this in an approach-retreat fashion or as a side-to-side movement. Again, we recommend three or four spurts of 15 to 20 seconds each.

You may wish to increase or decrease the amount of time spent in this drill, but it should be practiced daily. The foot-fire movement is recommended to stimulate defensive thought and increase foot quickness.

Dribbling in the Chute

A second drill which has been helpful to us, especially for guards, is dribbling in the chute. This drill requires a lane 15 to 20 feet wide and the length of the floor. The offensive player has the opportunity to practice the control or protected dribble.

The defensive player works on position while changing direction and stressing proper footwork. A hand up or to the side is permitted, but no fouling is allowed. You should make sure that proper body position and footwork are executed. This drill is excellent for getting your guards used to playing defensive pressure all over the floor. Diagram 4 shows the relative position of the offensive player (0) and the defender (D).

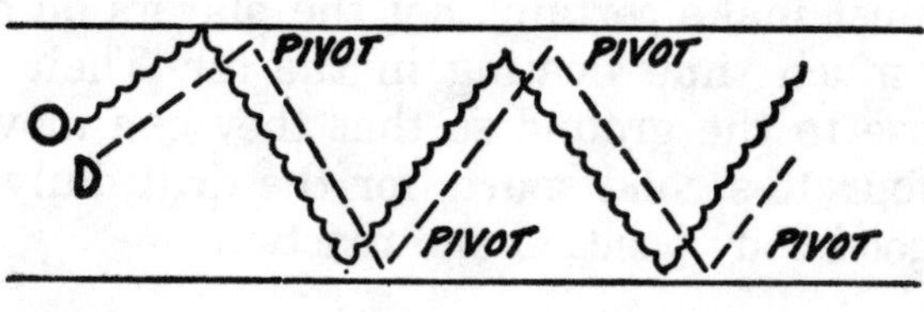

Diagram 4

Points to Stress

On offense, have the dribbler pivot and change hands on the dribble when he gets to the sideline. On defense, a pivot is used on the change of direction to allow good balance and proper position. The players exchange places when they reach the end of the floor. Two or three repetitions are suggested.

Five-Man Defense

Our next drill is the five-man defense. The object of the drill is to teach proper positioning with respect to the ball along with defensive alertness and adjustment. Players must realize that they must continually adjust to the ball and movement of the man they are guarding. The drill begins with the five offensive players in a 2-1-2 set. The defensive players guard their offensive responsibilities and foot fire when their men get the ball. Other players, who are guarding players without the ball, adjust.

At first, the offense is told to stay in their area of the floor. This allows the coach to see if the defense is adjusting properly. Once this has been established, the offense is allowed to move anywhere and attack the basket.

The points of stress are proper positioning and helping the post area (if you are two passes from the ball).

The defensive players will play defense until they get three steals or loose balls before the offense can get a shot. Then we switch positions. This helps teach appreciation for good team defense.

Conclusion

This discussion and the drills described here have served as a basis for teaching defense to our players. Since defense is half the game, we believe it is important to spend a good share of practice time in this area. The rewards are not always as glamorous as in offense, but good defense can lead to steals, fast breaks, and quick baskets.

We have tried to include some of the drills and philosophy of defense that we have found helpful and successful over the years. Basic drills are certainly an aid in coaching defense, but you, in your own way, must communicate the importance of defense to your players.